the psychology of closed mindedness

Essays in Social Psychology

General Editors: MAHZARIN BANAJI, Harvard University, and MILES HEWSTONE, University of Oxford

Essays in Social Psychology is designed to meet the need for rapid publication of brief volumes in social psychology. Primary topics will include social cognition, interpersonal relationships, group processes, and intergroup relations, as well as applied issues. Furthermore, the series seeks to define social psychology in its broadest sense, encompassing all topics either informed by, or informing, the study of individual behavior and thought in social situations. Each volume in the series will make a conceptual contribution to the topic by reviewing and synthesizing the existing research literature, by advancing theory in the area, or by some combination of these missions. The principal aim is that authors will provide an overview of their own highly successful research program in an area. It is also expected that volumes will, to some extent, include an assessment of current knowledge and identification of possible future trends in research. Each book will be a self-contained unit supplying the advanced reader with a well-structured review of the work described and evaluated.

Published titles

Van der Vliert: *Complex Interpersonal Conflict Behaviour*
Dweck: *Self-Theories: Their Role in Motivation, Personality, and Development*
Sorrentino & Roney: *The Uncertain Mind: Individual Differences in Facing the Unknown*
Gaertner & Dovidio: *Reducing Intergroup Bias*
Tyler & Blader: *Cooperation in Groups: Procedural Justice, Social Identity, and Behavioral Engagement*
Kruglanski: *The Psychology of Closed-Mindedness*

Titles in preparation

Biernat: *Standards and Expectancies*
Crisp & Hewstone: *Crossed Categorization, Stereotyping, and Intergroup Relations*
Dunning: *Self-insights*
Jost: *A Theory of System Justification*
Mackie: *Emotional Aspects of Intergroup Perception*
Semin & Fiedler: *The Linguistic Category Model*
Turner: *Social Identity Theory and Self-Categorization*

For continually updated information about published and forthcoming titles in the Essays in Social Psychology series, please visit: **www.psypress.com/essays**.

the psychology of closed mindedness

ARIE W. KRUGLANSKI

PSYCHOLOGY PRESS
NEW YORK • HOVE

Psychology Press
29 West 35th Street
New York, NY 10001
www.psypress.com

Published in Great Britain by
Psychology Press
27 Church Road
Hove, East Sussex
BN3 2FA
www.psypress.co.uk

Psychology Press is an imprint of the Taylor & Francis Group.
Printed in the United States of America on acid-free paper.

10 9 8 7 6 5 4 3 2 1

Library of Congress Cataloging-in-Publication Data

Kruglanski, Arie W.
   The psychology of closed mindedness / Arie W. Kruglanski.
     p. cm. — (Essays in social psychology)
   Includes bibliographical references and index.
   ISBN 0-86377-580-2 (hardback : alk. paper)
   1. Prejudices. 2. Social perception. I. Title. II. Series.
   BF575.P9K77 2004
   153.4—dc22

                  2004009956

CONTENTS

PREFACE

This book constitutes a sequel to my 1989 volume (*Lay epistemics and human knowledge*) and it describes what has been the most productive program of research to date, based on my lay epistemic theory. Actually, my explorations and those of my colleagues into the need for closure construct commenced (with the Kruglanski & Freund, 1983 paper) several years before the *Lay epistemics* book made its appearance, and this early work is indeed summarized in that volume. But it was not until after 1989 that our theorizing and experimentation on closed mindedness gathered steam, facilitated by several federal grants devoted to the topic, our development of the need for closure scale (Webster & Kruglanski, 1994), and the interest, enthusiasm, and energy of numerous collaborators in the United States and abroad.

Thus, when an invitation came to spend the 1998/1999 academic year at the Center for Advanced Study in the Behavioral Sciences (Palo Alto, CA), it seemed an auspicious moment to gather the closed mindedness research findings scattered across various journal publications and present them in a unified framework. Based on my experience with the previous volume, the writing of which frustratingly languished over almost a decade, I decided to be disciplined this time and to complete this work in one uninterrupted sweep. As witnessed by the date of the present writing (March 2003) I didn't actually succeed in this endeavor to an amazing extent, though the amount of drag has been lower than before (hence, there is hope!). Though as a social psychologist I am no stranger to the power of the situation, like other mortals I too rather succumbed to the phenomenon, and instead of tenaciously adhering to my writing schedule, I allowed myself to be distracted by the many inevitable exigencies arising in the course of normal laboratory life. Grants had to be written (and rewritten), papers based on data collected by talented and enthusiastic graduate students and post-docs had to be submitted (and revised), editorial duties had to be discharged, and conferences had to be attended (well, not quite "had to be," but they were too much fun to turn down). In short, even though most chapters for this book were completed in a draft form during the 1998/1999 year as intended, numerous other matters asserted their priority, and only now with the aid of another extended foray outside my home university (enabled by the Alexander von Humboldt Forschungspreis), I find myself able to bring this project to a close at long last.

This book is in essence about human minds and their connection to other human minds. The importance of these matters has been powerfully brought home for me by my own decades-long experience as a scientist. The ideas explored in this book, their initial inspiration, the derivation and testing of their implications, and their ultimate interpretation, all owe an immense amount to other people, great colleagues and gifted collaborators whom it has been my good fortune to encounter and whose thought and work put an indelible imprint on all aspects of the present endeavor. To these colleagues and friends I am profoundly grateful. Tali Freund and Ofra Mayseless carried out important initial work in our erstwhile lab at Tel Aviv University; Donna Webster and Linda Richter gave it a new impetus after my relocation to the University of Maryland; Antonio Pierro, Lucia Mannetti, and Eraldo DeGrada put in motion a major research program on closed mindedness at the University of Rome ("La Sapienza"); and a series of international visitors, graduate students, and post-docs carried out substantial work on this topic during my visits abroad, their stay with me at College Park, and, subsequently, at their home universities. These talented investigators included Monica Rubini and Paola Rocchi of the University of Bologna, Ankica Kosic, Stefano Livi, and Antonio Chirumbolo of the University of Rome ("La Sapienza"), Dino Giovannini of the University of Modena, Malgorzata Kossowska of the (Jagielonski) University of Krakow, Agnieszka Golec of the Institute of Psychology in the Polish Academy of Science, Woo Young Chun of the University of Yonsei, Seoul, Ap Dijksterhuis of the University of Amsterdam, Mark Dechesne of the University of Nijmegen, James Shah (currently at the University of Wisconsin), John Jost (currently at Stanford University), and Erik Thompson (formerly of Washington University at St. Louis). Needless to say, they should not be held responsible for any statements and opinions contained in the present volume of which I alone am the author.

As already mentioned, this work was enabled by two invitations to spend time outside of my home university, for which I am very grateful indeed. One was to the Center for Advanced Study in the Behavioral Sciences at Palo Alto, California, which was supported by National Science Foundation Grant SBR-9022192. The other was an Alexander von Humboldt Forschungspreis (Research Award) that, concomitantly with a Distinguished Faculty Research Award from the University of Maryland, enabled my current stay at the University of Heidelberg in the extremely pleasant and stimulating company of Klaus Fiedler, my gracious host, and his coworkers.

Over the years, this work was facilitated by NSF Grants SBR-9417422, National Institute of Mental Health Grants RO1-MH52578, and 5R01M-H4612-02, an NIMH Research Scientist Award KO5/MH01213, and an early Deutsche Forschungs Gemeineschaft Grant (with Martin Irle) on Lay Epistemology and Social Behavior. I also thank Alison Mudditt (formerly of Psychology Press in the United States), who gently persuaded me to embark on this work, and Paul Dukes, her able successor, who patiently waited for its completion. Finally, but most importantly, my wife Hannah deserves my greatest thanks. She was unwaveringly there for better and for worse, a perfect partner in the wanderings, the intellectual journeys, and the many friendships that combined to produce this work.

I dedicate this book to the memory of Harold H. Kelley, my great mentor, role model, and friend. His creativity, insatiable curiosity about human social behavior, inspirational powers, and the supreme human values he lived by set forth an ideal for me to which I shall always aspire.

Arie W. Kruglanski
Heidelberg, Germany

ABOUT THE AUTHOR

Arie W. Kruglanski is a distinguished university professor at the University of Maryland and one of the most cited researchers in the field of social psychology. His interests have centered on the psychology of judgment and knowledge formation, as well as on the processes of group decision making, and goal formation and implementation. He has served as editor of the *Journal of Personality and Social Psychology: Attitudes and Social Cognition*, and of the *Personality and Social Psychology Bulletin*. Among other distinctions, he has received the Donald T. Campbell Award for Distinguished Scientific Contribution to Social Psychology, the Humboldt Foundation Life Achievement Award (Forschungspreis), and the National Institute of Mental Health Research Scientist Award KO5. His publications include over 180 scientific articles, chapters, and books in the field of social and personality psychology.

Mr. Kruglanski is the editor of two Psychology Press series: *Key Readings in Social Psychology* and *Principles of Social Psychology*; and a coeditor of a new series of upper-level texts called *Frontiers of Social Psychology*.

Introduction

Two quintessential features of humans as a species are our strong cognitive and social proclivities. Relative to other organisms, we seem to think a lot, and do so in concert with others of our kind. That is why *social cognition*, a discipline devoted to the crossroads of thought and social interaction processes, may afford invaluable insights into core properties of human nature.

Departing from that premise, the present volume forays into a wide range of psychological phenomena and explores them from a social-cognitive perspective. At the heart of this investigation lies the phenomenon of closed and open mindedness, of key importance to the ways in which our thoughts, often inchoate and unwieldy, congeal to form clear-cut subjective knowledge. As we shall see, an understanding of closed and open mindedness is useful not only to furthering our comprehension of how we reason and go about forming our judgments, attitudes, and opinions, but also to how we relate to and interact with fellow human beings, how we function in groups, and how we relate to groups other than our own.

As highly sentient creatures, we hardly budge without at least a degree of forethought, aimed at equipping us with a reliable knowledge base from which to launch intelligible conduct. However, objectively speaking, the cognitive activity underlying such a process has no natural or unique point of termination. It could be carried on indefinitely as we seek ever more information relevant to a given judgment or opinion. Yet our time is finite, and hence the search must be terminated at some point. On the other hand, truncating our deliberations arbitrarily, conscious of having left out considerable relevant information, wouldn't do very well either: Our judgments then might be highly uncertain and hence furnish a shaky base for actions and decisions. Yet act and decide we must, so what are we to do? It seems that Mother Nature (probably via the evolutionary process) came to our rescue with a simple solution: the capacity to occasionally shut our minds, that is, develop the sense of secure knowledge that obviates our felt need for further agonizing deliberation. Is the solution adequate? Does it always work? Does it invariably yield the intended results? The answer is a threefold no (whoever claimed that Mother Nature was a paragon of perfection?), yet our capacity for closed mindedness allows us to get on with our lives, rather than remain in an indefinite cognitive limbo, perennially buried in thought, as it were. Besides, our mental shutdown is hardly irrevocable. When its potentially adverse consequences become salient, we often seem capable of reopening the internal debate and appropriately adjusting our opinions.

Our closed mindedness potential has a plethora of significant social implications. For one, it implies that in thinking about others we may often stick to prior impressions or preconceived notions rather than flexibly altering our opinions whenever relevant new information turns up. This suggests an ingrained capacity for prejudice and stereotyping in our social judgments. Similarly, it implies the potential to jump to conclusions about others, and to form impressions based on limited and incomplete evidence.

Such closed mindedness effects are hardly limited to thinking about *others*; indeed, they encompass veritably all topics of human judgment, i.e., judgment and opinion-formation on various nonsocial issues as well (from nuclear physics to supply-side economics, foreign affairs, or marine biology, the safety of crossing the street, or the likelihood of reaching a corner ball in a tennis match). Moreover, they shape our relations with others in their role as informants or *sources* of information, as well as the *targets* of our judgments. Such informational sources are typically social, including live communicators, books, newspapers, or the media of electronic communication. The tendency to close our mind may then amount to creating a social closure, or a shared "reality" often via truncating social interactions and breaking off contacts with other people or groups, that is, by counting them out and proclaiming them as informationally irrelevant.

Alienating though such practices might appear, there seems no ready alternative way out of our epistemic cunundrum as serious consideration of everyone's opinion is clearly unfeasible. Thus, though we cannot informationally manage without inputs from *some of the people*, we also cannot manage with inputs from *all of the people*. We need to be selective about who we listen to and delineate the boundaries of our informational community. This provides a powerful (albeit not an exclusive) motivation for creating social groups, giving rise to the complex and often highly emotionally charged acts of inclusion and exclusion that setting such social fences typically entails.

In short, closed and open mindedness phenomena shed light on intricate linkages between fundamental aspects of our cognitive functioning and our social nature. My purpose in this book is to explore these linkages and investigate the fascinating cognitive/social interface they illuminate. My particular perspective on these issues is *motivational*. Specifically, this book centers on the *desire* for closed or open mindedness, how it may arise, and what cognitive and social consequences it may have. I start by outlining a theory in which the desire for closed and/or open mindedness is characterized in detail. This is followed by description of a systematic research program guided by the theory's predictions on individual, interpersonal, group, and intergroup levels of analysis. A final discussion recapitulates the major findings and highlights their implications for various human affairs.

Though in some sense closed mindedness is inevitable, this book focuses primarily on its negative consequences for a couple of reasons: One is that such negative consequences touch on some truly important failures of human judgment and social interaction. As we shall see, closed mindedness is relevant to problems of prejudice, communication, empathy, negotiation, or outgroup derrogation, among others. Understanding its role in contributing to these difficulties may constitute an important step toward approaching them constructively. Second, it is failures of various natural processes that often provide particularly poignant illustrations of their workings (Kahneman and Tversky, 1996), thus the study of negative consequences of closed mindedness could be particularly telling with regard to human epistemic processes. For the sake of balance, however, I discuss in the final chapter some of the more positive implications of closed mindedness and identify contexts where the positive or the negative consequences are more likely to appear.

☐ Summary

The phenomena of closed and open mindedness are at the heart of the interface between cognitive and social processes. Every intelligible judgment, decision, or action rests on a subjective knowledge base held with at least a minimal degree of confidence. Formation of such knowledge requires that we shut off our minds to further relevant information that we could always strive and often manage to acquire. The relation of closed mindedness processes and social cognition and behavior is two-fold. First, other people or groups of people often are the targets of our judgments, impressions, or stereotypes. Second, they are often our sources of information, and their opinions, judgments, and attitudes exert an important influence on our own. Thus, closed mindedness phenomena impact on *what* we think of others as well as *how* we think, in terms of the sources of information we take into account when forming our own opinions. The present volume highlights the motivational aspect of closed and open mindedness, discusses its antecedents and its consequences, and reports a body of empirical research exploring closed mindedness phenomena in a variety of domains.

CHAPTER

Motivational Bases of Closed and Open Mindedness

The tendency to become closed or open minded is intimately tied to one's epistemic motivations, that is, to the (implicit or explicit) goals one possesses with respect to knowledge. In a previous volume (Kruglanski, 1989) I distinguished between four types of such motivations classifiable on two orthogonal dimensions; the first, of closure seeking versus avoidance and the second, of specificity versus nonspecificity. The first distinction asks whether the individual's goal is to approach or avoid closure. The second distinction inquires whether the closure one is seeking or avoiding is of a specific kind or whether any closure or absence of closure would do. This classification yields a fourfold matrix of motivational types shown in Table 2.1: the needs for nonspecific or specific closure and the needs to avoid nonspecific or specific closure.

Two motivational continua. The four motivational types yielded by the foregoing classification can be thought of as quadrants defined by two conceptual continua. One continuum relates to the motivation toward nonspecific closure and ranges from a strong desire to possess or approach it (i.e., a strong need *for* nonspecific closure) to a strong desire to avoid it (i.e., a strong need *to avoid* nonspecific closure). The second continuum relates to the motivation toward a given or specific closure and it too ranges from a strong desire to possess it (i.e., a strong need *for* this specific closure), to a strong one to avoid it (i.e., a strong need *to avoid* this specific closure). In what follows we briefly characterize these four motivational types in turn.

TABLE 2.1. A Typology of Epistemic Motivations

		Closure Approach/Avoidance	
		Approach	Avoidance
Specificity/ Nonspecificity	Nonspecific	Need for a Nonspecific Closure	Need to Avoid a Nonspecific Closure
	Specific	Need for a Specific Closure	Need to Avoid a Specific Closure

Need for nonspecific closure. This particular need may be defined as the individual's desire for a firm answer to a question, any firm answer as compared to confusion and/or ambiguity. Consider a college admissions officer who desired to simply find out how well or poorly a given high school graduate did on her SAT exam in order to make the appropriate admission decision. Such motivation would represent a need for a nonspecific closure, because no particular content of an answer is preferred to any other. In other words, the need for a nonspecific closure is *nondirectional* or *unbiased* toward specific kinds of information. A computer user may wish to know how a particular software operates without harboring preferences for a particular mode of operation. An air traveler might wish to know the departure gate of her plane without leaning toward a specific gate, etc.

Need to avoid nonspecific closure. As its name implies, the need to avoid nonspecific closure is directly opposite to the need for nonspecific closure. The need to avoid closure pertains to situations where definite knowledge is eschewed and *judgmental noncommitment* is valued and desired. Occasionally, a lack of closure may be valued as a temporary means of keeping one's options open, and of engaging in further exploration in order to ultimately reduce the likelihood of an erroneous closure. At other times, however, the avoidance of closure may be seen as a permanently desirable state. Judgmental noncommitment may be cherished as a means of preserving one's freedoms and a romantic sense of adventure, whereas commitment may connote the doldrums of excessive predictability and a routinization of one's life.

Need for specific closure. A need for a specific closure represents a preference for a particular answer to a question characterized by some specific property (mostly its contents) that may be flattering, reassuring, or otherwise desirable. For instance, a student's mother may strongly wish to know that her child did well on the Scholastic Aptitude Test (SAT) so that she can hope to enroll her or him in a prestigious college. Such motivation represents a need for a specific closure because the mother desires a *particular* answer to her question and would not be equally happy with any answer (and in fact would be quite unhappy with some answers). Thus, by contrast to the need for nonspecific closure that is nondirectional and unbiased, the need for a specific closure represents a *directionally biased* influence on the epistemic process.

Need to avoid specific closure. Individuals may be motivated to avoid specific closures because of their undesirable (e.g., threatening) properties. The need to avoid a specific closure may occasionally represent the need *for* the opposite closure. For instance, the need to avoid a belief that one has failed an exam may be indistinguishable from one's desire to believe that one has succeeded. However, occasionally an individual may focus on the closure to be avoided without much attention to its opposite. One may wish for not losing without necessarily craving winning, or wish for not failing without necessarily dreaming of spectacular succeeding. For example, in collectivistic cultures it may be important to abide by the group norms and not fail in one's obligations to the group. On the other hand, standing out from the group by dint of markedly outperforming the other members may be frowned upon (Markus & Kitayama, 1991). In such a culture, the twin needs to avoid specific closure might develop simultaneously, that is, the need to avoid perceiving oneself as a failure, and the need to avoid perceiving oneself as a success. Tory Higgins's (e.g., 1997) work on regulatory focus draws the important distinction between *prevention* and *promotion* focus. In present terms, prevention focus might be thought of as the need to avoid the perception that one is endangered in some way, or is losing ground in some respect, hence representing the need to *avoid* a specific closure, whereas promotion focus might be thought of as the need to believe that one is attaining or has attained a given, desirable, state of affairs, hence representing the need *for* a specific closure.

☐ Antecedents of the Motivations toward Nonspecific and Specific Closure

Approach and avoidance of nonspecific closure. The assumption that an individual's motivation toward nonspecific closure lies on a continuum and hence may run an entire gamut from a strong need for closure to a strong need to avoid closure, may seem contrary to the modern era's emphasis on the values of clarity and cognitive consistency implying a pervasive human preference for "crisp" cognitive closure over wishy-washy ambiguity. This may not always have been so, however. Commenting on this very point, the sociologist Donald Levine (1985) remarked that "no one in the West before 1600 intended to cast the discussion of human affairs in the language of precise propositions. The best knowledge of human conduct, to be garnered through experience, travel, conversation, and reflection, was thought to be a kind of worldly wisdom about the varieties of character and regimes and the vicissitudes of social life" (p. 1). Furthermore, whereas the American culture is known for the premium it places on perspicuity and communicative directness, that is, on getting to the point, and saying what one means, there exist cultures that deliberately eschew excessive clarity. For example, "the Chinese language is ill-suited to making sharp distinctions and analytic abstractions; and Chinese speakers like to evoke the multiple meanings associated with concrete images. Traditional Chinese produced an ornate style that blends a complex variety of suggestive images and creates subtle nuances through historic allusions" (p. 22). Similarly, the cultivation of ambiguity characterizes the culture of traditional Java where "communication that is open and to the point comes across as rude, and ... etiquette prescribes that personal transactions be carried out by means of a long series of courtesy forms and complex indirections" (p. 23). In Somali discourse "a love for ambiguity appears particularly notable in the political sphere…" (and the Somali language) permits "words to take on novel shapes that accommodate a richness of metaphors and poetic allusions" (p. 24). Laitin (1977, p. 39) has noted in this connection that "A poetic message can be deliberately misinterpreted by the receiver, without his appearing to be stupid. Therefore, the person for whom the message was intended is never put in a position where he has to answer yes or no, or where he has to make a quick decision. He is able to go into further allegory, circling around the issue in other ways, to prevent direct confrontation…".

The foregoing sociological analyses confirm the assumption that human attitudes toward nonspecific cognitive closure indeed range from extreme laudation and idealization to explicit shunning and condemnation. I am assuming, furthermore, that the macro-level differentiation among cultures and historical periods in attitudes toward closure is paralleled by differences among persons and among psychological situations in the capacity to induce such attitudes. The latter emphasis lends the phenomena of closed and open mindedness a commonplace flavor and treats them as ubiquitous features of everyday life.

More precisely, I assume that the needs *for* nonspecific or specific closure are elevated by the perceived *benefits* of possessing such closures, and/or the *costs* of lacking them (Kruglanski & Webster, 1996; Webster & Kruglanski, 1998). Likewise, the needs to *avoid* nonspecific or specific closures are elevated by the perceived *benefits* of lacking and the *costs* of possessing such closures. Note that such a conceptualization asserts the functional equivalence of a wide variety of possible cost and benefit factors assumed to impact the needs for nonspecific and specific closure, and in so doing makes strong assumptions about a common dynamic that numerous, in some ways quite different, states, characterized by different types of costs and benefits, may share.

For instance, the present analysis is compatible with notions about the role that family dynamics (e.g., a threatening ambivalence toward one's parents [cf. Adorno, et al. 1950]), social learning processes (cf. Altemeyer, 1981; Tomkins, 1963), or a generalized susceptibility to experiencing threat or anxiety in the face of uncertainty (Wilson, 1973) may play in the development of a need for nonspecific closure, by associating closure with positive benefits as a relief from anxiety. Additionally, however, our analysis allows for a similar role to be fulfilled by a host of quite different factors as well.

For instance, a potential *benefit* of closure may be the ability to act or decide in time to meet an important deadline (comparable to Jones and Gerard's (1968) notion of "unambiguous behavioral orientation"). Accordingly, the need for closure should be heightened under time pressure. An alternative benefit of closure is that it obviates the necessity for further information processing. If so, the need for closure should be heightened under a diverse set of conditions that render information processing subjectively difficult, laborious, or otherwise unpleasant. Some such conditions (e.g., environmental noise) may reside in the external context of information processing, whereas others (e.g., tedium and dullness of the cognitive task) may relate to intrinsic aspects of processing (Kruglanski, 1975). Yet other conditions may relate to the individual's psychological and physical states. For instance, we may find information processing particularly taxing and arduous when we are fatigued or low on energy, or when alcoholic intoxication limits our capacity for systematic thought. Accordingly, need for closure should be heightened by such seemingly diverse factors as environmental noise, task dullness, fatigue, or alcohol. Need for closure should also be heightened when closure is known to be valued by significant others because the possession of closure may earn us their esteem and appreciation. For example, if being self-assured and opinionated is valued by one's parents, one may well develop a motivation to become just such a person, i.e., acquire a strong need for (a nonspecific) closure. Finally, the need for closure should be heightened, simply, when judgment on some issue was required, compared to situations where the individual was at liberty to remain without a definite opinion.

As a mirror image of the above considerations, need for nonspecific closure may be lowered, and that to avoid such closure heightened, by conditions that highlight the costs of closure and extol the benefits of *openness*. In some circumstances the costs of closure may be rendered salient by a "fear of invalidity" stemming from concern about committing a costly error of judgment. Under these conditions the person may be prone to suspend judgment altogether or avoid premature closure.

Yet validity concerns do not necessarily clash with those of closure. Obviously, no one would consciously adopt a closure that she or he adjudged invalid. In fact, the common-sense notion of knowing connotes a sense of closure coupled with subjective validity. To know that one's name is John or that it happens to be Tuesday now means to have closures on these topics *and* simultaneously believe these closures to be true. Nonetheless, psychological concerns for closure and validity often arise fairly independently of each other. What is more important, they pull information processing in diametrically opposite directions. For example, where need for closure is elevated for some reason—for example, because of situational impediments to information processing like fatigue or noise—the individual may consider limited information, and/or rely on preconceived notions, prejudices, and cultural stereotypes in reaching social judgments. To the contrary, where need for closure is reduced—for example, by felt accountability for one's decisions, or by fear of the costs of making a false move—one might consider ample information before making up one's mind. Yet in the former case, the person may not be cognizant of sacrificing validity, and in the latter case, of postponing closure. Rather in both cases she/he may feel to have processed just the right amount of information to make a reasonably secure judgment. In other words, the epistemic dynamics prompted by the needs for closure and for its avoidance are not assumed to be consciously accessible to the knower, but rather to exert their effects implicitly and outside of awareness.

It is important to realize that validity concerns may not always lower the need for closure or foster openness to new ideas or information. If a particular closure appeared valid beyond reasonable doubt, for instance because its source (one's parents, an adored guru, or the printed page) appeared of impeccable credibility or indubitable "epistemic authority" (Kruglanski, 1989; Ellis & Kruglanski, 1992), validity concerns might magnify the tendency to embrace it rather than to avoid or postpone it until having considered ample further information.

The need for nonspecific closure may be lowered, and that to avoid closure heightened, for other reasons as well. When the task is intrinsically enjoyable and interesting, for example, individuals may wish to immerse themselves in its exploration for the sheer pleasure of it, and prolong the enjoyment to the extent possible rather than undercutting it by driving for the bottom line. Who has not experienced the frustration of asking an expert (e.g., a statistical consultant) a seemingly simple question only to see him/her delve into a complicated analysis with only a minimal relation to the original query? The expert in this case may relish the process of searching for an answer much more than the answer itself, hence she/he may prolong the process to the inquirer's consternation.

The need for closure may be lowered where any conceivable closure seemed potentially difficult, problematic, or dangerous. For instance, in a conflict among friends one may be motivated to refrain from deciding who is "right," for this may risk undermining the relationship with at least one of the parties. Also, in negotiating a conflictual situation one may frame some of the more difficult issues ambiguously so that progress may be achieved, and positive momentum built, on the basis of matters that are simpler or easier to deal with. Indeed, the expression of any definite opinion or preference (e.g., on aesthetic, ethical, or political issues) might be offensive to at least some individuals. Hence, one may refrain from expressing or even forming an opinion when in the company of strangers whose tastes and preferences are unknown. One may be more likely to form opinions in the presence of intimate friends with whom one feels safe, hence free to be one's own self and to speak one's uncensored mind.

Of course, some strong-headed individuals may form clear-cut and often extreme opinions regardless of the delicacy of the situation, whereas other, particularly cautious, persons may feel uncomfortable about rendering a definite judgment and prefer to suspend it in even the safest of environments. As already noted, people may exhibit considerable individual differences in their tendencies to approach and avoid cognitive closure. To tap such individual differences, Donna Webster and I (Webster & Kruglanski, 1994) have developed the Need for Closure Scale and established its reliability and validity. The scale has been translated into several languages (Cantonese, Croate, Dutch, French, German, Hebrew, Italian, Japanese, Korean, Mandarine Chinese, and Spanish); hence, it affords the cross-cultural investigation of issues associated with closed and open mindedness.

Since its publication a decade ago, Webster and Kruglanski's (1994) scale appears to have held up well both structurally and functionally, across its various translations and the heterogeneous contexts in which it has been applied. Nonetheless, work on this scale continues in order to further improve its psychometric properties and to reduce its length so as to make its application less laborious and time consuming.

In summary, individuals' motivational attitudes toward nonspecific cognitive closure may be induced by a wide range of factors. Some of these may have to do with persons' relatively stable dispositions (Webster & Kruglanski, 1994) or with cultural norms or mores prevalent in a given society (Hofstede, 1980; Levine, 1985). Others may relate to mundane everyday circumstances (e.g., time pressure, boredom, noise, or fatigue). In this latter sense, far from being esoteric or restricted, the phenomena of closed and open mindedness form a pervasive feature of everyday life.

Approach and avoidance needs for specific closures. A plethora of diverse factors may render a given closure desirable or undesirable. Some may be situation specific, others may reflect relatively stable tendencies of the person, yet others may characterize entire societies or cultures. A situationally desirable closure may relate to the individual's needs, wishes, and desires in a particular context. A high premium one places on career advancement, for example, may render agreement with one's boss desirable; the contents of that agreement would then depend specifically on the boss's opinion on a given issue at a given time and a given place. To a (situationally) hungry individual, the belief that food is forthcoming might represent a desirable closure, and to a lonely person—that company and social support are forthcoming. Some desirable closures may derive from widespread cultural values, such as freedom, democracy, courage, family, or a slim figure. Others may originate from one's personal upbringing and socialization history, e.g., the desirability of beliefs that one is economically well off, independent, strong-willed, assertive, etc.

Similarly, one's need to avoid specific closures may stem from a variety of sources. Thus, reactance against an attempt to usurp one's freedoms (Brehm, 1966) could identify the usurper's suggestion precisely as the closure to be avoided. Antisocial thoughts, e.g., sexual or aggressive fantasies about forbidden figures such as one's parents, may also represent closures one strives to avoid or defend against.

Occasionally, different undesirable or different desirable closures may conflict with each other—e.g., the desirable beliefs that (1) one is realistic about one's limited potential and (2) one will be extremely successful in whatever task one chooses to pursue (cf. Swann, 1990). In such a case, the stronger of the two motivations will have the upper hand. For instance, research by Murray and Holmes (1997) suggests that persons with low self-esteem may wish more to avoid disappointments than to believe they are truly appreciated by someone. Such persons may distrust their dating or marital partners and doubt their love, devotion, and respect for themselves.

Individual differences in wishful thinking. Because of various temperamental or socialization factors, individuals may differ in the degree to which their judgments are impacted by approach or avoidance motivations toward specific closures. As a first step toward tapping such stable individual differences Sigall, Kruglanski, and Fyock (1999) developed a wishful thinking scale on the basis of Weinstein's (1980) study of unrealistic optimism. In his research, Weinstein asked college students to compare the likelihood that each of 42 life events (e.g., being fired from a job or gaining statewide recognition in one's profession) would happen to them as opposed to other students at the college of the same sex as the respondent. The results indicated that overall there was a very strong tendency for participants to be unrealistically optimistic. Individuals estimate that they would be more likely than others to experience positive life events, and less likely than others to experience negative life events. The wishful thinking scale (Sigall, Kruglanski, & Fyock, 1999) largely derived from Weinstein's questionnaires affords the computation of a wishful thinking score for each separate individual. The score reflects the degree to which the individual perceives the likelihood of positive events occurring for him or her as higher, and of negative events as lower, than to other similar persons (college students). As Sigall, et al. (1997) have shown, wishful thinking is not the same as optimism (e.g., Scheier & Carver, 1985). Whereas optimism represents general positivity, both with respect to oneself and with respect to others, and does not generally differentiate between gradations of outcome-positivity/negativity, wishful thinking is sensitive to such gradations; hence it differentiates between positive/negative outcomes occurring to oneself versus similar outcomes occurring to others. Research by Sigall et al. demonstrated that wishful thinking (as a dimension of individual differences) affects persons' tendencies to overestimate their academic grades in college, reduces their responsiveness to corrective feedback about their exam performance, and induces the tendency to underestimate the amount of time an unpleasant task may take, and hence to unduly procrastinate prior to getting started.

It is unclear at the present time whether the wishful thinking effects observed by Sigall et al. (in press) reflect a stronger degree of (approach or avoidance) *motivation* toward specific desirable or undesirable closures or a greater degree of cognitive *bias* at the same degree of motivation. These precise mechanisms underlying wishful thinking effects may be profitably explored in subsequent research.

☐ Consequences of Motivations toward Nonspecific and Specific Closure

Need for Nonspecific Closure: Urgency and Permanence Biases Leading to Seizing and Freezing

How might it feel to want a nonspecific closure? How might it affect the way we go about our affairs and what impact might it have on ourselves and others around us? Given that an individual's need for closure is heightened, two fundamental consequences may ensue. First, the person may experience a sense of *urgency* about reaching closure. Second, once an initial closure was formulated, the individual may adhere to it come what may and treat it as relatively *permanent*. The sense of urgency may prompt the tendency to *seize* quickly on any notion that promises closure. A person under a heightened need for closure may wish to have closure immediately. Any postponement of closure is experienced as bothersome, and the individual's overriding sense would be that he or she simply cannot wait. This may induce a kind of mental impulsivity in which one leaps to conclusions on the basis of skimpy evidence, renders judgments in terms of top-of-the-head notions, often reflecting prevalent societal stereotypes and prejudices, shoots from the hip in communicating to others rather than carefully adopting one's messages to the listeners' perspectives, and so forth.

The craving for permanence may induce the tendency to *freeze* upon an extant closure, but also to prefer a potentially lasting closure over a transient, context-specific closure. Individuals under a heightened need for closure may thus try to form an enduring, stable closure, and abhor the specter of having to part with closure. Both the sense of urgency and the quest for permanence reflect the simple notion that when the need for closure is aroused, the absence of closure is aversive. Individuals may wish to terminate this unpleasant state quickly (displaying the urgency tendency) and to keep it from recurring (displaying the permanence tendency).

Belief Crystallization and the Demarcation of Seizing from Freezing

In an important sense, the seizing and freezing tendencies represent diametrically opposed epistemic attitudes: seizing signifies an openness to novel ideas, whereas freezing denotes closed mindedness, and hence the reluctance to seriously entertain them. Indeed, the need for closure may foster each of those contradictory tendencies in different circumstances. Whether seizing or freezing will ultimately occur should depend on whether the individual possessed crystallized closure to begin with. A person who lacked closure would, under a heightened need for closure, seize upon cues that promise its attainment, whereas a person who had closure would freeze upon it.

An early study by Zajonc and Morrissette (1960) provides evidence that the degree to which beliefs are crystallized and held with certainty is inversely related to the tendency to change them in light of new information. Participants in this research estimated the number of bomb craters in aerial photographs. Change in stimulus or change in feedback (alleged judgments of experts) constituted the informational manipulations intended to induce change. It was found that persons whose judgments prior to the informational change were held with high subjective certainty changed only if their uncertainty level increased. Let us assume that high subjective certainty was partly driven by participants' need for closure (Kruglanski & Webster, 1996). Accordingly, it would appear that high need for closure participants whose beliefs became less firm for some reason were those who seized upon the new information, whereas those whose beliefs remained firm froze on those judgments and held onto them at length. Of course, Zajonc and Morrissette (1960) did not manipulate or assess either the participants' firmness of beliefs or their need for closure, and hence they could not investigate whether these two variables interacted in the predicted way to effect seizing and freezing.

Two studies by Kruglanski, Webster, and Klem (1993) attempted precisely such manipulations using a persuasion context to look at cognitive change. We formed dyads consisting of a naive participant and a confederate posing as a participant. The experimenter introduced the study as one concerned with the workings of legal juries. Each participant (and allegedly also her or his partner) were presented with the essentials of a legal case (a civil suit involving an airline company and a lumber company). For half the participants, the materials also included an alleged legal analysis allowing them to form a fairly definite opinion in favor of the defendant or the plaintiff. No legal analysis was given the remaining participants, who therefore lacked a firm informational base for their opinion.

The experimental design was a two-by-two factorial with two degrees of the need for closure orthogonally crossed with whether the participants possessed or did not receive the legal advice, and hence whether they possessed a firm opinion on the issue they were confronting. We assumed that participants who received clear-cut legal advice would form a relatively firm judgment as to the case involved, whereas those who did not would have a substantially lower confidence in their views. The need for closure in this experiment was manipulated via environmental noise: In the noise condition, participants carried out the experimental tasks in the presence of considerable noise emitted by a rickety computer printer. In the control (quiet) condition, the printer remained inactive. Based on the logic outlined earlier, we assumed that the presence of noise would make information processing more laborious and costly, and hence that it would elevate participants' need for closure.

Participants read the case materials, recorded their opinion (or hunch) concerning the appropriate verdict, and discussed the issue with a confederate who took a position opposite to the participant's. The finding supported our notion that the crystallization of beliefs determines whether need for closure would effect the seizing on early cues, or the freezing on preexisting opinions. Where the materials given our participants lacked the legal analysis, and hence a basis for a crystallized opinion, they tended to be more persuadable under noise versus no noise. That is, they tended to shift more from their prediscussion verdicts toward their partners' views, and took less time to argue the issue with her or him. To the contrary, where the participants' materials included the legal analysis, affording the formation of a fairly secure opinion, they were less persuadable or more resistant to persuasion under noise (versus no noise).

The second study conceptually replicated the first with one major variation. Rather than using noise as a situational induction of the need for closure, we assessed this need via our individual difference measure (Webster & Kruglanski, 1994). The findings again yielded the predicted interaction. In the presence of the legal opinion, high (versus low) need for closure participants argued with the confederate more and tended to be less persuaded by this individual, whereas in the absence of such opinion, they argued less and were more persuaded.

Vermeir, Van Kenhove, and Hendrickx (2002) used consumers' choice behavior to investigate the amount of information sought prior and subsequent to a crystallization point. These investigators used a simulated store environment and had their participants repeatedly choose a brand within one of two low involvement product categories (detergents and margarines). The crystallization point was operationally defined as the moment following which the participant began to use the same decision rule (e.g., on the basis of price) consistently until the last choice was made. It was found, first, that fewer low (versus high) need for closure participants ever reached the crystallization point. Furthermore, whereas the high need for closure individuals sought more product-relevant information before versus after the crystallization point, no such difference emerged for low need for closure participants.

These findings demonstrate that the road leading from need for closure to close mindedness isn't a straightforward one. In the absence of preexisting opinions, persons under a high need for closure may be quite open minded and eager to gather information and to be influenced by novel suggestions. It follows that high need for closure persons might be obedient followers in some respect: They may quickly accept a leader's commandments if these pertain to new matters or at least do not clash with their preexisting views. But high need for closure individuals can also be particularly obstinate and refractory to arguments if these are at variance with their preexisting views. We shall revisit these possibilities at a later juncture.

The need to avoid nonspecific closure. It is of interest to consider what the experience might be like at the other end of the nonspecific closure continuum denoting a high need to avoid closure. It seems plausible that persons in such a motivational state should be inclined to deeply process or seize upon any new information *if* prior evidence threatened the formation of a definite closure. Inasmuch as closure is anathema to such persons, they should welcome any relevant information implying the need to rethink, and hence reopen, their judgmental commitments. On the other hand, if prior information was internally inconsistent, ambiguous, or vague and hence impeded the formation of closure, persons with a high need to avoid nonspecific closure should be relatively unmotivated to consider further information that might alter their comfortable current state of epistemic noncommitment. In a sense then, persons with a high need to avoid nonspecific closure may be said to freeze upon their noncommitment where current information justified it, select environments where ambiguity might reign in *permanence*, and seize with *urgency* upon new relevant information if prior evidence did begin to point to a definite opinion. In other words, whereas persons with a high need *for* nonspecific closure should be open minded in the absence of a prior opinion and closed minded in its presence, persons with a high need to avoid nonspecific closure should be closed minded in the absence of an opinion and open minded in its presence, or (preemptively) in its threatened presence.

Specific closure needs. What might the consequences be for the knowledge formation process of a need to have or to avoid a specific closure? Ample evidence from the domain of motivated reasoning (for discussions see e.g., Dunning, 1999; Kruglanski, 1999; Kunda, 1990; Kunda & Sinclair, 1999) as well as from cognitive dissonance research (Aronson, 1992; Cooper & Fazio, 1984, Harmon-Jones & Mills, 1999; Steele, 1988) suggest that specific closure needs introduce bias toward conclusions congruent with such needs. That means that individuals with a specific closure needs would tend to freeze on their prior knowledge if such knowledge was congruent with their needs and, to the contrary, would be quick to unfreeze their judgments if those were incongruent with their needs. Several different processes might mediate such effects. Thus, Ditto and Lopez (1992) obtained evidence that individuals may curtail the processing of information if the information supported their preferred judgments, and to prolong information processing if the initial information was contrary to their preferred judgments. It is also possible that ambiguous information is construed in a way that reinforces the desired conclusions (Kunda, 1990). Research by Sinclair & Kunda (1996) also suggests that specific closure needs may activate from memory information likely to support individuals' preferred judgments and, to the contrary, inhibit available knowledge structures inconsistent with such judgments. In some of their studies, for example, the investigators induced in participants the motivation to disparage or to think highly of an individual by suggesting to them that this person thought of them well or poorly. To accomplish this, participants completed a (fictitious) test allegedly assessing their leadership ability. Then they were shown a video recording of either a positive or a negative evaluation of their performance given by someone characterized as a manager in training. This person was either a mainstream individual (a white man) or a member of a potentially negatively stereotyped group (in one experiment this was a white *woman*, whereas in another study it was a *black* man). The main dependent variable in these studies was the evaluation by participants of the managers in training performance.

The investigators reasoned that the stereotypes of women as well as of black people contained negative elements in the domain of performance. Female managers are sometimes stereotyped as less interpersonally competent and less meritorious at work than are male managers (Heilman, Block & Martel, 1995). Black persons, too, are often stereotyped as less intelligent than whites, and black managers are considered less competent than their white counterparts (Landau, 1995). If directional motivation to negatively evaluate someone who had thought ill of oneself induces the tendency to recruit from memory cognitions supportive of such derogation, the woman and the black assessor should be evaluated less positively than the white assessor because of the availability in memory of negative stereotypes of women and blacks that could be activated by the motivation. That is exactly what happened. The woman and the black assessor, but not the white assessor, were disparaged after providing negative feedback but not after providing positive feedback. Subsequent studies found no such tendencies among detached observers, lacking the participants directional motivation, who were exposed to the same videotape of the evaluation that the actual participants received.

These results provide compelling evidence for the activation of cognitions consistent with one's directional motivations.

A note on reality constraints. Do motivational effects on human judgment (of both the nonspecific and specific varieties) know any limits? Or can one conclude what one will regardless of circumstances? A quick reflection seems to deny that the latter is the case. After all, we often enough receive bad news that we accept as such, and we all too frequently form specific closures whose contents are opposite of desirable. Thus, we typically accept professors' decisions failing us on exams, editors' actions rejecting our articles, or study sections determinations denying funding to our grant proposals. Wish however we may, we cannot conclude that we are doing well if painfully compelling evidence is clearly to the contrary. Nor can we form nonspecific closures without some supportive evidence. That is precisely why we seize on such evidence wherever it can be found, for without it no closure could be compellingly attained. Kunda (1990) coined the term *reality constraints* to indicate the limits of motivational effects. According to this notion, motivation can bias cognition when reality is ambiguous or "elastic" (Hsee, 1995) but not when it is obvious and clear cut.

However appealing they may seem at first blush, the reality constraints or elasticity ideas are difficult to reconcile with cases where (what to some might appear) thoroughly obvious realities are substantially bent in the service of motivational interests. The grief and bereavement literature, for example, tells us about persons who stubbornly deny the death of their dear ones (Stroebe & Stroebe, 1987). Similarly, some terminally ill patients are known to "cling to straws" by denying the seemingly incontrovertible evidence as to the inevitability of their own demise, and the inhabitants of areas prone to earthquakes and other natural disasters often display a cheerful "all is well" attitude that puzzles outside observers. Are these cases special exceptions that prove the rule of reality constraints? Yes and no. Yes, they are special for other people in the same circumstances might have accepted the reality of the terrifying news. But no, there is an alternative to concluding that those latter persons were unaffected by motivation because of reality constraints. Rather, they may have been impacted by a different type of motivation (e.g., a strong accuracy motivation that may have overridden their desire to deny the bad news or sweep it under the rug; Kruglanski, 1989b). What this boils down to is a kind of motivational contest; whatever motivation prevails will bias the judgmental conclusion in a motivationally congruent way. Persons whose directional motivation is more powerful than their accuracy or closure motivation will distort realities that to the rest of us might appear incontrovertible simply because our accuracy motivation may happen to be stronger than their accuracy motivation or because our directional motivation may be weaker than their directional motivation. If this view is correct, whether a given directional motivation will exert a judgmental bias and how extensive it will be (e.g., whether it will override the reality constraints) may depend on the relative strengths of one's directional and nondirectional motivations rather than on a confrontation between motivated cognition and reality.

This does not mean that informational clarity and ambiguity do not matter, but informational clarity or ambiguity themselves are in the eye of the beholder rather than representing objective features of the external stimulus. What may be eminently clear to one person may be ambiguous to another person, and these differences, too, may be dependent on motivation. An individual may find a given bit of information ambiguous because it is incongruous with that person's preferred closure. Such person may expend efforts to generate alternatives to a given interpretation of the information given, so as to ultimately dilute its impact and end up being unsure about the information's meaning. In short, motivational effects not only affect the interpretation of ambiguous information, but also determine whether given information is perceived as ambiguous, thus insinuating themselves at various levels of information processing phenomena.

☐ Summary

The tendency to become closed or open minded is intimately tied to one's epistemic motivations. These are classified as lying on two orthogonal continua: (1) of seeking versus avoiding closure, and (2) of the sought or avoided closure being nonspecific or specific. This twofold classification yields four distinct motivational types: (1) need for nonspecific closure, (2) need to avoid nonspecific closure, (3) need for specific closure, and (4) need to avoid specific closure. I assume that each of those needs is determined by the perceived benefits of attaining its desired end state, and the costs of failing to attain it. Because such benefits and costs are likely to vary widely across persons, situations, or cultures, the epistemic motivations for (or for the avoidance of) nonspecific and specific closures may have a plethora of determinants. The general consequences of epistemic motivations may be understood in terms of the induced tendencies toward seizing and freezing, that is, of intense and extensive information processing aimed at attaining the desired epistemic end state (of forming or dissolving nonspecific or specific closure), and of reluctance to continue information processing once such state is attained.

Specific Manifestations of Closure Needs in Information Processing Activites

How do the various epistemic motivations impact the way individuals approach information on their way to judgment? The discussion in the previous chapter suggests that two separate phases may be distinguished in this regard, those of knowledge-formation and of knowledge-maintenance. During the first phase there could be different degrees of seizing on judgmentally relevant information, and during the second phase, different degrees of freezing, both varying across persons and situations. The present chapter, therefore, addresses the specific ways in which the needs for (and for the avoidance of) nonspecific and specific closures may manifest themselves in information-processing activities aimed at the formation of judgments on various topics.

☐ Knowledge Formation: Need for Closure Effects

1. *Extent of Information Processing.* Because of the proclivity to seize and freeze on early notions, persons under a heightened need for closure may

process information less extensively and carefully and generate fewer competing hypotheses to account for the data they have available. Despite this curtailment in information processing, or perhaps *because* of it, persons under a heightened need for closure may feel particularly assured of their judgments, even though objectively these may have been based on a rather superficial exploration. Such a paradoxical sense of confidence may stem from the tendency of high-need-for-closure individuals to refrain from generating competing alternative interpretations of known facts, and to regard their own perspective as the sole valid one under the circumstances.

Individuals under high need to avoid closure, to the contrary, may process information extensively and consider numerous alternative possibilities to any given hypothesis. Thus, the higher the individual's need for closure, the briefer the extent of information processing in which they would engage. As a mirror image, the higher the individual's need to avoid closure, the stronger would be their tendency to process information extensively.

Whether persons with high (versus low) needs for specific closure would engage in extensive information processing should depend on the conclusions yielded by their initial information processing. Individuals whose initial information processing yielded a desirable conclusion would probably stop their information processing right there and then, generally speaking, whereas ones whose initial information processing yielded an undesirable conclusion would probably be inclined toward a more extensive informational probing (Ditto & Lopez, 1992). Individuals with a high need to avoid a specific closure would probably refrain from extensive information processing if they lacked closure on the critical topic, or if they held closure other than the one they were attempting to avoid. To the contrary, individuals with a high need to avoid a specific closure may process information quite energetically and extensively if the early information threatened to indicate just the closure they were most inclined to avoid.

2. *Cue utilization.* If individuals under heightened need for nonspecific closure seize and freeze on whatever first pops into their mind (assuming it is perceived as relevant to the judgmental topic), their judgments should be driven predominantly by early informational cues and less by later information. For example, they should be quicker to form impressions of persons on the basis of initial encounters, and be rather reluctant to alter their views even if subsequent interactions suggest they should: if those initial encounters be positive, so should the perceiver's overall impressions, even if further data brought to light more negative aspects of the target's personality. Similarly, should those initial encounters be negative, so should be the overall impression, with little that the

perceived target could subsequently do to redeem his or her tarnished image. In other words, a person under a heightened need for nonspecific closure should be particularly prone to exhibit the classic judgmental bias known as the "primacy effect" (Asch, 1946).

A person under heightened need for closure may fall prey to another, albeit a conceptually related, source of judgmental bias. Whereas the notion of primacy effects applies when the information is presented sequentially to the perceiver, often the entirety of the information may be available concomitantly in a given setting with some of it being more salient or more accessible than the rest of it. In such circumstances, the salient or accessible information may play a dominant role in driving the perceiver's judgments, whereas the less salient or accessible information, consideration of which requires a bit of digging or conceptual effort, may fail to be taken sufficiently into account. For instance, individuals under high need for closure may assume that anything a target person says or does authentically reflects what he or she thinks or feels because such a hypothesis may come to mind initially, failing to consider that this person's statements may simply reflect situational norms (e.g., of politeness) or situational constraints (e.g., the boss's presence). In other words, an individual under a heightened need for closure may be particularly prone to exhibit what social psychologists have called the "fundamental attribution error" (Ross, 1977): ascribing the actor's behaviors to her/his personality or attitudes and underestimating the power of the situation to elicit such behaviors from most people regardless of their unique proclivities, personalities, or attitudes.

In making numerical judgments, the high-need-for-closure individual may be overly influenced by initial figures and fail to conduct the necessary calculations to arrive at more exact estimates. In a technical language, the high-need-for-closure individual may be particularly likely to "anchor" on early estimates and fail to adequately adjust his or her judgments (Tversky & Kahneman, 1974) in the light of further evidence. A person with a high need for closure may be more likely to rely on his or her stereotypes and prejudices rather than on available individuating information. That is because such stereotypes may constitute "top of the head" notions, i.e., they may represent highly accessible concepts (that one could seize and freeze upon), whereas detailed consideration of case-specific information may require laborious data gathering and mental effort.

Whereas stereotypes and prejudices may be chronically accessible (Higgins, King, & Mavin, 1982), that is, constitute categories that often come to mind, some ideas may be activated momentarily in given situations. Reading a newspaper article about automobiles, say, may activate thoughts about one's own car and the need to replace it. A glance at one's desk may activate ideas about one's daily tasks, and a visit with a sick friend may increase the accessibility of one's own health concerns. The present theory suggests that such momentarily accessible ideas would also tend to be embraced and relied upon more by individuals under high (versus low) need for closure. Because critically confronting them with alternative possibilities may prolong ambiguity and delay closure, accessible constructs may exert a particularly dominant influence on judgments of high-need-for-closure individuals.

The seizing and freezing tendencies of high-need-for-closure individuals may go well beyond cognitive events occurring in persons' heads, and importantly imbue these individuals' interpersonal relations and social attitudes. Consider decision-making procedures in a group setting. Because they desire to have closure quickly, high-need-for-closure individuals may prefer authoritarian over democratic decision-making processes in groups of which they are members: In an authoritarian structure, it is the leader's decision that matters. This promises a briefer, simpler deliberation stage than in a democratic structure where, ideally at least, each member's opinion is discussed and seriously considered. Thus, high-need-for-closure individuals may treat their superiors very differently than their underlings. They may show considerable deference to those higher up in the social or organizational hierarchy and be rather dismissive and impatient to those lower down on the organizational totem pole. Moreover, in the absence of a clear hierarchy to begin with, high-need-for-closure individuals may be quick to generate one on their own. They may vie for leadership positions where their expertise and knowledge appear to warrant it, yet be quite ready to follow the lead of others where insecure about their competence in a domain.

The proclivity to seize and freeze on early notions is relevant to such fundamentally social phenomena as empathy and communication. Both phenomena hinge on one's ability to put oneself in another's shoes, that is, view the situation from the perspective of another. This ability actually forms the basis for one's capacity to emotionally identify with others, to experience the approximate feelings she or he experiences, and to appreciate the reasons for such feelings. Similarly, in interpersonal communication it is essential to tailor one's messages to the assumptions and understandings of one's interlocutors, or else the communication may fail and one's messages may fail to register with one's audience. The reason that the need for closure may obstruct these processes is that the early notions that pop into mind are likely to emanate from the individual's own perspective, often quite distinct from that of his or her listeners. Under high need for closure, individuals may adhere to those early ideas, i.e., seize and freeze upon them—rather than adjusting their perspective by taking into account the unique vantage point of the other, quite possibly distinct from one's own. Thus, persons under heightened need for nonspecific closure may be both less empathetic to others dissimilar from themselves and less capable of effectively communicating with such persons.

☐ Need to Avoid Closure Effects

As already noted, persons with a high need *to avoid* nonspecific closure may exhibit information-processing biases opposite in direction to individuals with a high need *for* such closure. In other words, the higher their need to avoid nonspecific closure, the lesser should be the individual's tendency to seize on initial cues and to base their judgments on them. On tasks where some kind of judgment is ultimately required, individuals with a high need to avoid closure are likely to postpone the inevitable and engage in extensive information processing to forestall judgmental commitment for as long as possible. Accordingly, they may be relatively unaffected by early cues and be unlikely to succumb to primacy effects in impression formation. Similarly, they may be less likely than their high-need-for-closure counterparts to assimilate judgments to accessible constructs (e.g., to widespread stereotypes), to anchor numerical judgments on initial estimates, and/or commit the fundamental attribution error by assuming that an actor's deeds or pronouncements necessarily reflect that person's authentic attitudes or dispositional tendencies.

Based on the same logic, persons with a high need to avoid nonspecific closure should prefer democratic over autocratic leadership and decision-making styles, and be less deferent to their superiors and less dismissive of those perceived as on a lower rung of the social ladder. Finally, individuals with a high need to avoid closure should be more capable of empathy and be better at communicative skills, all else being constant, than their high-need-for-closure counterparts.

☐ Specific Closure Effects

The knowledge formation process of individuals with a high need for a specific closure or for the avoidance of specific closure should considerably depend on what initial information may have reached them and whether it was congruent or incongruent with the desired or avoided closure. If the initial information was congruent with a desirable conclusion or constituted other than an undesirable conclusion, an individual high (versus low) on the need for (or for the avoidance of) that particular conclusion should cease information processing relatively soon. To the contrary, if the initial information was incongruous with a desirable conclusion or represented just the conclusion one would rather avoid, this would motivate a relatively extensive information-processing effort (Ditto & Lopez, 1992).

In other words, individuals with a high need for a specific closure or with a high need to avoid a specific closure would tend to base their judgments on early cues. They should exhibit primacy effects in impression formation (Asch, 1946), tend to engage in stereotyping, manifest dispositional attribution biases or fundamental attribution errors, etc. By the same token, individuals with high (versus low) such needs should be less prone to primacy effects, stereotyping, or dispositional biases if the contents of conclusions yielded by such processes were incongruent with their desired conclusions or represented conclusions they wished to avoid.

Furthermore, individuals with specific closure needs should be empathetic with regard to individuals who supported their desired conclusions or avoided their undesired judgments, and lack in empathy toward individuals holding views contrary to the ones they wished to form or views representing conclusions they wanted to avoid. They should also support autocratic leaders or majorities whose views match their own, and be in favor of democracy, instead, if the leaders' or the majority's opinions ran counter to their preferred conclusions.

☐ Knowledge Maintenance Processes: Need for Nonspecific Closure Effects

1. *Consensus Strivings.* Persons under a heightened need for a nonspecific closure may not only be quick to form their opinions, but may also be loathe to part with them because this would bring about renewed ambiguity. In anticipation of possible future challenges to their opinions, persons under heightened need for closure may be biased in favor of judgments that promise a priori to minimize them. Thus, they may seek out consensual opinions unlikely to elicit disagreement from significant members of their social group, and/or may be attracted to interaction partners unlikely to disagree with their views, for instance, individuals known to share their own attitudes and opinions or ones known to be "yeah sayers" unlikely to articulate dissent. Of course one may not realistically expect to agree with all of the people all of the time. That may be one of the reasons why people draw distinctions between members of the in-group, whose judgments matter subjectively and "deserve" to be

taken into account, and members of various out-groups whose judgments and opinions are neglected for all intents and purposes and treated as irrelevant to one's own views. Because high-need-for-closure individuals are particularly bent on attaining consensus, they may be particularly attuned to the in-group versus out-group status of given individuals. They may be particularly warm and positive toward the in-group members, insofar as they depend on them for consensus, and they may sharply demarcate them from out-group members irrelevant to their closure concerns.

2. *Linguistic abstraction.* Whereas consensus may refer to stability across persons (Kelley, 1967), persons under a heightened need for closure may also desire stability across situations. In other words, they may crave global knowledge that holds across many different contexts and prefer it over specific, situationally circumscribed knowledge (Swann, 1984). An unobvious implication of such tendency toward globalization may express itself in the use of language. Specifically, a person under heightened need for closure may prefer general trait labels in describing another individual (e.g., that she is intelligent, friendly, or assertive) rather than depicting more concretely how she or he acted in a particular context (e.g., that she did well on an exam, lent one a helpful hand in cleaning a friend's flat, or returned a bottle of corked wine at a restaurant).

Particularly interesting is the possibility that abstract language may have unforeseen interpersonal consequences. Abstract depictions of another individual may promote a sense of deindividuation in regard to that person in that they tend to place him or her in broad, impersonal categories that neglect this individual's unique properties. Such use of abstraction, furthermore, may elicit reciprocal abstraction by establishing a conversational norm as to the appropriate level of pitching the dialogue. The end result might be a formal, impersonal discourse promoting a sense of estrangement and alienation.

3. *Conservatism.* Finally, but not least important, the quest for permanence and the tendency to freeze on extant knowledge may induce a general resistance to change among high-need-for-closure individuals and the tendency to perpetuate the status quo whatever it might be (Jost, Glaser, Kruglanski, & Sulloway, 2003a, b). Does that mean we are likely to find a greater preponderance of political conservatives among high- (versus low-) need-for-closure individuals? Not necessarily, because for a person living in a liberal regime, the status quo may in fact mean liberalism. Nonetheless, all else being equal, the *contents* of conservative ideologies may be intrinsically more appealing to high-need-for-closure individuals than the contents of liberal ideologies because conservative ideologies explicitly applaud the values of tradition and are reticent

toward change. By contrast, in its fundamental commitment to freedom, liberalism supports the potentiality for change, openness, and the belief in progress (and hence, inevitably, change). All else being equal then, the contents of the conservative rather than the liberal ideology should be relatively more appealing to individuals under a heightened need for closure.

☐ Effects of the Need to Avoid Nonspecific Closure

Persons with a high need to avoid closure should be more likely to deviate from the group consensus or to support a breech of consensus by other group members. They may do so because consensus defines a firm social reality for group members, justifying definite opinions that individuals with a high need to avoid closure are trying to eschew. To avoid stable epistemic commitments that hold over numerous situations, individuals with a high need to avoid closure should be disinclined to think in terms of broad generalizations or to employ abstract linguistic categories with transcendental implications. As a further consequence, individuals with a high need to avoid closure may be less likely to exhibit in-group favoritism and out-group derogation to the extent that these stem, at least in part, from social reality concerns (Shah, Kruglanski, & Thompson, 1998; Kruglanski, Shah, Pierro, & Mannetti, 2002). Also, because of their relative lack of enthusiasm for group consensus, individuals with a high need to avoid nonspecific closure are likely to prefer democratic to autocratic decision-making structures because the former allow a plurality of voices to be heard.

☐ Specific Closure Needs

Just as with the need for an nonspecific closure, that for a specific closure should also give rise to freezing tendencies on various cognitions. But there is an important difference: Whereas nonspecific closure concerns may prompt unselective freezing on *any* definite knowledge that happened to form, that for a specific closure should be highly selective in this regard. It may promote a freezing only if the early notions were motivationally desirable. Should they be undesirable, however, high need for a specific closure should work in the opposite direction, working against freezing. In other words, the need for specific closure may promote closed *or* open mindedness *contingently* rather than *generally*, giving rise to one or the other depending on the circumstances. Imagine a situation wherein one's desired closure was the belief in a clean bill of health at one's annual check up. Such pleasing news may be frozen upon, rendering one rather inattentive to subsequent information that might qualify somewhat the positive initial diagnosis (e.g., that one's cholesterol level is within the normal range, but that one should watch one's diet and exercise more because of other risk factors present in one's profile). By contrast, an individual facing a negative initial bit of information may become particularly attentive, and open minded to subsequent information hoping that it will assuage the initial impact of the bad news.

Needs for specific closure may significantly imbue one's relations with other individuals. To the extent that a given closure was desirable to a person, he/she may well freeze upon it, believe it firmly, and strive to uphold it. This might promote a highly favorable attitude toward similarly minded others and a negative attitude toward dissimilarly minded ones whose views threaten to undermine the individual's cherished opinions.

Whereas the need for a nonspecific closure may invariably induce the striving for epistemic permanence, needs for specific closure may do so *contingently*, as a function of the type of closure being formed. If such a closure was desirable (e.g., if it appeared that one succeeded in a task), one would be likely to cast it in relatively permanent terms, e.g., attribute it to such global and general constructs as one's ability. If the evidence seemed to favor a negative judgment however, (i.e., if it appeared that one has done poorly) one might prefer instead a transient, situationally specific, closure, e.g., that one's performance outcome was low because of some transient state (of fatigue, illness, or negative mood) or a situational factor (noise, poor visibility, a biased referee). Such contingent tendencies may express themselves in the language whereby one describes desirable versus undesirable events, where the former would be expressed more abstractly than the latter.

Similar considerations apply to conditions under which a need for specific closure would promote a desire for consensus in a group versus favoring a plurality of opinions. This too should depend on the desirability of the emerging consensus. Should such consensus be congruent with one's goals (e.g., if everyone in the group seemed to accept one's favorite proposals), consensus per se should be appealing and evoke positive thoughts about togetherness (e.g., "we must act as a unit," "our decisions should be unanimous"). However, should the emerging consensus run counter to one's opinions (e.g., the rival recommendations were gaining the upper hand) one might feel rather negatively about it, seeing it, for example, as a sign of herd-like conformity, or obsequious political correctness. In such circumstances one might feel more enthusiastic about a pluralism of viewpoints and intellectual independence.

Individuals high on the need to *avoid* a specific closure may experience the impulse to freeze on extant opinions if they do not represent the dreaded closure. However, if the extant opinion did constitute, in fact, such reprehensible closure or if the extant information did seem to warrant it, the individual may seek to undermine such an opinion or unfreeze it by urgently seizing upon information inconsistent with it, whatever else such information might imply.

In group contexts, individuals under high (versus low) need to avoid a given closure should support the consensual opinion if it is innocuous or nonthreatening. However, if it is in fact threatening, they should be supportive of deviancy and dissent. As to the tendency toward generality and abstraction (reflecting the permanence bias), it should be manifested by individuals high on the need to avoid a specific closure to the extent that their current opinion was nonthreatening, whereas if it was threatening or otherwise undesirable, individuals high on the need to avoid closure should manifest the tendency toward concretization instead.

☐ Summary

Human cognitive functioning includes the capacity to shut off our minds and avoid the processing of new information potentially relevant to our judgments in a way that requires their rethinking and possible alteration. Such shutting of the mind fulfills an essential function without which knowledge formation and intelligent decision making would be virtually impossible. Whether one's mind will remain open or closed in given circumstances should depend on two types of epistemic motivations having to do with (1) nonspecific and (2) specific, cognitive closure. With regard to either, there exists a continuum of motivational attitudes ranging from a strong approach motivation represented by the need *for* nonspecific or specific closures, all the way to strong avoidance motivations represented by the needs *to avoid* nonspecific or specific closures.

The present theory assumes that the epistemic motivations toward nonspecific and specific closure can result from a wide variety of factors that are, therefore, *functionally equivalent* and should give rise to similar, motivationally based effects. It is assumed that all epistemic motivations (whether specific or nonspecific and whether of the approach or avoidance type) can originate in a plethora of circumstances that render a given closure subjectively beneficial or costly to the individual. Such factors may relate to the particular situational context in which the person finds her/himself, socialization environments that imprint relatively lasting tendencies on her/his personality, and broad cultural contexts that imbue entire collectives of people with specific, stable, inclinations. The present theory assumes that irrespective of its specific origins, once a given epistemic motivation is in place, its consequences (experiential, cognitive, or social) will be identical. In general, such consequences have to do with the degree of readiness to alter one's current epistemic states (of either the presence or the absence of cognitive closure) by the processing of new information, i.e., seizing, or the reluctance to do so, i.e., freezing.

Such seizing and freezing tendencies may give rise to a variety of effects on different levels of social psychological analysis: (1) on the intrapersonal level having to do with individuals' judgments, (2) on the interpersonal level affecting one's rapport with others (e.g., as regards empathy or communicative efficacy), (3) on the group level (e.g., via consensus seeking or predilections toward autocratic versus democratic decision making structures) and (4) on the intergroup level (e.g., as reflected in ingroup favoritism and out-group derrogation). Research relevant to these consequences is considered in subsequent chapters. First, however, let us see how closed and open mindedness phenomena were addressed in prior psychological analyses.

Prior Psychological Analyses of Closed and Open Mindedness

A major thesis of this volume is that issues of closed and open mindedness are fundamentally important to cognitive and social processes related to knowledge formation. If so, one might surmise that prior psychological theorists of various kinds would have addressed them to some considerable degree. Is that actually the case? The answer appears to be yes and no. Whereas prior theorists did indeed touch upon these matters, their conceptual framing of the issue of closed and open mindedness was typically very different from the present framing, as were the suggested theoretical underpinnings of the relevant phenomena, their presumed antecedent conditions, and their hypothesized consequences. Nonetheless, it is of interest to review such past work in light of the present perspective. The purpose of this chapter is to carry out an admittedly cursory review of prior relevant treatments starting with the seminal work of Jean Piaget.

☐ Piaget

Piaget's concepts of assimilation and accommodation echo, in some sense, the notions of closed and open mindedness. From this perspective, assimilation represents closed mindedness as it entails glossing over the unique aspects of an informational stimulus, and locating it within a preexisting intellectual frame or cognitive class (as in "X is a dog," i.e., member of the "dog" category). Accommodation, correspondingly, represents openness and sensitivity to the unique features of the new information (as in noticing what kind of dog X is, its color, shape, gender, or breed).

Flavell (1963) put it as follows: "Assimilation ... refers to the fact that every cognitive encounter with an environmental object necessarily involves some kind of cognitive structuring of that object in accord with the nature of the organism's existing intellectual organization. To adapt intellectually to reality is to construe that reality, in terms of some enduring construct within oneself ... The essence of accommodation is ... a process of adapting oneself to the variegated requirements or demands which the world of objects imposes upon one" (p. 48).

Piaget does not address circumstances or variables that affect the relative strength of assimilation or accommodation processes. Rather, in his framework "they (are) simultaneous and indissociable as they operate in living cognition. Adaptation is a unitary event, and assimilation and accommodation are merely abstractions from this unitary reality..." (Flavell, 1963).

For Piaget, smooth joint functioning of assimilation and accommodation represents how a cognitive ensemble containing closed systems of activity is nonetheless open to, and interactive with, the environment. Such conception of normal functioning depicts cognitive stability, and has relatively little to say about the possibility of a genuine cognitive change or alteration of prior schemas under the impact of new information. By contrast, in the present theoretical framework, stability is coordinated to closed mindedness and change to open mindedness.

A different Piagetian sense of closed and open mindedness, expressly referring to cognitive change, is that of equilibration (Piaget, 1975/1985). According to this concept, a schema is assumed to endure "to the extent that assimilation and accommodation are in equilibrium, that is—to the extent that the modifications introduced into the scheme through accommodation are effected without loss of continuity in functioning" (Chapman, 1988, p. 291). The possibility of change derives from disequilibria that occasionally arise and stimulate cognitive activity aimed at reequilibration. Such disequilibria reside in contradictions that the cognitive system may encounter, and that produce perturbations within it. Piaget attached considerable importance to these disequilibria noting that "one of the sources of progress in the development of knowledge must be sought in disequilibria as such ... (because) disequilibria alone force the subject to go beyond his current state and strike out in new directions" (p. 10).

Piaget identified three distinct ways in which an organism may react to perturbatory inconsistencies. In alpha reactions, the most primordial of the lot, perturbations are simply ignored or removed. Beta reactions are somewhat more refined entailing, as they do, a differentiation into subtypes, one of which continues to display the property originally assumed to characterize the class as a whole, and another now assumed to display the opposite property. Finally, gamma reactions represent the most complete and thoroughgoing reactions involving as they do "the anticipation off possible perturbations. Insofar as these possible variations are fully integrated into the system, they lose their character of perturbations and simply become potential transformations of the system" (Chapman, 1988, p. 297). According to Piaget, the progression from alpha to gamma reactions does not necessarily track the stages of cognitive development, and can take place at different developmental levels, from the sensorimotor to the operational stage.

☐ Cognitive Consistency Theories

Piaget's notions of equilibration, perturbation, and reequilibration are strongly reminiscent of the cognitive consistency theories in social psychology. In that work, too, a state of cognitive imbalance (Heider, 1958), incongruency (Osgood & Tannenbaum, 1958, or dissonance (Festinger, 1957), (among other similar notions) closely akin to Piagetian disequilibrium, is assumed to arouse a motivation (or need) aimed at the restoration of equilibrium (balance, congruity, or consonance). The cognitive consistency theorists typically assumed that the drive toward consistency is universal and that it is aroused by the appearance of a cognitive inconsistency (i.e., a salient logical contradiction among an individual's conscious beliefs; cf., Kruglanski & Klar, 1987; Kruglanski, 1989, pp. 86–100). In Festinger's (1957) formulation, moreover, the magnitude of the motivational arousal due to an inconsistency is partially determined by the importance to the individual of the clashing cognitions, even though the importance concept was never precisely defined in Festinger's formulation.

The modes of inconsistency reduction discussed by the cognitive consistency theorists also bear a strong resemblance to Piaget's notions. Thus, Abelson (1959, 1968) proposed that inconsistency may be resolved via several different modes including denial, bolstering, differentiation, transcendence, and rationalization, wherein denial strongly resembles Piaget's alpha reaction, differentiation the beta reaction, and transcendence the integrative solution of Piaget's gamma reaction.

☐ The Motive to Resolve Uncertainty

Kagan's (1972) analysis of the motive to resolve uncertainty is explicitly tied to notions of cognitive consistency, such as balance, equilibrium, or dissonance (p. 57). However, whereas the cognitive consistency theorists did not elaborate extensively on why inconsistency is aversive, other than invoking the need or drive toward consistency, Kagan made an important step in relating inconsistency to uncertainty-arousal, the resolution of which he viewed as a primary motive or the "wish to know" (p. 54). As he put it: "uncertainty leads to a primary motive to resolve it, and if no appropriate responses are available, distress, anxiety, fear, shame or guilt may occur" (p. 54). In fact, Kagan went so far as to assert that, "most of the popular motives normally ascribed to children and adults by novelists or psychologists in Western culture, such as achievement, affiliation, power, dependency, nurturance, or succorance, can be derivatives of a primary motive to resolve uncertainty and alleviate subsequent affective distress"(p. 54).

In his emphasis on uncertainty resolution, Kagan fundamentally anticipated the present epistemic approach to closed mindedness. In particular, our key construct of the need for nonspecific closure denotes a desire for firm knowledge, highly akin to Kagan's (p. 54) concept of the "wish to know." Those important similarities notwithstanding, unlike the present theory, Kagan's and Piaget's analyses, as well as the cognitive consistency theories imply that a state of openness (1) is forced or imposed upon the individual by discovery of an inconsistency among her or his cognitions, (2) is psychologically aversive, particularly where the cognitions are important to the individual (Festinger, 1957), and (3) leads to a motivational need state aimed at reducing the unpleasant inconsistency (i.e., by restoring consonance, balance, or equilibrium) and resolving the uncertainty.

In contrast, the present analysis suggests that a motivation for (a nonspecific or specific) cognitive closure may often antedate (rather than follow) the discovery of an inconsistency. For example, according to the present theory, the desire to have closure may be prompted by the need to make an important decision or undertake an action. The desire for closure may also be fostered by various contextual conditions or momentary states, such as the state of fatigue or conditions of time pressure or noise. All of these may precede the receipt of any information on a topic, including the receipt of any inconsistent information. Similarly, the desire to believe that some impatiently awaited news (about the result of one's annual check-up, a panel's decision on one's grant, or a marriage proposal) will be desirable or congruent with one's wishes, representing a need for a specific (desirable) closure, requires no prior cognitive inconsistency for it to exist and be strongly felt.

Finally, unlike Kagan, Piaget, and the cognitive consistency theorists, the present analysis does not assume that states of open mindedness, the absence of a cognitive commitment, or inconsistency are invariably unpleasant or aversive. In fact, it envisages circumstances where such states might be strongly desired and strived for. The present concept of the need to avoid nonspecific closure represents a state in which judgmental noncommitment, continued uncertainty, and ambiguity, far from being unpleasant and threatening, may feel rather appealing and comfortable to an individual and represent the person's preferred epistemic end state.

☐ Seeking and Rejecting Information

Seeking information. The notions that humans pervasively experience the wish to know, and hence generally crave cognitive closure, has been embraced by other theoretical conceptions in social psychology of more recent vintage than the cognitive consistency theories. Though quite different in focus, these formulations continued to subscribe to the notion that persons generally crave stable and coherent knowledge and do not put their mind to rest until they possessed it.

This view seems common to social psychological formulations addressing such seemingly opposite phenomena as the quest for, versus the rejection of, information. Festinger's (1954) theory of social comparison processes, for example, stresses the quest for, or openness to, certain kinds of information (cf. Sorrentino & Roney, 1999). Festinger postulated a drive to assess our abilities and opinions prompting the comparison with (similar) persons capable of affording the requisite assessment. Trope (1975, 1986), similarly, emphasized people's desire for self-assessment that assists them in making the right choices, and hence ultimately mediating positive outcomes leading to self-enhancement: The self-assessment need prompts the search for diagnostic or veridical information; even if in the short run it may represent bad news (e.g., by revealing one's low ability in some domain), it may afford the opportunity to correct one's mistakes thus improving one's likelihood of attaining the desired objectives.

It is of course likely that both the need of self-assessment and that of self-enhancement would vary widely across situations and persons. For some people, or for most people in some situations, the truth about oneself may represent the overriding concern regardless of its consequences.

For other people, and/or for most people in some situations, judgmental consequences (e.g., their implications for one's self-esteem) may loom more importantly than the truth (albeit not necessarily at a conscious level). If so, the question as to which motive is the prepotent one (i.e., the self-assessment or the self-enhancement motive), may not have a general answer. Rather it may all depend on the person and/or on the situation.

The contextual dependency of various motivations for information processing (e.g., the need for accurate assessment) is highlighted in recent theories of persuasion and attitude change (Chaiken, Liberman, & Eagly, 1989; Petty & Cacioppo, 1986; Kruglanski & Thompson, 1999 a, b). These formulations typically assume that in situations characterized by the recipients' high personal involvement in an issue, that is, where holding the correct attitude or opinion matters to the recipients, they will be strongly motivated to safeguard the accuracy of their attitudinal judgment, which in turn may prompt a relatively thorough and meticulous information-processing activity. By contrast, in situations characterized by low personal involvement, the motivation for accuracy would be lower, with corresponding reduction in the extent of informational search and elaboration.

Rejection of information. Some social psychological theories have stressed peoples' avoidance of specific types of information. Swann's (1990) self-verification theory, for example, highlights people's avoidance of self-disconfirming information or information inconsistent with one's view of oneself. According to Swann, stability of self-conception is needed for the maintenance of subjective assurance essential for everyday living. In support of this theory, Swann and his colleagues have demonstrated that even when peoples' self-conceptions are negative, they often avoid information that contradicts them (e.g., Swann & Pelham, 1988; Swann, Wenzlaff, Krull, & Pelham, 1992).

Note that even though Swann's theory stresses the avoidance of (self-disconfirming) information, whereas the self-assessment notions of Festinger (1954) or Trope (1975) stress the quest for, or approach to, information, all three conceptions assume individuals' general desire for secure knowledge (i.e., closure) on some topics. To the extent that such closure was absent—attempts to form it were assumed to prompt an informational quest, whereas if it was present already, attempts to maintain it were assumed to prompt the avoidance of potentially undermining information threatening to usher in uncertainty and ambiguity. By contrast, the present approach assumes that the need for closure can vary, and that rather than universally wishing to attain or maintain closure, in some situations people would be motivated to actively eschew it as noted earlier.

☐ Notions of Closed and Open Mindedness in Freud's Theorizing

The structural analysis of the psyche. Though Sigmund Freud was not directly concerned with issues of closed and open mindedness, his work alluded to these and related matters in several ways. First, his structural division of the psyche into the id, the ego, and the superego represents a psychological framework that constrains the ways in which information enters consciousness. Information incompatible with societal values (located in the superego), e.g., about hostile or sexual feelings toward one's parents (located in the id), will be repressed and kept outside the gates of our conscious mind. In a different way, our wishes and fantasies originating in id-based impulses are prevented from ensconcing us in a cocoon of dreamlike irrealities by forces of the ego that keep our mental gates open to society and the world. In this sense then, the ego is related to open mindedness, whereas the id and the defenses against its impulses represent forms of closed mindedness.

Mechanisms of defense. Whereas the id, if let to have its way, would give rise to specific closures desirable from its primordial perspective, Freud's notion of defense mechanisms highlights a specific type of closed mindedness stemming from the need to avoid specific closures (Kruglanski, 1989). Such closed mindedness consists in the filtering out of certain types of ideation through a resource-depleting repression. For instance, in discussing the notion of taboo Freud writes:

"The prohibition does not merely apply to immediate physical contact but has an extent as wide as the metaphysical use of the phrase 'to come in contact with.' Anything that directs the patient's thoughts to the forbidden object, anything that brings him into intellectual contact with it, is just as much prohibited as direct physical contact" (Strachey, 1955, Vol. XIII p. 27). And on the resource-depleting nature of repression, Freud writes, "the ego (is) obliged to protect itself against the constant threat of a renewed advance on the part of the repressed impulse by making a permanent expenditure of energy, an anticathexis, and it thus (impoverishes) itself" (*Sigmund Freud, An Autobiographical Study*, p. 30, in Strachey, 1955, Vol. XX).

Ambivalence. Whereas the notion of defense mechanisms represents a kind of closed mindedness, Freud's notion of ambivalence represents a kind of emotional open mindedness if by that term is meant an affective incertitude and the inability to decide between opposite emotional responses toward significant others. The notion of ambivalence has been the cornerstone of Freud's psychoanalytic theory, and has been commented on and analyzed by various interpreters (e.g., Merton, 1963, 1976; Levine, 1977, 1985; and Smelser, 1998).

Smelser (1998), for example, notes the original use of the ambivalence concept by Bleuler in 1910, and its subsequent influence on Freud, who used it pervasively (e.g., in his Interpretation of Dreams, analysis of sadomasochism, or theory of the oedipal relations between child and parent). According to Smelser, Freud's "prototypical setting for the development of ambivalence is the young child, who is dependent on his or her parents in many ways—for survival as an organism, as authorities on what to think or do, and emotionally dependent on them because it loves them. Childhood entails a type of enslavement from which one cannot escape. The child objects of ambivalence are those by whom he or she is entrapped—parents and siblings. Adolescence is the protracted experience of partial escape, a period in which ambivalence toward parents and siblings is repeatedly 'acted out', sometimes in extreme ways ... The escape is never complete, however. The enslaved child inside us never totally sheds its ambivalence toward parents and siblings, and this ambivalence finds expression in recurrent 'transference' to authorities, colleagues, subordinates, loved ones, friends, gods, demons, heroes, and scapegoats" (pp. 8–9). In short, ambivalence, or the inability to reach or sustain emotional closure toward important figures in one's interpersonal environment, represents a kind of openness that plagues most of our significant social relations, according to Freud.

To summarize, Freud's theorizing did not focus directly on issues of closed and open mindedness. Nonetheless, his work did touch upon certain kinds of closed mindedness, such as avoidance of specific types of information leading to undesirable (ego threatening) closures, and the kind of affective open mindedness immanent in the notion of ambivalence. The impact of psychoanalysis on the topics of closed and open mindedness is not restricted to Freud's own theorizing, however. Various subsequent interpretations of psychodynamic notions served as the theoretical backdrop for several individual-difference constructs whose relevance to these topics was much more focal and direct than was Freud's original work. The individual difference approach to closed and open mindedness is examined next.

☐ Individual Difference Approaches to Closed and Open Mindedness

Der Gegentypus. Issues of closed and open mindedness came into the limelight during the advent and subsequent defeat of Nazism and fascism, as psychologists of various stripes attempted to defend or explain the political ideologies leading to the globe-shattering events of World War II. Arguably, the first such effort was that of Erik Jaentsch (1938), the Nazi psychologist, who in his volume *Der Gegentypus (The Antitype)*, identified the orientation toward cognitive clarity as a significant personality variable. Jaentsch's work regarded the traits of consistency, stability, firmness, and decision-making confidence as the hallmarks of normalcy and good mental health rooted in the individual's perceptual functioning. According to Jaentsch, the perceptual process of a normal, psychologically healthy individual is characterized by a stable coordination between objectively determined points in space and their corresponding locations on the retina. In stark contrast, the antitype manifests a notable lack of such coordination. His/her spatial perception is labile and fleeting, and these perceptual characteristics are paralleled by cognitive and social liberalism. For Jaentsch, the antitype represented a morbid psychological disposition and a menace to the purity of the German culture and public life (cf. Levine, 1985, p. 12). His own conception of cognitive clarity as the epitome of sanity was much in accord with the Nazi ideology and in stark contrast with the Gestalt theoretic emphasis on the essential ambiguity of perceptual processes, which Jaentsch vigorously criticized.

A reversal of Jaentsch's position was articulated in a postwar magnum opus on the authoritarian personality published in 1950 by Adorno, Frenkel-Brunswik, Levinson, and Sanford. In counter-distinction to Jaentsch's emphasis, the work on the authoritarian personality saw excessive quest for clarity and the tendency to perceive the world in unambiguous "black-white" terms as a sign of a deep-seated pathology. I turn now to briefly consider this work and the subsequent research that it inspired.

☐ Authoritarianism

The work on the authoritarian personality represented a confluence of two streams of thought: (1) Frankfurt-school inspired Marxist theories of ideology and social structure, and (2) Freudian theories of child rearing and personality development. Accordingly, Adorno et al. (1950) proposed that harsh parenting styles encouraged by economic stringencies led entire generations to repress hostility toward authority figures and supplant it by excessive deference and idealization coupled with exaggerated conventionalism and hostility toward societal scapegoats and cultural deviants (like Jews, homosexuals, or people of color). Parental harshness and strict disciplinary styles were assumed to engender particular difficulties for the offspring in passages through the oral and the anal stages of psychosexual development, fomenting a sense of basic mistrust and hence resistance to novel or unconventional ideas. The authoritarian personality, according to Adorno et al., represented a conjunction of nine traits: (1) conventionalism defined as the rigid adherence to conventional middle-class values, (2) authoritarian submission or submissive, uncritical attitudes to idealized moral authorities of the in-group, (3) authoritarian aggression or the tendency to be vigilant to infractions of conventional norms and the inclination to condemn, reject, and punish the perpetrators; (4) anti-intraception, involving the opposition to the subjective, the imaginative, and the tender minded; (5) superstition and stereotypy, rolling together mystical beliefs about people's destinies and the inclination to think in rigid categories; (6) power and toughness, that is, the preoccupation with the dominance-submission dimension of human relations, exaggerated assertion of one's own strength, and identification with power figures; (7) destructiveness and cynicism in regard to human affairs; (8) projectivity of one's own wild and dangerous impulses onto the perceptions of other people and external events; and (9) sex or a preoccupation with and concern about alleged unconventional and hence untoward sexual behavior on the part of others. A measure designed to tap these various tendencies was labeled the F-scale (for fascism).

In support of their theoretical notions, case studies carried out by Adorno et al. found that high authoritarians, as assessed by the F-scale, showed evidence of both the putative developmental causes of the authoritarian personality and of their psychological effects. As to putative causes, high authoritarians tended to describe their home environment as relatively severe and threatening, "and their family relationships as based on clearly defined roles of dominance and submission. Family relationships (were) characterized by fearful subservience to the demands of the parents and by an early suppression of impulses not acceptable to them" (p. 385). The educational objectives of parents of high authoritarians tended to be highly conventional. "What is socially accepted and what is helpful in climbing the social ladder is considered 'good' and what deviates, what is different, and what is socially inferior is considered 'bad'" (p. 385). This, in turn, was assumed to produce a strong and largely unconscious ambivalence toward one's parents, and externalization of the superego "with the punishing and rewarding authority seen as being outside rather than inside of oneself" (p. 454).

As to alleged psychosexual effects, Adorno et al. predicted and obtained a (an insignificant) trend showing that high scorers on a measure of authoritarianism (the F-scale) rejected erotic orality. High authoritarians tended "to defend themselves against both the direct oral urge, e.g., indulgence in food, drinking, smoking, etc, as well as its various sublimations (including) indulgence in talking, artistic interests, etc." (p. 447). High authoritarians were also found to reject the anal syndrome, and exhibit responses known technically as anal reaction formations including rigid moralistic patterns of behavior as well as excessive emphasis on, and preoccupation with, such issues as money, neatness, "good clean life and hard work." (p. 448).

In Adorno et al.'s work, the F-scale correlated 0.73 with ethnocentrism, 0.53 with anti-Semitism, and 0.52 with conservatism. The subsequent years have seen a proliferation of research with the F-scale in a wide variety of correlational studies. In the 1950s, the scale was found to correlate with misanthropy, nationalism, and militarism (see Eckhardt & Lentz, 1971, p. 22). Kohlberg (1964) reported that the F-scale correlated –0.52 with moral maturity, and in a comparison of British fascists with British communists, it turned out that the former obtained a higher mean score on the F-scale (Brown, 1965, pp. 527–528). In the 1960 election, Kennedy supporters were found to be less authoritarian than Nixon supporters (Leventhal, Jacobs, & Kurdika, 1964). Furthermore, high authoritarians tended to vote Republican in the United States and tended to sympathize with the political right in England and in India (Hanson, 1975).

The F-scale was extensively reviewed and commented on (e.g., see Rokeach, 1960; Rosenberg, 1965; Scott, 1965; Shils, 1954; Christie & Jahoda, 1954, Titus & Hollander, 1957; Eckhardt, 1991). Altemeyer (1981, 1988) undertook an exhaustive critique of authoritarian personality research and put forth his own model of right-wing authoritarianism in response to what he saw as serious conceptual and measurement problems associated with the previous work. The conceptual part of the critique was aimed at the perceived imprecision and vagueness of the authoritarian personality model. The model of authoritarian personality assumed a conjunction of as many as nine traits yet, in fact, even more psychological constructs are involved in Adorno et al.'s (1950) list. For example, stereotypy and superstitiousness are hardly the same trait, yet they are rolled into one in Adorno et al.'s conception. Altemeyer (1981) similarly questioned the isomorphism implied in Adorno et al.'s work of "'power' and 'toughness' and of 'destructiveness' and 'cynicism'" (p. 15). Furthermore, the wording of the trait concepts did not give a specific enough sense of what the traits were meant to represent. As Altemeyer put it "Calling conventionalism 'the rigid adherence to conventional, middle class values'... does not give a very specific idea of what the trait is supposed to be" (p. 15).

From the methodological perspective, Altemeyer (1981) argued that many of the items on the F-scale were intended to simultaneously tap several of the constituent traits of the authoritarian personality. Further methodological critiques of the F-scale, such as susceptibility to response sets, led Altemeyer to conclude that "the test measures very little which is identifiable and comprehensible" (p. 25).

As an alternative, Altemeyer (pp. 147–148) proposed his construct of "right wing authoritarianism" including the "covariation of three attitudinal clusters:

1. Authoritarian submission—a high degree of submission to the authorities who are perceived to be established and legitimate in the society in which one lives;
2. Authoritarian aggression—a general aggressiveness, directed against various persons, which is perceived to be sanctioned by established authorities; and
3. Conventionalism—a high degree of adherence to the social conventions which are perceived to be endorsed by society and its established authorities."

Altemeyer's measurement tool for tapping this threefold construct was the Right Wing Authoritarianism Scale that in numerous studies was found to "have scientifically important relationships with most of the authoritarianism criteria under consideration" (p. 213), such as continued acceptance of the home religion, preference for right-wing political parties, harsh punishment of peers in learning situations, high degree of punitiveness toward lawbreakers, and acceptance of violations of the law by authority figures.

As to the developmental origins of right-wing conservatism, Altemeyer criticized the psychoanalytic approach of Adorno et al. (1950) for a lack of adequate evidence. As he put it: "the early childhood origins of authoritarianism may be taken for granted in our culture today, and the theory might be valid. But there is little scientific support for it so far" (p. 254). As an alternative, Altemeyer (1981) proposed a social learning approach to account for the evolution of the authoritarian attitude cluster. Especially, he proposed that people acquire authoritarian attitudes "(a) from other people, through direct tuition and through imitation; and (b) through their own experience with the objects of these attitudes. The determinant of what attitude is learned is the reinforcement the person receives for learning the attitude … and the reinforcement he receives from his interaction with the object of the attitude, according to principles of social learning theory" (Bandura, 1977).

Whether in its original, Adorno's et al.'s (1950) version, or its more recent version developed by Altemeyer (1981, 1988, 1996), the concept of authoritarianism shares obvious common features with that of closed mindedness. The tendencies toward idealized, moralistic thinking in black-and-white terms and rigid categories, rabid conventionalism and the tenacious adherence to societal norms, worship of authority, the differentiation between persons on dimensions of power and status, the tendencies toward prejudice and stereotyping—all cohere with the present theoretical notion of closed-minded individuals who crave clear-cut knowledge of their social realities, rooted in the firm foundation of the prevailing consensus (hence conventional). Such individuals may indeed be aggressively intolerant of breaches in their worldviews perpetrated by dissenting minorities, liberal types, or members of various out-groups.

As to the putative antecedents of the authoritarian personality, I view both the psychodynamic notions and the social learning hypotheses as tapping possible contributing factors in the development of a closed-minded psychological system. It is quite possible, from the present perspective, that parental harshness and disciplinary strictness could encourage the perception that there are right and wrong ways of doing things, and that knowledge of the former represent belongs with authority figures and is encrypted in social norms. This may well encourage a generalized quest for clarity and the eschewal of ambiguity and confusion. Furthermore, it is quite possible that authoritarian attitudes and closed-minded dispositions are also acquired via social learning from significant others in one's environment who espouse such attitudes and dispositions and reinforce them in others.

☐ Intolerance of Ambiguity

Closely related to authoritarian personality research, yet distinct from it both methodologically and substantively, was Frenkel-Brunswik's work on the intolerance of ambiguity. In an abstract published in the American Psychologist in 1948, she reported a study with 100 adults and 200 children, 9 to 14 years of age having to do with attitudes toward ethnic prejudice. Frenkel-Brunswik argued that ambiguity tolerance constitutes a general personality variable manifesting itself in relation to prejudice, but also to a broad range of further social and cognitive variables.

As she put it, individuals intolerant of ambiguity: "are significantly more often given to dichotomous conceptions of the sex roles, of the parent-child relationship, and of interpersonal relationships in general. They are less permissive and lean toward rigid categorization of cultural norms. Power-weakness, cleanliness-dirtiness, morality-immorality, conformance-divergence are the dimensions through which people are seen ... There is sensitivity against qualified, as contrasted with unqualified, statements and against perceptual ambiguity; a disinclination to think in terms of probability; a comparative inability to abandon mental sets in intellectual tasks, such as in solving mathematical problems, after they have lost their appropriateness" (Frenkel-Brunswik, 1948a).

In subsequent papers, Frenkel-Brunswik (1948b, 1949, 1951) developed further the theory of ambiguity tolerance and elaborated its antecedent conditions and its manifold consequences. As to the antecedents, she viewed ambiguity tolerance in Freudian terms as the consequence of an underlying emotional conflict between strong ambivalence toward one's parents, involving feelings of hostility in combination with glorification tendencies developed in partial reaction to the hostility. The primordial ambivalence toward the parents was assumed to generalize to ambivalent attitudes toward sex and to one's own social identity.

The consequences of low ambiguity tolerance were hypothesized to include the tendencies to seek certainty by clinging to the familiar, by distorting the meaning of information, and by imposing on it simplistic cliches and stereotypes. In a recent review of ambiguity-tolerance research, Furnham and Ribchester (1995) list the following additional consequences claimed for the intolerance of ambiguity: "Resistance to reversal of apparent fluctuating stimuli, the early selection and maintenance of one solution in a perceptually ambiguous situation, inability to allow for the possibility of good and bad traits in the same person, acceptance of attitude statements representing a rigid, black-white view of life, seeking for certainty, a rigid dichotomizing into fixed categories, premature closure, and remaining closed to familiar characteristics of stimuli" (p. 180).

Thus, the ambiguity tolerance construct represents a combination of psychodynamic antecedents and a wide range of consequences encompassing perceptual and cognitive processes but also a host of social and ideological attitudes (e.g., in regard to authority, power, or cleanliness). Arguably, it is this richness of implications that accounts for the considerable and persistent interest in this concept over the 50 years since its introduction.

A considerable amount of research on ambiguity tolerance was conducted in various parts of the world between the late 1950s and the mid-1970s (e.g., Block & Block, 1950; Bhushan, 1970; Eysenck, 1954; Feather, 1969, Sidanuis, 1978). This work employed a wide variety of measurement techniques. Frenkel-Brunswik herself assessed ambiguity tolerance (AT) from case study material obtained in interviews. Block and Block (1950) measured AT by the number of trials a participant took to establish an individual norm in the autokinetic situation. A number of questionnaire measures of AT were devised, the first being Walk's A Scale, reproduced by O'Connor (1952). Other similar tests were devised by Saunders (1955) and Eysenck (1954). Among the most widely used such instruments was a scale developed by Budner (1962), including 16 items designed to tap the various dimension of ambiguity tolerance identified in the previous literature. Various other measures of ambiguity tolerance were devised (see Furnham & Ribchester, 1995, for a review). For instance, Kreitler, Maguen, and Kreitler (1975) presented 45 participants with several different tasks, yielding 12 different measures of ambiguity tolerance. On the basis of their data they found three distinct classes of ambiguity tolerance behaviors: intolerance of (1) situations admitting of multiple interpretations, (2) situations that are difficult to categorize, and (3) situations involving contradictions and conflicts.

The notion of ambiguity tolerance has been applied in the domain of organizational behavior. Keenan and McBain (1979) measured ambiguity tolerance by the Budner (1962) questionnaire and found that for individuals with a high intolerance for ambiguity, role ambiguity was negatively correlated with job satisfaction but positively correlated with tension at work. Along the same lines, Frone (1990) found in a meta-analysis that ambiguity tolerance moderates the relationship between role ambiguity and strain. Bennet, Herold, and Ashford (1990) found a negative relation between ambiguity tolerance and the tendency to seek feedback in organizations. Furnham and Ribchester (1995) summarized this work by concluding that, "Where good research has been done with representative samples and robust and realistic dependent measures, AT has proven to be a highly predictive individual difference varible. Clearly individuals with low AT appear to be more sensitive to stress, more risk averse, and more sensitive to particular kinds of feedback" (p. 193).

AT has been occasionally regarded as a characteristic of organizational climates. In this vein, Furnham and Gunter (1993) observed that some organizations may be (implicitly) selecting persons who are low or high on ambiguity tolerance, and this may imbue their organizational climate in specific ways. Furthermore, various organizations (e.g., the military), may have structure and/or subscribe to values that encourage intolerance of ambiguity, whereas other organizations (e.g., political parties or reading clubs), may encourage substantial tolerance of ambiguity. Little research has examined these possibilities empirically, however.

Furnham and Gunter's (1993) theorizing about organizational climates that vary on the tolerance/intolerance of ambiguity dimension echoes the present notion that the need for closure may be aroused situationally. More generally, the intolerance of ambiguity concept is akin in many ways to that of the need for closure and the numerous presumptive correlates of the intolerance of ambiguity are similar to various need for closure effects described in Chapter 2. Thus, in a way the present work is continuous with the AT tradition, though it extends it well beyond its putative dynamic antecedents, allowing as it does for its acquisition via social learning, and emphasizing the possibility of situational inductions of ambiguity tolerance or intolerance. Furthermore, the present framework is more explicit and systematic than ambiguity tolerance theory about the multiple consequences of the need for closure deriving them from the urgency and permanence tendencies aroused by the need for closure.

☐ Uncertainty Avoidance

The notion that attitudes toward ambiguity may characterize larger social entities underlies Hofstede's (1984) work on uncertainty avoidance across cultures. Whereas notions of uncertainty and ambiguity may not be fully isomorphic, the affinity between the two is considerable as Hofstede acknowledged. Hofstede's thesis has been that all societies deal with various natural uncertainties to which they are exposed. They invoke laws to deal with uncertainties stemming from the behavior of other people, and they turn to religion to provide unambiguous answers in domains that transcend common or scientific knowledge.

Hofstede devised an uncertainty index based on responses to three questions on (1) rule orientation, (2) stability of employment, and (3) stress. He then rank ordered 40 countries according to their uncertainty avoidance scores, and demonstrated that uncertainty avoidance is related to such important social tendencies as lower ambition for advancement; bias in favor of specialists over management positions; a preference for large over small organizations; placing greater positive value on organizational loyalty; eschewal of competition among employees and the preference for group decisions and consultative management over individual decisions; dislike of being employed by a foreigner; and resistance to change. Finally, Hofstede speculated that uncertainty avoidance at the level of culture impacts the personalities of members: individuals socialized in an uncertainty-avoiding culture may develop an inclination to avoid uncertainty as well, whereas ones socialized in less-avoidant cultures would be more tolerant of uncertainty.

Conceptually, uncertainty avoidance is highly similar to the need for nonspecific closure. Furthermore, Hofstede's notion that cultural values and goals may determine the degree to which uncertainty is perceived as bothersome fits well with the present notion that the need for closure could be a function of a wide set of factors among which cultural values and objectives may certainly be included.

☐ Conservatism

Another concept related to intolerance of ambiguity and authoritarianism is conservatism. The study of this construct commenced with the work of Lentz who was primarily interested in character and ethical development defined as the concern for the welfare of others (1929). Based on a questionnaire measure, Lentz (1930, p. 539) concluded that "conservatism for certain purposes can be considered a general trait" unrelated to intelligence or acquiescence. Validation studies showed that "People who call themselves conservative or middle of the road and who have not changed their church or who did or would vote for Hoover or Smith or Roosevelt, or who are enrolled in the small denominational colleges, make respectively higher conservative scores on the test than those who rate themselves as radical or who have changed their church or who would or did vote for Norman Thomas or who are enrolled in the large universities" (p. 1).

Eysenck (1955) reported that 77% of the highest class in England voted Conservative, while only 8% voted Labor. By contrast, only 20% of the lowest class voted Conservative, but 52% voted Labor. He developed a two-factor theory of social attitudes including the dimensions of conservatism-radicalism and tough mindedness-tender mindedness. Eysenck's conservatism notion included "favorable attitudes toward patriotism, Sunday observance, capital punishment, the church, harsh treatment of criminals, a belief in the inevitability of war, and in the reality of God. At the other extreme were found a cluster of radical beliefs favouring Communism, Pacifism, birth control, divorce reform, sexual freedom, and a belief in evolution" (pp. 118–119). And in a later work, Eysenck and Wilson (1978) asserted that "there can be no doubt that conceptions like the authoritarian personality, dogmatism, Machiavellianism, ethnocentricity, tough mindedness, ... overlap to a considerable extent" (pp. vii–viii).

General expectation of positive things from oneself and others may foster an openness to new ideas. A theory of conservatism based on such a notion was developed by Sylvan Tomkins (1963) who hypothesized a strong link between general affective positivity and ideology. Tomkins hypothesized that "how positively or how negatively a human being learns to feel about himself and about other human beings will determine his general posture toward the entire ideological domain" (1965, p. 97). In support of these notions, Tomkins (1963) reported significant positive correlations between a positive trust in human nature (whereby "human beings are basically good") and humanistic philosophy of science, a preference for democratic government, empathy, permissive discipline, faith in feelings, and variety, on the one hand; and between a generalized distrust (whereby "human beings are basically evil"), a positivistic philosophy of science, a preference for punitive government, lack of empathy, directive discipline, fear of feelings, and hierarchical selectivity.

A different theoretical underpinning of conservatism was postulated by Wilson (1973). Wilson's thesis was psychodynamic to some extent and it held that conservatism is "a generalized susceptibility to experiencing threat or anxiety in the face of *uncertainty*" (p. 259). Accordingly, "conservative attitudes serve a defensive function. The conservative attitude syndrome serves an ego defensive function, arising as a response to feelings of insecurity and inferiority, and a generalized fear of uncertainty" (pp. 261, 265). Using the known groups approach, Wilson validated his C-scale (i.e., conservatism) by successfully discriminating between socialists and conservatives, religionists and scientists, as well as humanists and members of the Salvation Army. Furthermore, the C-scale correlated significantly with authoritarianism (0.68), with rigidity (0.51), and with dogmatism (0.39). Wilson further found that conservative parents tended to produce conservative children (p. 258), and that the "conservative syndrome ... (includes) religious dogmatism, right-wing political orientation (in Western countries), militarism, ethnocentrism, intolerance of minority groups, authoritarianism, punitiveness, anti-hedonism, conformity, conventionality, superstition and opposition to scientific progress" (p. 257).

Eckhardt (1991) viewed conservatism research in terms of its affective, behavioral, cognitive, ideological, and moral correlates. As he put it, "Affectively, the conservative tends to be optimistic, leadership-oriented, conformist, disciplined, extroversive, and misanthropic. Behaviorally, the conservative tends to support capitalism and to go to a conventional church. Cognitively, the conservative tends to be dogmatic, positivistic, rigid, intolerant of ambiguity, and to hold hereditary theories of human behavior. Ideologically, the conservative tends to be capitalistic, militaristic, nationalistic, and prejudiced. Morally, the conservative is authoritarian, bureaucratic, censorious, religious, punitive, conformist, and law-and-order oriented" (p. 108).

Though the notion of conservatism is related to the need for closure, there are important differences here as well. The similarity between the two notions hinges on strivings for permanence the need for closure is assumed to induce and that imply adherence to existing notions and defense of the status quo—corresponding to key aspects of conservatism (for discussion see Jost, Glaser, Kruglanski, & Sulloway, 2003 a, b). The main difference is that conservatism has been typically thought of as an ideology that is a set of positions on various content-related issues (e.g., capitalism, religiosity, punitivity). The need for closure, by contrast, refers to a content-free tendency to seize and freeze on any relevant notions that happen to be accessible. In that regard, a person with a high need for closure may well be a rigid (or conservative!) liberal, if liberal notions were accessible in her or his environment (Jost, Kruglanski, & Simon, 1999). More about this later.

☐ Dogmatism

Even though Adorno et al.'s (1950) explicit concern was with authoritarianism of the right, the major operationalization of the concept, the F-scale, was criticized for neglecting the authoritarianism of the left. Partly in reaction to this alleged asymmetry, Rokeach (1960) developed the dogmatism scale meant to provide a value-free measure of authoritarianism. The dogmatism scale contained items tapping double-think subscription to logically contradictory beliefs, denial of contradictions in one's belief system, a narrow future orientation and a strong orientation toward authority. According to Rokeach, dogmatism is indicative of closed mindedness that contrasts with an open minded attitude allowing one "to distinguish information from source of information and to evaluate each on its own merits" (p. 396).

Rokeach (p. 420) found that dogmatism loaded .71 on a general factor on which the following were also loaded: authoritarianism (.78), ethnocentrism (.73), rigidity (.68), right opinionation (.64), conservatism (.49), paranoia (.47), anxiety (.44), and self-rejection (.41). Barker (1963) further found that high scorers on the dogmatism scale tended to be intolerant of ambiguity, given to stereotypes, opinionated, and submissive to authority.

A certain amount of discussion revolved around the question of whether dogmatism or authoritarianism can characterize the left end of the political spectrum (Eysenck, 1955, 1969; Rokeach, 1960) even as they characterize the political right. Eckhardt (1991) summarized the debate as follows: "So far as 'authoritarianism' is used in the strict sense to refer to fascists or prefascists then, by definition, there are no 'authoritarians' on the left, who are, again by definition 'equalitarians'. However, if 'authoritarianism' is used in a more general sense to refer to dominance-submission relations, then of course there are authoritarians of the left and center as well as of the right" (pp. 114–115). In other words, at any point of the political left-right spectrum, there seems to exist considerable variability in the degree to which people exhibit dogmatism, conceptual rigidity, or authoritarianism. Yet on the average, authoritarianism and dogmatism are higher as one moves from the political left to the political right. I shall revisit this particular asymmetry at a later juncture.

Rokeach's (1960) work on the dogmatism scale was closely linked to his more general theorizing about open versus closed belief systems. Indeed his conceptual framework was quite elaborate and distinct in some ways from the theoretical rationale given for kindred individual difference concepts like authoritarianism or conservatism. As he expressed it: "a basic characteristic that defines the extent to which a person's system is open or closed … (is) the extent to which the person can receive, evaluate, and act on relevant information received from the outside on its own intrinsic merits, unencumbered by irrelevant factors in the situation arising from within the person or from the outside … Irrelevant internal pressures that interfere with the realistic reception of information are unrelated habits, beliefs, and perceptual cues, irrational ego motives, power needs, the need for self-aggrandizement, the need to allay anxiety, and so forth … irrelevant external pressures (are) particularly the pressures of reward and punishment arising from external authority, for example, as exerted by parents, peers, other authority figures, reference groups, social and institutional norms, and cultural norms … The more open one's belief system, the more should evaluating and acting on information proceed independently on its own merits, in accord with the inner structural requirements of the situation. Also, the more open the belief system, the more should the person be governed in his actions by internal self-actualizing forces and the less by irrational inner forces …" (pp. 57–58).

According to Rokeach furthermore, "all belief-disbelief systems serve two powerful and conflicting sets of motives at the same time: the need for a cognitive framework to know and to understand and the need to ward off threatening aspects of reality. To the extent that the cognitive need to know is predominant and the need to ward off threat is absent, open systems should result. But as the need to ward off threat becomes stronger, the cognitive need to know should become weaker, resulting in more closed belief systems …" (p. 67). All this implies a negative relation between the need to know and closed mindedness. However, Rokeach was not entirely consistent in the role he accorded to the need to know, for in another passage significantly anticipating the present theory, he also wrote: "if the closed or dogmatic mind is extremely resistant to change, it may be so not only because it allays anxiety but also because it satisfies the need to know …" (p. 68) clearly implying a positive relation between the need to know (or to have firm cognitive closure) and closed mindedness.

Furthermore, Rokeach's analysis implies that there is a way of objectively assessing the intrinsic merits of the information—and that the contents of a source's pronouncements are necessarily more relevant or diagnostic, with respect to the matter at hand than information about the source's perceived characteristics (hence the closed-minded persons who attend more to the source than the contents are likely to be in error more than the open minded persons with the opposite emphasis). By contrast, the present analysis views informational relevance as a largely subjective rather than objective matter (see Kruglanski & Thompson, 1999a, b; Erb, Kruglanski, Chun, Pierro, & Spiegel, 2003). From this perspective, the source's statements and/or its characteristics could constitute information types that some individuals would view as subjectively relevant to given conclusions. For individuals who believe that "experts are right," for example, the expertise of a source would be highly relevant to accepting the conclusions advocated, no less so, if not more, than the intrinsic features of the message. As discussed earlier, closed and open mindedness in our framework refer to the readiness to process novel information—not to the kind of information processed.

☐ Openness to Experience

McCrae (1996) recently argued that of the five basic dimensions of personality (the so-called Big Five), Openness to Experience is the most relevant to understanding social and interpersonal phenomena. According to McCrae and Costa (1992), Openness relates to the "breadth, depth, and permeability of consciousness, and in the recurrent need to enlarge and examine experience" (p. 2). Openness to Experience is conceived of as a broad and general dimension that manifests itself in the vividness of fantasy, artistic sensitivity, depth of feeling, behavioral flexibility, intellectual curiosity, and unconventional attitudes, all assessed by the openness facets of the Revised NEO Personality Inventory (NEO-PI-R; Costa & McCrae, 1992).

On the basis of behavior genetics research (Loehlin, 1992), the results of which attest to strong heritabilities and little influence of shared environments on children's subsequent adult personalities, McCrae (1996) suggests that the predispositions toward openness or closedness may be inherited rather than learned. An important correlate of openness is the willingness to consider new cultural ideas and new ways of living. In this vein, Yik and Bond (1993) found a relatively high correlation (r=.40) between Hong Kong students' tendency to rate themselves as "extremely Westernized" versus "extremely Chinese" and their openness to experience scores. The Openness to Experience facets were also significantly and negatively correlated (rs ranging from –.21 to –.64, Trapnell, 1994) with political conservatism as assessed by the Wilson-Patterson Conservatism scale (Wilson & Patterson, 1968), and Altemeyer's (1981) right-wing authoritarianism.

Costa and McCrae (1978) reported significant negative correlations ranging from –.20 to –.61 between Openness to Experience facets and Levinson and Huffman's (1955) Traditional Family Ideology scale. Furthermore, whereas there is no evidence for concordance of personality among couples on neuroticism, extraversion, agreeableness, or consciousness, there is clearly such evidence with regard to openness. There is also evidence of concordance in perceived Openness in oneself and an ideal friend (Cheng, Bond, & Chan, 1995). Furthermore, Openness is related to vocational interests (Holland, Johnston, Hughey, & Asama, 1991) suggesting that it is also related to the development of professional and friendship ties between people.

In short, the personality dimension of Openness to Experience seems relevant to a broad range of social phenomena including political attitudes, interpersonal choices and relations, and the reactions to cultural innovations and social change. It is clearly a significant factor of interest that should be studied more broadly in reference to a variety of social psychological research.

It will be of particular interest to study the relations between Openness to Experience and the need for closure. The fundamental conceptual commonality between the two is obvious in that both relate to the positive acceptance versus rejection of new information. But there also exist some substantial differences in the ways in which these constructs have been conceptualized. Whereas Openness to Experience is thought of primarily as a heritable personality dimension, the need for (nonspecific) closure is thought of as a psychological state that varies not only as a function of personality, but also as a function of the situation and of culture (Hofstede, 1980). The need for closure is thought of as a motivational construct, whereas openness is defined in terms of "individual differences in the structure and functioning of the mind" (McCrae, 1996, p. 1, emphasis mine). Finally, need for closure theory makes certain specific assumptions as to the mediating mechanisms of need for closure effects relating to the urgency and permanence tendencies this need may evoke. By contrast, the Openness to Experience concept is less committed (at least thus far) to specific mediating mechanisms of its putative effects.

☐ Uncertainty and Certainty Orientation

An intensive research program highly relevant to issues of closed and open mindedness was launched over a decade ago by Richard Sorrentino and his colleagues (Sorrentino & Short, 1986; for a recent review see Sorrentino & Roney, 1999). Like the previous approaches considered in this chapter, Sorrentino also emphasized individual differences. Specifically, he defined a continuum of uncertainty orientation at one end of which "are those who find uncertainty a challenge. These people are called uncertainty-oriented, as approaching and resolving uncertainty has become part of their way of thinking about the world. At the other end of the continuum are those who view uncertainty as something to be avoided. These are people (who are) certainty oriented, as clinging to the familiar, predictable, and certain, are their particular ways of thinking about the world..." (pp. 3–4). According to Sorrentino and Roney, both the certainty- and the uncertainty-oriented persons wish to attain certainty. But whereas the uncertainty-oriented persons approach uncertainty in order to resolve it, the certainty-oriented persons avoid it altogether.

Like several previous authors reviewed in this chapter, Sorrentino and Roney view the etiology of uncertainty and certainty orientations from a psychodynamic perspective. Specifically, they regard the uncertainty-oriented individual "as one who likely made it through the oral, anal, and phallic stages of development relatively successfully, developing a basic trust in the world, a sense of autonomy, and a desire to explore new worlds" (p. 4). By contrast, "the Certainty Oriented (individual) likely did not make it through the oral, anal, and phallic stages of development relatively successfully. Consequently, this person developed a basic mistrust in the world, a lack of a sense of autonomy, and a desire to adhere to predictable and familiar worlds ... this person is oriented toward maintenance of present clarity about the self and the environment" (p. 7).

Sorrentino and Roney assume that the wish to resolve uncertainty is independent of the desire for clarity and predictability. And an individual's standing on the uncertainty orientation continuum is assumed to be the result of these two tendencies. One of these, nUncertainty, is measured via a projective technique of sentence completion (Atkinson, 1958). The second is assessed via Cherry and Byrne's (1977) measure of authoritarianism. Based on these measures, an uncertainty orientation score is calculated for each individual by subtracting her/his standardized score of authoritarianism from a standardized score on nUncertainty. Sorrentino's rich research program has uncovered a wide variety of ways in which the uncertainty- and certainty-oriented individuals differ, e.g., in their degree of interest in self-discovery, the readiness to deal with self-discrepancies, reactions to self-discrepancies, attention to ambiguous situations, rigidity of cognitive structures, reactions to persuasion, behavior in achievement situations, trust in interpersonal relations, attachment styles, reactions to leadership styles, exposure to health-threatening information, and more (for a review, see Sorrentino & Roney,1999).

Sorrentino's theoretical framework differs from the present one in several respects. Whereas he views both the certainty- and the uncertainty-oriented individuals as ultimately motivated to arrive at a clear knowledge and in this sense to achieve closure, our work defines a motivational continuum in persons' desire for closure at one extreme of which individuals are, in fact, motivated to avoid closure. Moreover, Sorrentino's work treats uncertainty and certainty orientations exclusively in individual difference terms, whereas the present approach views the desire for closure (or closure avoidance) in terms of their epistemic functions that can be evoked situationally as well as differentially by various personality types or cultures. Finally, Sorrentino views the developmental antecedents of uncertainty/certainty orientations in psychodynamic terms, whereas the present theory assumes a wide variety of possible antecedents of closed and open mindedness related to their perceived costs and benefits for given individuals and/or in given situations.

☐ Summary: Prior Psychological Treatments of Closed Mindedness and the Present Framework

In summary, the concepts of closed and open mindedness have received a fair amount of consideration in the psychological literature. Admittedly, the different programs of research reviewed in this chapter accorded these concepts varying degrees of emphasis or direct attention. In the work of Piaget and Freud, they are touched upon rather tangentially and indirectly, as they are in the cognitive consistency theories (e.g., of Festinger, 1957; Heider, 1958; or Kagan, 1972) and analyses of information-processing motivations for self-assessment (Festinger, 1954; Trope, 1975, 1986) or self-verification (Swann & Pelham, 1988; Swann et al. 1992). Issues of closed and open mindedness are more focal to research on authoritarianism (Adorno et al. 1950), conservatism (Eysenck, 1955; Eysenck & Wilson, 1978; Tomkins, 1963; Wilson, 1973), dogmatism (Rokeach, 1960) and certainty and uncertainty orientations (Sorrentino & Roney, 1999).

As a possible consequence of such differential centrality, different treatments of closed and open mindedness varied in the degree of elaboration accorded these concepts. Theorists to whose work these phenomena were peripheral (like Piaget, Freud, or the cognitive consistency theorists) did not elaborate much on circumstances likely to affect them, whereas authors to whose work they were more central (like Adorno et al. 1950 or Rokeach, 1960, for example) provided more detailed analyses of such conditions.

The substance of analyses relevant to closed mindedness also differed widely. The cognitive consistency theorists, for example, postulated a need for consistency (cf. Festinger, 1957; Heider, 1958), or uncertainty reduction (Kagan, 1972) as a major mechanism responsible for closure strivings. Such need was assumed to be aroused by a situational encounter with a cognitive inconsistency, particularly if the cognitions involved were important to the individual (Festinger, 1957).

In contrast to the situational analyses offered by the cognitive consistency theorists, the various individual-difference approaches viewed tendencies toward closed or open mindedness as a matter of personality style (e.g., Adorno et al. 1950; Rokeach, 1960). Accordingly, they identified a wide heterogeneity of notions, largely influenced by psychoanalytic theorizing, to account for individuals' socialization to closed- versus open-minded functioning. In this vein, Adorno et al. invoked parental harshness and strict discipline as the critical antecedents of authoritarianism, Frenkel-Brunswik (1948) invoked ambivalence toward one's parents as a critical causal factor behind the intolerance of ambiguity, Hofstede (1984) invoked societal norms and laws as critically relevant to uncertainty avoidance, Tomkins (1962) stressed the learning of generalized positive or negative attitudes toward self and others as the underlying factor of conservatism, Wilson (1973) viewed conservatism as the consequence of susceptibility to anxiety and threat in the face of uncertainty, Rokeach (1960) invoked the presence of threat, and the pressures of reward and punishment by authority figures as the developmental cause of dogmatism, and Sorrentino (e.g., with Short, 1986; with Roney,1999) emphasized the successful passage through the oral and the anal stages of psychosexual development as the responsible factor for the forging of certainty versus uncertainty orientation.

The different approaches to closed and open mindedness also differed in their emphasis on one versus the other, and on the adaptive value they attached to each. Jaentsch (1938), for example, viewed open mindedness as a symptom of psychological morbidity. From an entirely different perspective, various social psychological theories (e.g., the cognitive consistency models, self-assessment, social comparison, and self-verification notions) also emphasized the quest for closure (or firm knowledge) as the typical or normal tendency for most humans. Other approaches took the opposite stance and pronounced closed mindedness as a somewhat pathological, maladaptive state of mind (cf. Adorno et al. 1950; Rokeach, 1960; Sorrentino & Roney,1999).

As the foregoing analysis makes clear, the present perspective on closed and open mindedness differs substantially from prior pertinent notions in several major respects. First, its point of departure recognizes that both closed and open mindedness are essential to knowledge acquisition. Accordingly, some degree of open mindedness is necessary to gather relevant information for decision making and actions, but some degree of closed mindedness is also necessary lest one remain buried in thought and unable to make a cognitive commitment imperative for getting on with the task at hand. From that perspective, whereas excessive closed or open mindedness could be detrimental in some contexts, neither state in and of itself should be considered psychologically healthier or more adaptive than the other.

Second, the present treatment offers a more general as well as more specifically elaborated analysis of closed and open mindedness than most prior approaches. Accordingly, several different cases of closed and open mindedness are presently distinguished depending on their motivational bases (having to do with needs for and for the avoidance of specific and nonspecific closures). Also, compared to most prior notions, the present framework offers a broader conception of the antecedent conditions of closed and open mindedness. Whereas the prior approaches focused on a rather narrow set of putative antecedent conditions of those states having to do with specific motives (e.g., to allay anxiety or threat), the present conception is based on the perceived benefits or costs of closure or the lack of closure; hence it admits the potential relevance to the development of closed versus open mindedness of a broad universe of circumstances having to do with socialization variables or the family dynamics stressed by some theorists (e.g., Frenkel-Brunswik, 1948; Sorrentino & Roney, 1999) as well as societal norms stressed by other theorists (like Hofstede, 1984). However, beyond variables contributing to the development of closed and open mindedness as relatively stable personality dispositions, the present analysis accords major attention to a wide variety of situational circumstances that may evoke powerful momentary tendencies toward closure or the avoidance of closure on a daily basis and from most individuals.

Finally, to a greater degree than most of its predecessors, the present analysis elaborates the rationale behind the manifold consequences of closed- versus open-minded states by deriving them from two motivational tendencies, those toward urgency of attaining closure and permanence in maintaining it. The subsequent chapters consider such consequences in greater detail.

Intrapersonal Effects of Closure Needs

As epistemic motivations, the various closure needs form part and parcel of an individual's experience, as private and "up close and personal" as such experience can get. Indeed, many of the effects of needs for closure occur proximally and determine individuals' psychological reactions to their informational environments. Such reactions can often, though not invariably, have a social psychological flavor. In the present chapter, I specifically review need for closure studies on social and nonsocial phenomena treated at the intra-individual level of analysis. These encompass events transpiring within the individual's mind including personal perceptions, cognitions, and feelings.

What often imbues such phenomena with a social psychological significance is that to an appreciable extent they deal with other people. As a social species, we passionately observe, wonder, and have feelings about others; we are interested and intrigued in the kinds of persons they are, we probe their values and opinions, assess their capabilities and motivations, and ponder their fates and personal histories. Need for closure theory is relevant to such phenomena in two interrelated ways having to do with (1) the extent of processing information about others, and (2) the tendency to weigh some such information more than others.

As noted in previous chapters, the present theory suggests that in forming judgments about others, one will seek less information before crystallizing an impression if one experiences at the moment, a heightened need for a nonspecific closure. By contrast, the extent of information processing under a high need for a specific closure should depend on the content of the early information. If it is desirable, information processing should be curtailed, whereas if it is undesirable, it should be prolonged. Let us consider now some empirical evidence bearing on such hypotheses.

Nonspecific effects. Restriction of predecisional search for information was examined in a study by Webster, Richter, and Kruglanski (1996), which manipulated need for closure via mental fatigue. Specifically, fatigue was expected to raise the need for closure, as mentally fatigued individuals should seek closure to avoid further information processing that may appear laborious, and hence subjectively costly to those persons. Psychology students carried out an impression-formation task in which each played a personnel manager faced with a hiring decision. Students were randomly assigned to complete the task either before or after a normal class period, or following a final examination. Those conditions were designed to produce low and high degrees of mental fatigue, respectively. Manipulation checks provided evidence that: (a) the fatigue induction was successful (that is, participants tested either before or after a normal class reported a lower degree of fatigue than those tested after the final examination); and (b) fatigue varied positively with a need for closure: the higher the need for closure as indexed by various checks, the higher the fatigue. As part of the impression-formation task, participants were presented with a list of materials often used in the evaluation of job applicants and were asked to indicate which of those items they would like to review prior to their own evaluation of the candidate. The list consisted of a variety of relevant items, including resume, references, transcripts, and a personal statement. Information about the number of pages involved in each document was also provided. As expected, individuals experiencing a relatively high (versus low) need for closure requested significantly fewer pages of relevant information prior to forming their impression of the job candidate. Furthermore, when some participants were held accountable for their judgments (a manipulation designed to lower their need for closure), they requested significantly more pages of information than those who were not held accountable.

The extent of information processed en route to knowledge formation was also examined in an earlier experiment by Mayseless and Kruglanski (1987, Study 2). Participants identified barely visible digits appearing on a screen of a tachistoscope. Need for closure was heightened for some participants by informing them that mental concentration and intelligence are positively correlated with the ability to form unambiguous, clear-cut opinions. Those instructions were designed to heighten the need for closure by enhancing the perceived value of closure. The need to avoid closure was aroused in other participants with accuracy instructions and the promise of extra-experimental credits for correctly identifying 9 out of 10 digits. Those instructions were designed to increase participants' tolerance of ambiguity and their propensity to entertain various possibilities regarding a digit's identity. A neutral control condition was also included in which no motivational induction was attempted. All participants were given the opportunity to operate the tachistoscope an unlimited number of times. Results indicated that, as expected, the extent of informational search, operationally defined as the number of times participants operated the tachistoscope, was lowest in the need-for-closure condition, intermediate in the control condition, and highest in the need-to-avoid-closure conditions.

Specific closure effects. The extent of information processing is often affected by the desirability of the specific closure implied by the early evidence. Where such a closure is desirable, e.g., where one's research supports one's favorite hypothesis, or where one's annual check up eventuates in a clean bill of health—one's tendency may be to stop information processing right there and then, and accept the desirable conclusion as valid. However, should the implied conclusion turn out to be threatening, unpleasant, or otherwise undesirable, one's tendency may often be to resist the undesirable conclusion and engage in a vigorous search for further information, hopefully capable of overturning the negative news. Elisabeth Kubler-Ross (1969, p. 38, cited in Ditto and Lopez, 1992, p. 568) wrote in this context about the reactions of a patient just informed of his/her terminal condition. The first reaction is typically disbelief and the assumption that an unfortunate mix-up must have occurred. This is often followed by an extensive search for additional opinions and further professional counsel. Resignation to the sad news is the last phase and it comes after a lengthy effort to prove it incorrect.

Ditto and Lopez (1992, Study 1) conducted research to investigate the relation between desirability of information and the extent of its processing. In one experiment, participants assessed which of two students was more intelligent, expecting to subsequently work with the student they had judged as the more intelligent. One of the students was portrayed as likable and the other one as unlikable. The assessment was to be made on the basis of the students' prior performance, which was made available to the research participants. It was found that participants required less information to determine that a dislikable student was less intelligent than that he was more intelligent. That is, where the initial information suggested that the dislikable target was intelligent, participants considered significantly more information to accept that conclusion as valid than where the initial information suggested that the dislikable target was unintelligent.

In another study, Ditto and Lopez (1992, Study 2) provided some participants with information that they suffered from a fictitious medical condition called "TAA enzyme deficiency," whereas other participants were told they did not suffer from this particular deficiency. It was found that participants led to believe that they suffered from the deficiency took significantly longer on the average to decide that their TAA test was complete (hence that its results were informative) than did the no-deficiency participants.

☐ Hypothesis Generation

As we try to arrive at a judgment or to form an opinion, we often generate a number of alternative hypotheses to account for known facts, and proceed to choose among them on the basis of further relevant information. Imagine a wife trying to interpret her husband's unusually complimentary remarks. Could it be that he is trying to win her over to a plan she has long opposed (e.g., concerning a costly trip abroad in the company of his buddies)? Could it be that his satisfaction at work is "spilling over," given that his long-awaited promotion just came through? Could it be that a death of a close friend reminded him of the brevity of life and inspired him to count his blessings and appreciate what he has? Could it be all of the above?

The seizing and freezing tendencies evoked by the need for (nonspecific) closure may appreciably affect the tendency to keep generating such alternative hypotheses versus curtailing their generation relatively early on. The relationship between the need for closure and hypothesis generation was specifically examined in an experiment by Mayseless and Kruglanski (1987, Study 3). Participants were shown photos of parts of common objects, such as a comb or a toothbrush. These photos were enlarged and taken from unusual angles to disguise their true identity. On each of several trials, participants listed as many hypotheses as possible concerning an object's identity and finally selected what they deemed as the most likely identity. Need for closure was aroused in some participants by stressing that clear-cut opinions are related to intelligence and mental concentration. Need to avoid closure was induced in other participants by informing them that mental concentration and intelligence are related to correct visual recognition. A neutral condition was also included in which no motivational induction was attempted. As expected, results indicated that participants in the need-to-avoid-closure condition generated more hypotheses on the average than participants in the neutral control condition, whereas participants in the need-for-closure-condition generated fewer hypotheses on the average than did the control group.

Specific closure effects. It is easy to extrapolate the logic of specific closure needs to the phenomenon of hypothesis generation. Specifically, the more motivationally desirable the early hypotheses are that come to one's mind, the fewer alternative hypotheses one might generate. To the contrary, the less motivationally desirable the early hypotheses, the greater the number of alternative hypotheses one might generate. Imagine a male whose overriding specific need was ego enhancement. Imagine further that an attractive female co-worker at the office just smiled at our protagonist. If the first explanation that came to his mind was that she found him appealing, he may well cease generating further explanations and accept the current one as fact because it was so pleasing and satisfactory. On the other hand, if the first explanatory hypothesis that popped into this person's mind for some reason was that she is ingratiating because of his status and power, he may continue generating further explanatory possibilities, finding the current explanation rather disappointing.

Consistent with this analysis, in research by Ditto and Lopez (1992, Study 3) all participants were presented with information that they possessed a (fictitious) TAA enzyme, but the healthfulness of this alleged condition was varied. Some participants were informed that TAA presence was healthy as it reduces the likelihood of a pancreatic disease. Other participants were informed that the TAA presence was unhealthy as it increases the likelihood of such a disease. The main dependent variable was the amount of recent irregularities in participants' lives they cited as potentially biasing the test results. It was found, as expected, that participants given the "unhealthy" diagnosis generated a significantly greater number of such biasing factors, hence producing more numerous alternative explanations of the test results than participants given the "healthy" diagnosis.

Ditto, Scepansky, Munro, Apanovitch, and Lockhart (1998, Study 3) drew one further, intriguing derivation from the notion that individuals will engage in an extensive informational search if the initial data returns should yield an undesirable conclusion, or specific closure. Specifically, such research indicates that the individuals may not arrive at desirable conclusions on a whim; rather, in order to accept them, they need to ground them in subjectively compelling evidence. One implication of such an assumption is that the search for further evidence may fail, after all, to yield the desired preference-consistent information, in which case the negative conclusions would have to be accepted whether one liked it or not.

Participants in the Ditto et al. (1998, Study 3) research were all informed that they tested positive for the TAA enzyme. However, whereas half the participants were led to believe this was good news because the enzyme fulfills a positive function (reducing the likelihood of a pancreatic disease), the remaining half were led to believe it was bad news because the enzyme is detrimental to one's health (increasing the likelihood of a pancreatic disease). Participants were then offered an alternative explanation for why the test yielded the result that it did. They were told, specifically, that false readings could sometimes be caused by unusually high or low blood-sugar levels. Some participants were informed that such false readings are reasonably likely, and others that they are possible but unlikely. It was found that when the TAA was portrayed in positive terms, the probability of the alternative interpretation of the test results did not make a difference. In other words, the favorable diagnosis was perceived as equally accurate irrespective of the probability of the alternative interpretation. By contrast, where the diagnosis was unfavorable (i.e., when the TAA was portrayed in negative terms), the probability of the alternative interpretation did matter. When such explanation was depicted as probable, participants rated the test as rather inaccurate, but when it was depicted as improbable, participants rated the test as accurate despite the negative implications of such a judgment for their future health.

☐ The Noncomplementarity Effect

The noncomplementarity effect refers to a tendency to ignore the implications that changes in one interdependent component of a conceptual system have for the remaining components. For example, in judging the likelihood of each alternative in a set of mutually exclusive and exhaustive alternatives, people often vitiate the fundamental mathematical assumption that the probabilities in such a set must sum up to unity. Thus, when the probability of one alternative is altered on the basis of evidence, the probability of the remaining alternatives isn't adjusted appropriately (Robinson & Hastie, 1985; Sanbomatsu, Posavac, Kardes, & Mantel, 1998; Sanbomatsu, Posavac, & Stasny, 1997; Van Wallendael, 1989; Van Wallendael & Hastie, 1990).

Noncomplementarity may be observed in other interdependent conceptual systems as well, such as market-share estimation. For example, information that influences the estimates of market share for one firm, may have no effect on subjective market share estimates of competing firms. This is true despite the logical interdependencies and the constant sum nature of market shares whereby if the market share of one firm increases (or decreases), the market shares of the remaining firms must decrease (or increase) complementarily. Recently Houghton and Kardes (1998) argued that such noncomplementarity effects might represent an instance of seizing and freezing under a heightened need for nonspecific closure. Specifically, under need for closure, the estimator may restrict her/his consideration of a focal alternative; that is, seize and freeze upon the implications of the evidence for changes in that alternative, and fail to consider what implications these have for the remaining alternatives.

In a study designed to test these ideas, Houghton and Kardes (1998) had participants estimate market shares with limited information. Specifically, information for the year 1992 was provided about R&D (research and development) expenditures, assets, and profits relative to the industry averages with regard to a focal firm, HON Industries, and three to seven other companies. The participants considered this information and then provided market share estimates for the focal and the alternative companies.

Subsequently, participants were told that, "in the beginning of 1994, HON Industries (the focal company) was implementing a change in strategy. Specifically, HON was increasing (or decreasing) R&D expenditures, or increasing (decreasing) sales force size" (Houghton & Kardes, 1998, p. 315). Participants were then asked to estimate the market share for HON Industries as well as for the remaining, nonfocal, firms.

The main dependent variable of interest was the degree to which participants with high versus low need for cognitive closure (as assessed by Webster and Kruglanski's, 1994 Need for Closure Scale) revised their estimates in regard to the focal versus the nonfocal companies. As predicted, the noncomplementarity effect was significantly more pronounced when participants' need for closure was high (versus low). The noncomplementarity effect was also significantly reduced when the number of alternative companies was high (seven) versus low (three) presumably because the greater the number of the alternatives, the greater their saliency (Tversky & Koehler, 1994). Houghton and Kardes (1998) summarize these results by noting that "myopic reasoning processes in managerial judgment and decision making are especially likely in industries comprised of a relatively small set of competing firms or when concerns about closure—due to individual differences in decision making styles or due to situational pressures—is high" (p. 319).

Specific closure effects. The differential tendency to attend to the focal versus the alternative entities underlying the noncomplementarity effect might be affected also by needs for specific closure. Specifically, the concentration of attention on the focal alternative, and hence the noncomplementarity effect, might be greater if that alternative was of particular concern to the estimator. In a market share estimation paradigm, this might be so if the focal alternative represented the estimator's own firm or if the implied shift in market share due to the new information was particularly desirable to the estimator (e.g., it represented an important increase versus a decrease in profits). Similarly, the noncomplementarity effect might be reduced if desirability considerations shifted the estimator's attention to the nonfocal alternatives. These possibilities could be explored in future research.

☐ Subjective Confidence

An ironic consequence of reduced hypothesis generation before forming a judgment may be heightened subjective confidence despite limited consideration of alternatives. If individuals under high need for closure are less aware of competing judgmental possibilities, they may be more confident that the possibility they select is the correct one. Indeed, elevated judgmental confidence under heightened need for closure has been manifest in numerous studies that operationally defined this particular motivation in a variety of ways, such as via instructions stressing the desirability of voicing clear-cut opinions (Mayseless and Kruglanski, 1987), via time-pressure (Kruglanski & Webster, 1991), by varying the interestingness/dullness of the judgmental task (Webster, 1993), and by increasing the difficulty of information processing by introducing environmental noise (Kruglanski, Webster, & Klem, 1993). These findings suggest that attainment of subjective certainty is indeed possible in the absence of extensive information processing. In fact, our research demonstrates that the restriction of information processing under heightened need for closure often goes hand in hand with elevated confidence.

These findings echo the everyday observation that true believers, ideologues, and various authoritarian types are often extremely confident in their opinions as well as intolerant of alternative views (cf. Jost, Glaser, Kruglanski, & Sulloway, 2003 a,b). However, while one might have surmised that the dismissal of alternative views follows the commitment to one's chosen opinion, the present analysis implies the opposite causal sequence, whereby the arrested generation of alternatives, possibly due to enhanced need for cognitive closure, enhances one's confidence in the hypotheses that one did generate.

Specific closure effects. The implications for confidence of the needs for a specific closure are readily inferable: If the early hypotheses were congruent with one's wishes, one would likely abstain from generating alternative hypotheses, and hence end up with a high degree of confidence that these hypotheses are valid. By contrast, if the early hypotheses ran counter to one's wishes, one may confront them quickly with competing alternatives, undermining the confidence in those unpleasant possibilities. I am unaware of research specifically looking at these phenomena. Their probing might thus need to be undertaken by future work.

☐ Type of Information Sought

The suppression of hypothesis-generation under a high need for closure (Mayseless & Kruglanski, 1987, Study 3) may also affect the type of information sought, not merely its amount. This notion was specifically examined in a study (Kruglanski & Mayseless, 1988) that required participants to evaluate whether a target person belonged to a given professional category. Individuals under high need for closure were expected to prefer prototypical information about the category, e.g., information on whether the individual possessed the prototypical features of an architect (interest in visual aesthetics, mathematical ability, creativity, elegant lifestyle), while attempting to test the focal hypothesis that he/she was an architect. By contrast, individuals experiencing a need to avoid closure were expected to prefer diagnostic information (Trope & Bassok, 1983) capable of discriminating among different possibilities regarding the target's professional affiliation. For example, when testing the focal hypothesis that a target is an architect, a person under high need to avoid closure might generate the competing alternative that he/she might be a painter instead, and proceed to seek diagnostic information with regard to the architect versus the painter possibilities. Thus, our knower might prefer information about mathematical ability and elegant lifestyle (presumed characteristic of architects but not of painters), rather than information about creativity and interest in visual aesthetics (presumed common to both). Indeed, the results of the Kruglanski and Mayseless (1988) research indicated that participants under high need for closure were more likely to seek information about prototypical features of the professional category, whereas participants under need to avoid closure were more likely to seek diagnostic information.

The restriction of hypothesis generation under high need for nonspecific closure implies that high-need-for-closure individuals may be less creative than their low-need-for-closure counterparts. In support of this notion, recent work by Rocchi (1998) found that Italian participants high (versus low) on a dispositional need for closure generated figures and objects rated as less creative by external observers. This and other similar work is described in greater detail later.

Specific closure effects. Again, it is easy to extrapolate these findings to specific closure effects. Consider a situation where the focal hypothesis tested by a knower was agreeable to this individual, hence representing a desired closure. For instance, the person may be testing the (pleasant) hypothesis that a new acquaintance genuinely likes her. Because of its agreeable nature, the tendency to generate alternatives to that hypothesis is likely to be weak. As a consequence, our knower is likely to seek out prototypical information having to do with evidence of genuine liking by the other. (Did she/he smile at me? Did he/she indicate an interest in further encounters? Did she/he respond positively to my initiative in this domain?) Imagine, by contrast, that the person is testing the disagreeable hypothesis that the new acquaintance's somber expression reflects repulsion or disdain toward our knower. The latter might be motivated, indeed, to engender several alternatives to such an unpleasant possibility; for example, ponder whether the individual in question may not be feeling ill, whether he/she may not be reacting to some bad news he/she may have received, or whether he/she is not generally timid and withdrawn—all of which would explain her/his gruff manner during the encounter. The presence of such alternative hypotheses would prompt the search for diagnostic information capable of demarcating them from the focal alternative. The timidity/withdrawal hypothesis, for example, would imply the value of observing the target's behavior toward other new acquaintances. If he/she is indiscriminately gruff to others as well, the personal dislike hypothesis would be refuted. The illness or bad-news hypotheses would imply the value of observing the target's behaviors (toward oneself and/or others) in alternative situations not presumably characterized by the unfortunate features associated with the initial encounter (cf. Kelley, 1967).

☐ Cue Utilization

Nonspecific closure effects. As noted earlier, under a heightened need for a (nonspecific) closure, an individual may experience dual psychological tendencies: a sense of urgency about forming closure, and a desire for maintaining closure once it had been formed. The urgency tendency should dispose persons to quickly seize upon early cues and utilize them toward the formation of initial judgments. And the permanence tendency should dispose them to freeze, or to fixate or perseverate on those particular judgments. Substantial research on a variety of seemingly diverse social psychological topics has found support for these ideas.

Primacy effects in impression formation. A striking example of such effects is the classic primacy effect in impression formation. Order effects in impression formation, of which the primacy effect is an example, have long been of substantial interest to social psychologists, perhaps because they tellingly illustrate how the psychology of social judgments deviates from the dictates of pure reason. There is nothing, after all, in an item's location in the informational sequence (e.g., whether it comes early, late, or in the middle of an informational string) that should logically bear on its relevance, weight, or importance to the judgment being made. Yet order effects have been pervasively documented in social psychological studies beginning with research by pioneers such as Asch (1946) or Luchins and Luchins (1950) and continuing to the present (Kruglanski & Freund, 1983; Webster, Richter, & Kruglanski, 1996). As implied above, a primacy effect refers to the tendency to base one's social impressions on early information about that person, to the relative neglect of subsequent, equally relevant information. Thus, if the early information about a person was positive, whereas the subsequent information was more negative, a primacy effect would be revealed if the overall impression of that person ended up being positive on the whole. Similarly, if the early information was negative and it was followed by positive information, an overall negative judgment would indicate the presence of a primacy effect as well.

From the present perspective, primacy effects exemplify the seizing and freezing tendencies assumed to be manifest under a heightened need for closure. In such a motivational state, an individual may quickly grasp the early information and fixate on the judgment it implies, becoming relatively unaffected by, or impervious to, subsequent information that, objectively speaking, warrants being taken into account. If our analysis is correct, the magnitude of primacy effects should be augmented under a heightened need for (nonspecific) closure. This prediction was first supported in an experiment by Kruglanski and Freund (1983, Study 1). In that study, need for closure was heightened for some participants via a time-pressure manipulation designed to highlight the benefits of early closure, and reduced for the other participants via accountability instructions (Tetlock, 1985) designed to highlight the costs of premature closure. As expected, the magnitude of the primacy effect varied positively with time presure and negatively with accountability. This effect has been replicated in several studies that operationally defined the need for closure in diverse ways, including (again) time pressure (Freund, Kruglanski, & Schpitza-jzen, 1985; Heaton & Kruglanski, 1991), requests for global or undifferentiated impressions (Freund, Kruglanski, & Schpitzajzen, 1985), or scores on the Need for Closure Scale (Webster & Kruglanski, 1994). Finally, in a study referred to earlier, Webster, Richter, and Kruglanski (1996) operationalized the need for nonspecific closure via a mental fatigue induction and found that markedly stronger primacy effects were exhibited by fatigued participants than by their nonfatigued counterparts.

Specific closure effects. Though no specific evidence in the matter seems to exist, the need for a specific closure should increase the magnitude of primacy effects if the early information was congruent with the perceiver's salient motivation. Under such circumstances, the perceiver should seize and freeze on the pleasing judgments that such information affords, and pay less attention, and/or give less weight to, subsequent information. All to the contrary, if the early information was undesirable or incongruent with one's goal, the individual may be motivated to search further (Ditto & Lopez, 1992; Ditto et al., 1993) and hence be less prone to exhibit the primacy effect. Imagine a parent at a PTA meeting receiving information about how her/his child has done during the preceding semester, or a worker receiving feedback from a supervisor about her/his performance on the job. According to the present hypothesis, if such early information was positive, the individual may use it as a basis for her/his overall judgment: The parent may conclude her/his child has done rather well and tend to underestimate the importance and/or relevance of the subsequent, less positive, information. Similarly, the worker may feel that her/his boss is rather pleased with her/his performance and tend to minimize the significance of the subsequent, less glowing part of the evaluation. By contrast, if the initial information was negative, the subsequent information may be attended to much more carefully and systematically. Especially if the evaluative implications of such information were positive or agreeable, they may color one's overall judgment disproportionately and drown out the impression left by the initial, less sanguine information.

In addition, an intriguing asymmetry may exist between attention accorded the desirable and the undesirable information as a function of their relative ordinal position. The positive information may be paid considerable attention both if it preceded the negative information and if it followed it. By contrast, the negative information may be paid considerably greater attention when it preceded the positive information than when it followed it. The reason is that after receiving the desirable information, the individual may freeze on the judgment it implies and refrain from considering the subsequent undesirable information. By contrast, if the negative information came first, the individual would continue processing information in the hope of overturning its undesirable implications, and would therefore attentively consider the subsequent desirable information.

Anchoring effects. An important feature of the seizing and freezing effects is that they may characterize quite disparate social-cognitive phenomena, which superficially have little relationship with one another. For instance, the primacy effects may seem rather unrelated to a famous judgmental phenomenon known as the anchoring effect (Tversky &

Kahneman, 1974; Strack & Mussweiler, 1997). An anchoring effect occurs in situations where individuals are asked to render a numerical estimate of some kind, for example, to estimate the percentage of African nations within the UN, the length of the Yangtze River, or the average annual rainfall in Brazil. At issue here are judgments rendered under uncertainty rather than ones involving the retrieval of well-known (hence, subjectively certain) facts. In such circumstances, casual exposure to some seemingly irrelevant number in the context of a prior comparative question, (e.g., is the percentage of the African Nations in the UN less or more than X?) has been known to bias the final or absolute estimate in the direction of that number. Thus, if that anchor (yielded, e.g., by a spin of a roulette wheel) was high (e.g., 95%), the percentage of African members estimated to exist within the UN would be estimated as relatively high (say, 45%). By contrast, if the initial, and seemingly arbitrary, anchor was low (e.g., 15%) the absolute percent estimate would be relatively low (say 24%).

From the present perspective, the anchoring effect represents the seizing and freezing on an initial knowledge activated, and hence made accessible, by the anchor. A similar perspective is featured by Strack and Mussweiler (1997) in a recent analysis. In line with other accessibility effects, these investigators found that target knowledge activated by the anchor is used toward the rendition of judgments primarily if it is perceived as applicable to the judgment. For instance, if the anchor concerns length and the judgment concerns width, the anchoring effect is much attenuated. Similarly, where the original stimulus compared with the anchor was similar to the stimulus about which the absolute judgment was being rendered (e.g., participants indicated whether the mean winter temperature in the Antarctic was higher or lower than –50 degrees centigrade, and then had to estimate the mean winter temperature in the Antarctic) assimilation to the anchor was found to occur. However, if the two stimuli were different (i.e., after being asked the first question about the Antarctic, the second question involved an estimation of the mean temperature in Hawaii), a contrast from the anchor was found. Perhaps the most compelling evidence that the anchoring effect involves the use of activated knowledge was the finding that where the anchor was totally implausible, the latency of answering the first comparative question was shorter than where the anchor was plausible. However, in such a case, the latency of answering the second, absolute question was longer! This verifies that where the anchor is plausible, but not where it is implausible, the individual engages in elaborative processing, which activates considerable knowledge. Such knowledge may subsequently facilitate and hence shorten the latency with which the respondent answers the second question.

If the anchoring effect is a special case of seizing and freezing upon plausible (or applicable) activated knowledge, it should be appropriately augmented by a heightened need for closure. We submitted this idea to empirical test (Kruglanski & Freund, 1983, Study 3). To that end, we used a paradigm developed by Maia Bar-Hillel (1973) requiring participants to choose within pairs of events the one more likely to occur. Some pairs contrasted conjunctive events with simple events, while other pairs contrasted simple events with disjunctive events. A conjunctive event represents a union of several simple events with given probabilities. Hence, its probability is lower than that of its constituent events. A disjunctive event represents the exclusive occurrence of one among several possible events, (e.g., the probability that on two tosses of a coin, one would obtain two heads). Accordingly, its probability is higher than that of any of its constitutive events, (e.g., the probability that on a throw of a die, its upper face will show either a three or a two).

According to Bar-Hillel (1973), participants start the process with the probability of a constituent event. This provides a plausible ("in the ball park") anchor that participants then adjust upward (for disjunctive events) or downward (for conjunctive events). However, the adjustment is often insufficient (Tversky & Kahneman, 1974). This results in an underestimation of the probabilities of disjunctive events and an overestimation of the probabilities of conjunctive events. Such adjustment should be particularly limited under a heightened need for closure.

In our study, participants judged the probabilities of conjunctive and disjunctive events either under time pressure (assumed to elevate the need for closure) or without time pressure, and were either given or not given accountability instructions (assumed to lower the need for closure). As predicted, time pressure generally increased, and the accountability instructions decreased, the degree to which participants underestimated the likelihood of disjunctive events and overestimated the likelihood of conjunctive events.

It should be noted that need for closure effects should be considerably reduced if the anchor was in the implausible range (Strack & Mussweiler, 1997) for that particular judgmental domain. In such a case, there should be little elaborative activity to begin with, hence little generated knowledge that could be seized and frozen upon by the need for closure.

Specific closure effects. I know of no specific research that investigated the valence of the anchor in relation to its capacity to exert impact on subsequent estimates. Yet, if the anchor indeed represents or fosters the generation of an initial (plausible) hypothesis that may be seized or frozen upon, it might do so in part as a function of its desirability. Imagine an individual estimating the number of engineers in a given town. Suppose further that this estimator was himself/herself an engineer, and was contemplating relocation to the town in question. In as far as our individual might well be interested in finding employment, it would be to his/her clear advantage if the number of engineers was low (implying lower competition and higher demand for engineers) rather than high. If our analysis is correct, the impact of a low (hence, motivationally desirable) anchor on the final estimate should be more pronounced than the impact of a high (and motivationally undesirable) anchor.

The correspondence bias. A phenomenon that held particular fascination for social psychologists over the last three decades is known as the correspondence bias (Jones, 1979), or the fundamental attribution error (Ross, 1977). It refers to the attributor's tendency to over-ascribe an actor's behavior to her/his unique attitudes or personality, and underestimate the power of the situation capable of eliciting such behavior from most people. The effect was originally demonstrated in a study by Jones and Harris (1967) that required participants to judge the true attitude of a target person after reading an opinion essay allegedly prepared by this individual under either free-choice or under no-choice conditions. The intriguing finding was that even when participants learned that the target was given no choice in determining the contents of the essay, and was explicitly instructed by the experimenter to espouse a given position, they still estimated that his/her attitude corresponded to some degree to the one expressed in the essay.

Various theorists (e.g., Jones, 1979; Quatrone, 1982; Gilbert, Pelham, & Krull, 1988) speculated about the possible role that the anchoring and insufficient adjustment process may play in this particular bias. Specifically, when participants are asked to judge the target's true attitude, the most salient piece of evidence available to them is the behavior that has just occurred (i.e., the opinion endorsed in the essay). This may directly bring to mind the assumption that the behavior corresponds to the writer's authentic attitude. This initial hypothesis may serve as a kind of anchor that is subsequently adjusted in the course of a deliberative process that involves the consideration of some less salient (yet highly relevant) evidence, namely, that the behavior was situationally constrained. Because such an adjustment typically is insufficient (Tversky & Kahneman, 1974), the final attitude attribution would be biased in the direction of the anchor (i.e., the initial attitudinal hypothesis).

It seems plausible that such a deliberative adjustment process may require substantial cognitive resources and effort. Indeed, evidence suggests that the correspondence bias is substantially greater when the individual's cognitive capabilities are reduced (Gilbert, Pelham, & Krull, 1988). If adjustment requires significant cognitive effort, however, it should also be appropriately affected by the motivation to expend the effort. Evidence to that effect was adduced by Tetlock (1985), who found that the correspondence bias was reduced substantially when participants were made to feel accountable for their judgments. It seems, then, that accountability concerns may motivate participants to become more active and discriminating as information processors, leading to greater adjustment of the initial hypothesis and lowering the degree to which the final judgments tend to be anchored on it.

Now, as noted earlier, accountability (accuracy, evaluation apprehension, etc.) instructions may evoke in participants a "fear of invalidity" that may lower their need for closure. Similarly, a reduction in cognitive capability (Gilbert et al., 1988) may elevate such a need as it increases the laboriousness of information processing that would render the possession of closure advantageous. In short, just as with the primacy and anchoring effects discussed earlier, the correspondence bias may reflect the seizing and freezing on early hypotheses effected by the need for closure. This possibility was tested in a series of experiments by Webster (1993). Participants completed a typical attitude-attribution task in which they estimated a target's attitude after hearing her deliver a speech criticizing student exchange programs with foreign universities. The speech was allegedly prepared under high- or low-choice conditions. The need for closure was manipulated via perceived task attractiveness. Specifically, perceptions of the attitude-attribution task were varied by comparing this initial task to a subsequent task our participants were expecting to perform. In some conditions, this subsequent task (watching a new comedy video) was presented in glowing colors and was expected to be highly appealing. This made the initial attitude-attribution task seem unattractive by comparison. In other conditions, the subsequent task (watching a video of a lecture on multivariate statistics) was expected to be rather unappealing, which rendered the initial task attractive by comparison. Finally, in a control condition, the subsequent task was portrayed as very similar to the initial one, leading participants to perceive it as of the same, moderate, attractiveness.

Appropriate manipulation checks (e.g., items inquiring how important it was for participants to render a judgment quickly, and ones inquiring into participants felt confidence with respect to their judgments) showed that these task-attractiveness conditions were successful in producing the corresponding differences in the need for closure. Thus, the need for closure was highest in the unattractive task condition, lowest in the attractive task condition, and intermediate in the neutral control condition. More importantly, the correspondence bias appeared to be influenced by the need for closure in the expected manner. This bias was enhanced in the unattractive task condition relative to the control condition and reduced in the attractive task condition relative to the control condition. These results were replicated in a second study, where need for closure was operationally defined via scores on the Need for Closure Scale (Webster & Kruglanski, 1994).

Of particular interest, in a third study the pattern of results was completely reversed when initial cues implied a situational rather than an attitudinal attribution. In that study, attributors again read a negative essay on student exchange programs, allegedly authored by a participant in a prior research study. The description of the attributors' task made highly accessible the hypothesis that the target's essay writing was strongly influenced by the situation. To achieve that effect, the experiment was alleged to study the psychological experience of serving as a participant in an experiment. The putative objective was to develop methods of minimizing experimental error leading to invalid data. Specifically, participants were informed that because of a desire to gain a positive evaluation from the experimenter, some individuals might respond to subtle cues conveyed by her or him as to the appropriate ways to behave. The participants' task was to determine whether the target's behavior (of essay writing) was possibly the result of such situational pressures.

As in Webster's prior two experiments, the need for closure was manipulated via task attractiveness. Prior to reading the target's essay, participants reviewed an attitude survey the target had allegedly completed, which indicated that her opinion of student exchange programs was negative (congruent with the position espoused in the essay), positive (incongruent with the essay), or neutral (neither congruent nor incongruent). Participants then read the essay and responded to measures of the dependent variables. No differences due to task attractiveness appeared where the participants' attitude was incongruent with the essay. In that condition, the position espoused in the essay was predominantly ascribed to the situational influence (i.e., the experimenter's subtle cues). However, where the targets' alleged attitude was congruent with the essay, and hence capable of providing a perfectly plausible explanation of the writer's position, task attractiveness did make a substantial difference. Specifically, where the task was unattractive and hence likely to instill a relatively high degree of the need for closure, participants tended to attribute the essay's position to the situation more than participants in the neutral position who, in turn, attributed it to the situation more than participants in the task-attractive condition. Moreover, these differences were mediated by differences in need for closure, assessed via the appropriate manipulation checks.

☐ Cultural Differences in Lay Explanations, Reactions to Conflict, and Self- Presentation Strategies

Lay explanations. The above findings suggest that whether a dispositional or a situational attribution will be made depends jointly on the accessibility of a given attributional hypothesis and on the need for closure. In contexts where a dispositional hypothesis is particularly accessible, persons under a heightened need for closure will be more likely to make a dispositional attribution than their low-need-for-closure counterparts; and in contexts where a situational hypothesis is accessible, high- (versus low-) need-for-closure individuals will be more likely to make a situational attribution.

Recently, Chiu, Hong, Menon, and Morris (1999) examined the cross-cultural implications of this analysis. In prior work, these investigators found that as compared to Chinese subjects, North Americans tend more to explain social behaviors in terms of individual dispositions. By contrast, the Chinese more so than the North Americans, tend to explain social behaviors in terms of the group's dispositions. Chiu et al. (1999) reasoned that the North American cultural context primes (hence, renders accessible) the individual-disposition hypothesis as an explanatory construct for social behavior, whereas the Chinese cultural context primes the group-disposition hypothesis. If it is true that under heightened need for closure individuals tend to seize and freeze on any accessible hypothesis, it follows that high- (versus low-) need-for-closure Chinese should be more likely to make attributions to group dispositions, whereas high- (versus low-) need-for-closure North Americans should be more likely to make attributions to individual dispositions. Chiu et al. (1999) investigated these possibilities in three separate studies.The first of these replicated the basic finding of Menon, Morris, Chiu, and Hong (1998) that Hong Kong Chinese have a greater propensity to attribute social events to group rather than individual dispositions. A noteworthy feature of this replication was that rather than using vignettes (as in the Menon et al.'s 1998 work), participants reacted to descriptions of real-life events that have occurred in Hong Kong and had to do with pharmaceutical errors with adverse health consequences for the patients.

The second study assessed U.S. and Hong Kong participants' need for closure via the English version of the Need for Closure scale (Webster & Kruglanski, 1994) or its Chinese translation (Lam, Lau, & Chiu, 1998). The participants were ethnic Chinese recruited at a subway or train station in Hong Kong and non–Asian Americans encountered in the waiting area of a San Francisco domestic airport. They were presented a description of one of the pharmaceutical errors used in the first study, whereby mouthwash erroneously given as a fever medicine to children made many of them sick. Participants then responded to various attributional items, half of which depicted individual dispositional causes (e.g., "The assistant is incompetent," "The assistant is neglectful") and the other half, group-dispositional causes (e.g., "The clinic is incompetent in maintaining the proper use of medical products," or "The clinic has poor management"). As predicted, among Chinese participants the NFCS scores correlated positively with group dispositional attributions, and did not correlate significantly with individual dispositional attributions. By contrast, among American participants, there was a marginally significant positive correlation between NFCS and individual dispositional attributions and an insignificant negative correlation between the NFCS and group dispositional attributions.

The third study returned to the vignette format and manipulated the need for closure via time pressure (Kruglanski & Freund, 1983). Chinese and American participants were presented with a vignette about cattle escaping from an enclosed area and hitting a farmer. This information was presented in two forms; one where the agent was an individual (a specific bull that broke away), the other where the agent was a group (the entire herd broke away). No culture or agent effects were found under low time pressure. Under high time pressure, however, Chinese participants made significantly stronger dispositional attributions when the agent was the group, whereas the American participants made significantly stronger dispositional attributions when the agent was the individual.

Conflict resolution strategies. Fu, Morris, Lee, Chiu, and Hong (2003) investigated need for closure effects on preferred conflict resolution strategies of Hong Kong Chinese versus European Americans. Prior research has found that as compared with the Chinese, Americans have stronger preference for competitive over accommodating conflict management styles (Trubinsky, Ting-Toomey, & Lin 1991). In their first study, Fu et al. (2003) replicated this difference using Rahim's (1983) Conflict Management Style scale, but also found that it was significantly amplified by the need for closure assessed via (the original or translated) versions of the Webster and Kruglanski (1994) scale.

In their second study, Fu et al. (2003) investigated need for closure effects on another feature previously shown to separate Chinese versus American approaches to conflict resolution: the kind of mediation preferred by members of the two cultures. Prior (LeResche, 1992) work has indicated that whereas the Chinese prefer a mediator who is known and respected by both parties, the Americans prefer a stranger (assuming such individual to be capable of greater objectivity, and hence fairness in her or his approach to mediation). Fu et al. (2003) proceeded to test these notions via a vignette study portraying a workplace conflict in which two disputants argued about the origin attribution, and hence the accreditation, of an award-winning marketing scheme. Both disputants apparently agreed to mediation, but the question was what kind of mediation would they prefer. Participants were asked to put themselves in the disputants' shoes and to select their most preferred mediation type. Specifically, they were given the descriptions of four possible mediators, two of whom were well known to both disputants and respected by both, whereas the remaining two were unknown to either disputant. The statistical interaction between culture, need for closure, and mediator-type was significant. High-need-for-closure Americans significantly preferred the unfamiliar mediator rather than the familiar one, whereas high-need-for-closure Chinese exhibited a significant opposite pattern of preferences. Among low-need-for-closure participants, there were no significant cultural differences on mediator choice.

Self-presentation strategies. Another potential dimension of cultural differences between the Chinese and the Americans relates to their strategies of self-presentation. These differential strategies correspond to Paulhus' (1998) dual-mode framework of self-presentation, including self-deceptive enhancement (SDE) and impression management (IM). Lalwani, Shavitt, Johnson, and Zhang (2003) recently reported that individualists (an orientation typical of Americans and other Westerners) tend to present a positive self by the former mode (SDE), whereas collectivists (an orientation typical of the Chinese and other Asians) tend to do so via the latter mode (IM). In a recent study, Chiu, Ip, and Chen (2003) found that the need for closure (assessed via the Webster and Kruglanski, 1994 scale) moderated these differences for both Hong Kong Chinese and American participants. Specifically, whereas high-need-for-closure American participants significantly preferred the SDE strategy over the IM strategy, and the high-need-for-closure Chinese significantly preferred the IM strategy over the SDE strategy, these differences effectively disappeared for low-need-for-closure Americans and Chinese.

Reward allocation. Fu, Lee, Chiu, Morris, and Hong (2003) investigated cultural differences in the perceptions of reward-allocation procedures. Equity and equality allocational rules were presented via the appropriate scenarios. These scenarios depicted two co-workers, Alex and Pat, who collaborated on designing a new signaling system for a railway. In all conditions, Pat has done two times more work on the project than Alex. In one condition Pat, who was generally assigned the task of allocating the cash bonus the two workers received for their work, uses the equity rule to divide the money. In another condition, Pat employs the equality rule to do so. Participants (Hong Kong Chinese or Americans) were asked to rate the fairness of this procedure; the time it took them to respond to this measure was assessed. It turned out that participants who responded relatively quickly, attesting that they may have been under a high need for closure, demonstrated significant differences in perceived fairness of the allocational procedure consistent with their cultural norms. The Chinese rated the egalitarian procedure as fairer than the equity-based procedure, whereas the Americans rated the equity-based procedure as more fair. Participants who responded relatively slowly, attesting to a low need for closure, did not show culturally consistent preferences among allocational procedures. These findings were replicated in a second study in which the need for closure was measured via the Webster and Kruglanski (1994) scale, and where the participants were all Hong Kong Chinese, in whom either the Chinese or the Western cultural norms were primed via cultural icons. Participants who scored high on the need-for-closure measure (but not those scoring low on this measure) evinced culturally consistent preferences. Those exposed to the Chinese prime preferred the equality-based procedure over the equity-based one, whereas those exposed to the American prime displayed the exact opposite preference pattern.

Taken as a body, findings reviewed in this section support the present analysis that need-for-closure effects are essentially content-free, and that they depend on whatever inferential rules or cues are momentarily or chronically accessible. From that perspective, the need for closure was shown capable of magnifying the tendencies to render a wide variety of inferences, including situational, group, or personal attributions, positive versus negative impressions, etc. Of particular interest, the need for closure was shown to amplify the adherence to cultural norms, beliefs, and procedures across cultures as different in their contents as are those of the Americans and the Chinese. Of course, differences in belief systems may exist within cultures as well, and not only between cultures. For instance, members of the same culture may subscribe to distinct political ideologies, and as illustrated in a later chapter, the need for closure may moderate the extent of also those ideological differences.

Specific closure effects. How might the phenomena above be affected by the motivational desirability of specific closures? Take the correspondence bias. The critical variable should be, again, the extent to which the correspondence hypothesis was desirable or undesirable to the individual. Imagine a target person who, under considerable external pressure, expressed a public support for a given political candidate. To a supporter of that politician, the correspondence hypothesis, that this is the target's true opinion, would be highly desirable, and hence he/she would be unlikely to discount it. On the other hand, the politician's adversary may be reluctant to accept that hypothesis and be rather quick to notice the duress under which the target's support was elicited.

Or to take a currently salient example, consider the attributions made by various parties for President George W. Bush's administration's decision to launch a war on Iraq. From the present perspective, opponents of this administration (motivated to reach the specific closure that the administration was scheming and sinister in its aims) may well question the supposition that the readiness to go to war reflected the administration's genuine attitudes and concern about the danger posed by Saddam Hussein, and instead attribute it to various ulterior motives such as the U.S. economic interest in Iraq's oil fields. Supporters of the administration, on the other hand, motivated to reach a benign attribution, may take its pronouncements at face value and accept that its readiness to war reflects deep-seated values and ideological convictions.

Research by Ditto, Scepansky, Munro, Apanovitch, and Lockhart (1998, Study 1) tested empirically the hypothesis that preference-consistent dispositional inferences (that is, desired closures) will reveal the insensitivity to situational constraint information resulting in the typical correspondence bias (Jones, 1979). By contrast, preference-inconsistent information relevant to dispositional inferences will evoke sensitivity to situational constraints and initiate a more effortful cognitive appraisal. Male participants were given favorable or unfavorable evaluations by another alleged participant (a female accomplice). Half the participants were told the evaluator had been free to write whatever she desired, whereas the other half were informed that she had been instructed to write on the participant's most desirable or undesirable features. The results revealed an intriguing asymmetry in participants' sensitivity to the situational constraint information driven by the degree to which the target's alleged impressions were desirable or undesirable for the participants. Those among them who received the positive evaluation tended to infer that the evaluator had a positive impression of them, and they made that inference irrespective of whether the evaluator was or was not under a situational constraint to render a positive evaluation. A very different picture emerged when the evaluation was negative. When the evaluation was made in the absence of constraints (i.e., where the evaluator was given free hand as to what to write), her true impression was perceived to be quite negative. However, when the evaluator was explicitly instructed to focus on negative features, participants' perceived her true impression of themselves as significantly less negative.

Ditto et al. (1998) replicated the foregoing study adding, for half the participants a cognitive load manipulation introduced by a separate letter-counting task they had to perform while reading the evaluator's impression statement. The results in the no-load condition replicated those of the prior experiment. Participants given the positive impression perceived the evaluator's true judgment of them as equally positive irrespective of whether she was or was not subjected to a situational constraint to focus on the participants' positive characteristics. Participants in the negative impression condition, however, paid attention to the constraint and perceived the evaluators judgment as less negative in the constraint, versus the free-choice condition. The interaction between constraint and evaluation valence disappeared, however, where the participants were subjected to the cognitive load. In that situation, their inferences of the evaluator's opinion of them was positive in the positive feedback condition and negative in the negative feedback condition, suggesting that the increased motivation to process further information in the preference-inconsistent (i.e., the negative feedback) condition was counteracted by the decrease in cognitive capacity occasioned by the cognitive load.

Specific closure effects may manifest themselves in tendencies to adopt or reject culturally prescribed interpretations, strategies, and procedures. Thus, the desire to be accepted by a group of "cultural loyalists" may increase one's tendency to embrace the norms of one's culture, whereas a desire to gain acceptance to a society of foreigners may decrease such a tendency. For instance, the desire to curry favor with the mullah's regime in contemporary Iran may increase the authentic acceptance of their cultural dictates, whereas a commitment to the secular goals of professionalism and education may instill a tendency to rebel against those norms. Similarly, the desire to gain favors from the communist regimes in the former Soviet Union, or from the fascist regime in Hitler's Germany, may foster a genuine acceptance of the social and political ideologies propagated by their representatives, whereas a motivated disidentification with these particular regimes may instill a motivation to reject their ideologies as well.

Stereotype formation. The tendency to seize and freeze on salient or readily accessible information may underlie such central social psychological phenomenon as stereotype formation. Schaller, Boyd, Yohannes, and O'Brien (1995) investigated this possibility in a study that assessed the need for closure via the Personal Need for Structure measure introduced by Neuberg and Newsom (1993) and referred to earlier (for a fuller discussion of this particular measure see Kruglanski et al. 1997). Participants were presented with information about two fictitious groups (A and B) whose members' intelligence was presumably assessed via an anagram task. Participants were given information about the outcome (success or failure) of a given member's attempt, identified such member as belonging to group A or B, presented the actual anagram that contained either five letters (e.g., DLABE) or seven letters (e.g., YOCNEOM), and gave the correct solution of the anagram (e.g., BLADE, ECONOMY). The critical feature of this procedure was that the proportion of five- to seven-letter anagrams was not exactly the same for the two groups. Group A members attempted only 5 anagrams that were five letters long and 20 that were seven letters long. Group B members had these proportions reversed, as their anagram set included 20 that were five letters long and 5 that were seven letters long. The outcome information indicated that group A members solved all 5 five-letter anagrams and 5 of 20 seven-letter anagrams. Group B, on the other hand, solved 15 of the 20 five-letter anagrams (i.e., 75%) and none of the 5 seven-letter anagrams. Schaller et al. (1995) argued that "although Group A had a higher success rate on both five-letter and seven-letter anagrams, group B solved more total angrams" (Schaller et al. 1995, p. 546).

Assuming that the total number of anagrams solved represents a highly accessible bit of evidence for the groups' putative intelligence, and assuming that persons under high need for closure are likely to seize and freeze on such evidence and integrate it less with the less salient and more difficult to figure constraint information about length of the anagrams and relative success rate, they should decide that members of group B are more intelligent than those of group A, whereas a fuller analysis would reveal the opposite to be the case. This is precisely what was found. Participants falling below the median on PNS (i.e., persons with relatively low need for closure) formed accurate judgments and concluded that Group A was more intelligent than Group B. Those falling above the PNS median (those high on the need for closure), however, reached the opposite erroneous conclusion that Group B was the more intelligent of the two.

Schaller et al. (1995) replicated these results in a second study where in addition to need for closure assessment, accountability manipulation was introduced for some participants by leading them to believe they would have to explain and justify their judgments to another participant. From the present perspective, accountability instructions may arouse a fear of invalidity that may lower the individuals' need for closure (cf. Kruglanski and Freund, 1983). Consistent with this analysis, Schaller et al. (1995) concluded that, "at least on some measures, situationally induced accountability concerns did moderate the impact of PNS on the stereotype formation process" (p. 550).

Stereotype application. On 2 February 1999, an unarmed West African immigrant with no criminal record was killed by four New York City police officers, who fired 41 shots at him in the doorway of his Bronx apartment building. It is not entirely clear what brought about this tragic incident, but a strong possibility is that application of an aggressive African American stereotype under high need for closure played a significant part in the quickly unfolding events that led to the shooting. It was 12:45 A.M., the street was poorly lit, and the black man, Mr. Diallo, was loitering in the vestibule of the apartment "acting suspicious." The darkness may have rendered careful information processing difficult. Also, the police officers may well have been quite fatigued at that late hour, contributing to the costliness of information processing and elevating their need for closure.

What business might a black man have acting suspiciously at almost one in the morning? The first, stereotypic, idea that probably popped into the officers' minds was that it was surely an illegal business, and a dangerous one at that. If so, time was of the essence because a failure to act might be expected to result in tragic consequences for the policemen involved. Fatigue, costliness of information processing, and subjective time pressure might have conspired to produce a highly elevated need for cognitive closure in these individuals. Seizing and freezing on the idea that the suspect was dangerous, the policemen may have interpreted an innocent movement on the part of Mr. Diallo as a hostile gesture. One policeman may have interpreted the situation in that way and opened fire, and the rest may have accepted the social reality this action defined and followed suit.

From a social psychological perspective, an increased application of prevalent social stereotypes and prejudices to various social judgments represents a particularly striking case of seizing and freezing under heightened need for closure. General stereotypes prevalent within the culture (e.g., gender or age stereotypes, or stereotypes about particular social groups) constitute knowledge structures that may readily come to mind. This implies that they may be particularly likely to serve as bases for judging such stereotyped individuals when the knower is under high (versus low) need for closure. This possibility was first tested in an experiment by Kruglanski and Freund (1983), which examined the impact of ethnic stereotypes about the academic competence of Ashkenazi and Sepharadi Jews in Israel on the assignment of grades to students for a literary composition. The Ashkenazi Jews have their origins in Europe, and their stereotype in domains of competence and achievement is rather positive. The Sepharadi Jews have their origins in the Middle East and North Africa, and their corresponding stereotype is negative. Kruglanski and Freund (1983) had their subjects (students in a graduating class of a teachers' seminary) assign grades for a composition allegedly written by an eighth grader. All participants evaluated the same composition, but the author's name was varied. Some participants learned that her/his name was Blumenthal (suggesting an Ashkenazi origin), whereas other participants learned that her/his name was Aboutbul (suggesting a Sepharadi origin). Results indicated that the Ashkenazi and Sepharadi stereotypes were more likely to influence grade assignments when the evaluators were under a high need for closure (manipulated via time pressure) as compared to low need for closure (manipulated via accountability concerns). Specifically, when the writer's name was Aboutbul the composition was generally graded much lower (17 grade points out of 100!) than when it was Blumenthal. These differences disappeared, however, when the writers' need for closure was substantially lowered by an absence of time pressure combined with the presence of evaluation apprehension.

In subsequent similar research, time pressure was found to increase reliance on gender stereotypes (Jamieson & Zanna, 1989). Specifically, participants known a priori to have negative stereotypes about women in management were more likely to devalue the resumes of female (versus male) applicants for a management position when placed under high (versus low) time pressure. This effect occurred even though pretesting indicated that the information presented on the male and female resumes was essentially equivalent. Those findings support the notion that the need for closure leads to reliance on preexisting knowledge structures to the relative neglect of case-specific information.

The tendency to rely on stereotypes may impact memory over and above its influence on judgment. In research directed at this possibility, Dijksterhuis, Van Knippenberg, Kruglanski, and Schaper (1996) assessed participants' need for closure via the Dutch version of the Need for Closure Scale (Cratylus, 1995). In one study, Dutch undergraduates were presented with behavioral information about a negatively valenced group of soccer hooligans and were asked to form an impression of this group. Participants high in the need for closure recalled relatively more stereotype-consistent information, whereas participants low in the need for closure recalled more stereotype-inconsistent information. Furthermore, participants high in the need for closure judged the target group more stereotypically and perceived it as more homogeneous compared to participants low in the need for closure. These results were replicated in a second study, where the target group was positively valued, consisting of nurses.

Stereotyping and specific closure needs. Recent evidence suggests that judging persons in terms of prevalent stereotypes may be affected by the degree to which doing so may be congruent with one's needs for specific closure. For example, the motivation to reaffirm one's self-worth following a failure experience may lead one to apply a negative stereotype to another individual and thus to induce in oneself a feeling of superiority over her or him. In research conducted by Fein and Spencer (1997), participants were exposed to a failure or a success experience and were then given an opportunity to evaluate a fictitious job applicant who either was or was not a member of a stereotyped group (i.e., was or was not Jewish). It was found that following a failure experience, participants derogated the Jewish target but not the non-Jewish one, by judging her incompetent. Following success, however, participants did not differentiate between the Jewish and non-Jewish targets, disparaging neither. In other words, the failure experience may have introduced the motivation to self-affirm, which lent the status of a desirable closure to the judgment that one is superior to another individual. Because the negative stereotype (of the "Jewish American Princess" in this case) may quickly come to mind in response to the Jewish target, it may be seized and frozen upon by individuals whose prior failure experience might dispose them to view a negative evaluation of the target as desirable. But in the absence of such motivation (i.e,. following success), the tendency to seize and freeze on the negative stereotype would be weaker and the tendency to disparage the target would essentially disappear. It is also of interest that the mere motivation to reaffirm one's self-worth after failure is not enough in the absence of accessible constructs (in the case of a nonstereotyped target) that may allow one to do so.

Of course, failure experience is merely one among several possible sources of the motivation to reaffirm one's self-worth. Another such source could be awareness of one's own mortality, which according to Greenberg, Pyszczynski, Solomon, Rosenblatt, Veeder, Kirkland, et al. 1990) may induce the motivation to reaffirm one's value as an individual and boost the perceived meaningfulness of one's existence. Indeed, these investigators found that increasing one's mortality salience via a questionnaire specifically designed for that purpose increased the tendency of Christian participants to rate a Jew more negatively than another Christian and in this way to boost their perceptions of their own self-worth. A more extensive description of mortality salience research relevant to need for closure concerns is given in the last chapter of this volume.

Recent work by Kunda and Sinclair (1999) found further evidence that needs for specific closure may enhance the tendency to base judgments on prevalent stereotypes. These investigators report evidence that college students rated female professors who had assigned them low grades more negatively than they did male professors who had given them comparable grades; this difference disappeared when evaluating female and male professors from whom the participants received high grades. Presumably, the motivation in the former case was to maintain one's self-esteem in face of a negative evaluation (a low grade) by disparaging the evaluator. The negative female stereotype makes accessible a basis for such a disparagement on which the hurt evaluators may seize and freeze, and which is absent in the case of the male evaluators.

In similar subsequent research (described in Kunda & Sinclair, 1999) participants were experimentally motivated to disparage or think highly of a target by information that this person had evaluated them positively or negatively. The participants completed a test of their leadership ability and subsequently watched a videotaped evaluation of their performance, either positive or negative, delivered by the target portrayed as a management trainee who was either a member of a nonstereotyped group (i.e., a white man) or of a negatively stereotyped group (a white woman in one study, and an African-American man in another). It was found that the woman and the African-American man were disparaged after providing a negative evaluation, but not after providing a positive evaluation. These differences were absent when the evaluation was positive (hence, the tendency to disparage the evaluator was absent).

Spontaneous trait inferences. The notion that persons with a high need for closure will seize and freeze upon early cues suggests that they may make inferences rather readily, and from a relatively slight evidential basis. Furthermore, the notion that such individuals are biased in favor of stable knowledge, due to the permanence tendency, suggests that their inferences will often pertain to general or transcendental categories. Work by Moscowitz (1993) on spontaneous trait inferences is consistent with such an analysis. The notion of spontaneous trait inferences (introduced by Winter and Uleman, 1984) refers to the case where persons categorize behavior in terms of trait labels (e.g., "solving a mystery" is categorized as "being intelligent") in the absence of a conscious intention to do so. The research on spontaneous trait inferences (e.g., Moscowitz & Uleman, 1987; Uleman, Winborne, Winter, & Schechter, 1986; Newman & Uleman, 1989, 1990) typically uses the cued-recall procedure in which inferences made spontaneously at the encoding stage of information processing can be detected by assessing the degree to which they facilitate the accurate recall of the encoded behaviors. Participants read a series of sentences with instructions to memorize them for a subsequent recall test. Each of these sentences describes a target, characterized by a professional role, performing a behavior that strongly implies a trait (e.g., "the librarian helped the children cross a busy intersection" implies kindness). It is then shown that the traits, pretested to have no prior semantic links to the behaviors, serve as efficient retrieval cues for the behaviors suggesting that they were spontaneously inferred from the behaviors. If the need for closure disposes persons to seek knowledge and meaning wherever they can find it, they may be particularly likely to engage in the making of spontaneous inferences. That is precisely what was found. Using the Personal Need for Structure scale (Neuberg & Newsom, 1993) to measure the need for closure, Moscowitz (1993) found that high (versus low) PNS participants showed superior cued recall (but not overall recall) of the behaviors, suggesting that they spontaneously inferred the traits from the behaviors.

Mental accessibility of hypotheses. The argument that need for closure enhances the tendency to base judgments on prevalent stereotypes or that it often magnifies the tendency to over ascribe actors' behaviors to their attitudes or dispositions, critically assumes that such stereotypes or dispositional (attitudinal) hypotheses were highly accessible to the individual and that they tended to pop to her/his mind immediately upon his/her encounter with the stimulus. Two independently conceived studies, one by Ford and Kruglanski (1995), the other by Thompson, Roman, Moscovitz, Chaiken, and Bargh (1994), tested this assumption directly. Both sets of studies employed the priming paradigm employed by Higgins, Rholes, and Jones (1977) in which an ambiguous paragraph about an individual named Donald is interpreted in line with the prime. For example, if the description of Donald was ambiguous in regard to the traits adventurous/reckless, priming the word *adventurous* in a prior (and allegedly unrelated task) would disambiguate the description in a corresponding direction, as would priming the word *reckless*. In the Ford and Kruglanski (1995) study, participants who scored either high or low on the Need for Closure Scale (Webster & Kruglanski, 1994) received one of two primes during a memory task: either the negatively valenced adjective *reckless* or the positively valenced adjective *adventurous*. They then performed an impression-formation task that required them to characterize a target person with a single word after reading behavioral information about the target that was ambiguous with regard to the adventurous/reckless distinction. In one of the experiments (Study 1), the need for closure was manipulated via cognitive load, specifically via rehearsal of an eight-digit number while processing information about a target person. In the second experiment (Study 2), the need for closure was assessed via the appropriate scale (Webster & Kruglanski, 1994). The findings of both studies indicated that participants high (versus low) on a dispositional need for closure tended to characterize the target more in terms suggesting recklessness in the reckless prime condition, and adventurousness in the adventurous prime condition. Furthermore, where in Study 1 the need for closure was lowered via accuracy instructions, the differences between the two primes (i.e., the reckless and the adventurous primes) disappeared. Thus, consistent with the seizing and freezing notion, participants high on the need for closure exhibited stronger effects of priming than participants low on this need. Similar results were reported by Thompson et al. (1994). In their first experiment, participants given accuracy instruction tended less to assimilate the descriptions of Donald to the prime than subjects not given accuracy instruction. Furthermore, scores on the Personal Need for Structure scale (Neuberg &

Newsom, 1993) were positively correlated with the assimilative tendency. In their second experiment, Thompson et al. (1994) demonstrated that attenuation of the assimilative tendency under the accuracy condition was significantly reduced by the introduction of a cognitive load (i.e., a situational manipulation that may increase participants' need for cognitive closure).

Recency effects. If construct accessibility is what truly matters as far as the effects of information on judgments are concerned, the notion that need for closure invariably leads to primacy effects in impression formation has to be reexamined. Indeed, on reflection, it appears that under the appropriate circumstances need for closure may lead to recency effects instead. The moderator variable in this case may be the timing of the goal setting for the information-processing task. Specifically, it should matter whether the impression formation goal was set prior to the informational exposure or following it. When the goal of forming an impression existed from the start, judgments about the target may be formed on-line or in a piecemeal fashion, that is, as the relevant person-information is received. Under such circumstances, a heightened need for closure may indeed foster primacy effects prompted by seizing and freezing on the early information as soon as it became accessible. When the impression-formation goal was formed only following the informational exposure, however, judgments may be made from memory based on previously received notions deemed relevant to the present judgment. In such a case, the most recently received information is the most accessible (cf. Higgins, 1996). In a recent experiment, Linda Richter and I verified that this, indeed, is the case (Richter & Kruglanski, 1998).

Participants believed that they were involved in a study designed to investigate their linguistic abilities. Specifically they were to judge descriptive sentences for their grammatical structure and coherence. All the sentences depicted a job candidate named Phil. In one condition, the first 10 sentences described Phil via information that put him in a positive light, and the next 10 sentences described him in a negative light. In the other condition, the negative sentences came first and were followed by the positive sentences. Because our intention was to instill in our participants a comprehension goal and not an impression-formation goal, information about Phil was presented as a series of separate sentences that the participants were asked to judge for grammatical structure and coherence. Only after the participants rated each of the 20 sentences for those linguistic properties were they presented with a questionnaire that (among other things) inquired about their impressions of Phil.

Need for closure was elevated by means of time pressure and reduced by means of accuracy instructions. The results confirmed our analysis. As expected in a situation where the impression-formation goal was introduced following exposure to the stimulus information, participants' judgments were based on memory rather than being formed on-line in that a significant correlation obtained between positivity of recall and positivity of participants' impressions. Furthermore, participants under high time pressure manifested more pronounced recency effects than did participants under no time pressure. Finally, this difference was eliminated when an accuracy motivation was introduced, assumed to lower the need for closure.

☐ Summary

Simple though it may seem, the notion that social judgments are subject to the seizing and freezing tendencies under a heightened need for (nonspecific) closure serves to integrate a host of proximal social psychological phenomena on the intrapersonal level of analysis, reflecting how an individual thinks, feels, and acts with regard to others. These tendencies affect both the extent of information processing en route to judgment formation, and the weight attached to different informational items as a function of their mental accessibility. Curtailed extent of processing under heightened need for closure reduces the number of hypotheses generated prior to selecting one as valid and inflates the individual's confidence in its validity. The increased weight given informational items as a function of their accessibility may give rise to primacy as well as recency effects in impression formation, stereotyping and discrimination, assimilation to prime effects, and the correspondence bias in person perception. Our research indicates that all these seemingly disparate phenomena share a deep commonality. They refer to different contents of knowledge that are governed by the same epistemic process wherein the needs for closure (of both the nonspecific and specific varieties) play a pivotal part.

Interpersonal Consequences of the Closure Needs

Whereas Chapter 5 dealt with proximal need for closure effects affecting the individuals' psychological reactions to their informational environments, the closure motivations have distal effects as well, which affect how patterns of interpersonal relations may unfold. That may be so because our interactions with others are typically accompanied by continuous cognitive activity. We interpret the actions of others in terms of their meanings and intents; we attribute the outcomes that they produce to pertinent situational or personal factors (Nisbett & Ross, 1980); we try to understand their perspectives and to divine their unarticulated thoughts and true intentions. It is the judgments yielded by such deliberations that guide our actions and responses toward others, as well as affecting how we feel in given interpersonal situations. In short, the processing of information about one's interaction partners, and the formation online of judgments about their feelings, cognitions, and probable actions constitutes an inseparable part of social relations. The seizing and freezing tendencies fostered by a heightened need for nonspecific closure should transcend, therefore, intrapersonal phenomena occurring in the knowers' minds and impact important social effects at the interpersonal level of analysis. In the following pages I consider three such interactional phenomena to which the seizing and freezing tendencies seem highly relevant: (1) perspective taking and empathy, (2) audience design in interpersonal communication, and (3) interpersonal negotiations and bargaining.

☐ Perspective Taking and Empathy

According to Davis (1983), the common term empathy actually refers to two conceptually separate phenomena. Perspective taking is an aspect of empathy that involves an ability to see things from another person's vantage point. Empathic concern represents a different aspect of empathy referring to the extent to which we may express compassion, sympathy, or caring for another person (Davis, 1983). These two aspects of empathy are interrelated. Perspective taking is likely to affect empathic concern, as we are more likely to feel a concern for others if we understand their situation or appreciate their predicament.

The taking of another person's perspective may not be easy. Often it may require substantial cognitive effort because the first thing that typically comes to mind is one's own interpretation of the situation or one's own perspective. An inhabitant of New York, for example, may find it difficult to appreciate a visitor's strong affective reactions (of awe, fear, or wonderment) to the urban jungle of the city that never sleeps. An expert skier bursting with energy and excitement for the slopes may not readily appreciate the perspective of an exhausted novice who yearns for the crackling fire of the cozy chalet. Indeed, perspective taking may require correction, adjustment, and careful consideration of just exactly how another person may differ from oneself. All this may necessitate appreciable cognitive labor, especially if the person whose perspective one is attempting to divine differs from oneself substantially on various pertinent dimensions.

It is at this juncture that the individuals' epistemic motivations become relevant to perspective taking phenomena. If the need for nonspecific cognitive closure reduces the individual's readiness to expend mental effort into the processing of information, and if it disposes the individual to seize and freeze upon early notions, it may substantially reduce perspective taking and empathic concern when it comes to a person with a dissimilar perspective.

These ideas were examined in two experimental studies conducted by Webster-Nelson, Klein, & Irvin (2003). In this work, need for closure was operationalized in terms of mental fatigue. Participants in the high-fatigue condition were given difficult proofreading and reading-comprehension tasks. Those under low fatigue were given an uncomplicated reading task and, indeed, they reported being less fatigued than their counterparts in the high-fatigue condition. Furthermore, appropriate manipulation checks verified that the fatigued (versus nonfatigued) participants indeed experienced a higher need for closure. Following their completion of the fatigue portion of the experiment, participants went on to engage in a social perception task wherein they read information allegedly provided by another participant from a previous study. The participants' task was to form impressions of that target.

The target information depicted a negative social experience. Half the participants read a description in which the target reported suffering from chronic shyness, as well as feelings of disappointment and dejection after a specific failed attempt to socialize at a party. The remaining participants read the same description, only the target now reported feeling guilty and agitated after the social failure. The first variation described the kind of affect common among individuals with a chronic discrepancy between their ideal and actual selves (Higgins, 1987), that is, a discrepancy between their current realities and their hopes and aspirations. Such discrepancy was found in past research to result in dejection-type emotions. The second variation described the kind of affect typical of people with a chronic discrepancy between their actual realities and what they perceived as their duties and obligations (ibid.), signifying their ought selves. Such discrepancy was found in past research (see Higgins, 1987, for a review) to result in agitation-type emotions.

These two variations were used to manipulate the similarity between the participants and the targets, as participants were preselected on the basis of possessing one or the other kind of discrepancy. Thus, participants were exposed to information about a target who either expressed thoughts and feelings similar to how they might feel in the same situation or about someone who expressed thoughts and feelings different from how they might feel.

After having read the description, participants answered a number of questions. First, they evaluated the appropriateness of the target's response to the incident. This was designed to assess perspective taking. Further, they indicated the extent to which they felt compassionate, sympathetic, tender, warm, and soft-hearted with respect to the target. These questions were adapted from a measure designed by Batson et al. (1983) to assess empathic concern. Finally, they responded to manipulation checks that confirmed that the similarity manipulation was successful, and that this was equally so irrespective of the type of discrepancy possessed by the participants.

The main analyses indicated that perceived appropriateness of the response (reflecting perspective taking) was reduced by fatigue when the target was dissimilar from the participant. This condition represented a case when perspective taking would require cognitive effort, which fatigued participants (assumed to experience the need for closure) apparently did not make. No significant differences in perspective taking as a function of fatigue occurred when the target and the participant were similar. An identical pattern of findings emerged for the measure of empathic concern. Specifically, less empathic concern was reported by fatigued participants when the target was dissimilar to themselves, while no significant differences in empathic concern emerged when he/she was similar to the participants.

If perspective taking and empathic concern for dissimilar targets was reduced by the need for closure, lowering this need should appropriately reverse this effect. A second study tested just this possibility. In this experiment, need for closure was expected to be attenuated if individuals expected to be outcome-dependent on the target, since past research demonstrates that outcome dependency motivates people to make accurate judgments (e.g., Erber & Fiske, 1984) and accuracy concerns seem to lower the need for closure (Mayseless & Kruglanski, 1987).

The procedure of the second study was highly similar to the first with the exception that an outcome-dependency manipulation was now added. Half the participants believed they would be interacting with the target in the future as part of a peer-support program; the remaining participants had no such expectation. Appropriate manipulation checks confirmed that reported need for closure was significantly higher for fatigued versus nonfatigued participants. Also in accord with expectations, reported need for closure was significantly lower for perceivers in the outcome-dependent (versus nondependent) condition. These findings are consistent with the notion that outcome dependency should reduce the need for closure.

Of greater interest, the non-outcome-dependent participants behaved pretty much as did participants in the first study. Fatigued (but not nonfatigued) participants rated the target's affective response as significantly less appropriate when the target's discrepancy was dissimilar from the participant. No differences in rated appropriateness emerged when targets' affect and participants' discrepancies matched each other. The empathic concern data revealed the same general pattern. Fatigued (versus nonfatigued) participants exhibited significantly less concern and compassion toward the target's response when the targets' and participants' perspectives were dissimilar, yet no differences as a function of fatigue emerged when these perspectives were similar.

A very different data-pattern emerged in the outcome-dependent condition where no fatigue effects emerged on either perspective taking or empathic concern. It appears that despite their fatigue, outcome-dependent participants were quite capable of adopting the target's perspective and consequently experiencing empathic concern even when the target's perspective was quite dissimilar from their own. These findings are consistent with the notion that empathic deficits owing to fatigue are at least in part motivational in nature (that is, are related to the need for closure that fatigue may induce). Further analyses suggested that the effects of need for closure on empathic concern were mediated by perspective taking (Baron & Kenny, 1986). These findings support the notion that "seizing" and "freezing" on one's own perspective may play an important role in such a distinctly interpersonal phenomenon as is empathy.

Specific closure effects. Should needs for specific closure affect the phenomena of empathy? Our theoretical analysis suggests that they should. This could depend on the degree to which one's own perspective was pleasing and desirable as compared to the perspective of another individual. If it was pleasing and desirable, for instance, if one felt good about life and the world, one might be relatively disinclined to switch perspectives and to empathize with those with pessimistic thoughts and feelings about these topics. The literature on mood management processes (see Bless, Clore, & Schwarz, 1996, for a review) provides some indirect support for this notion. Specifically, it suggests that if one's current mood is happy and the information one expects to encounter is unpleasant, one may freeze on one's current ideas and refrain from further information processing. By contrast, if one's own perspective is rather negative and dreary, one might find it much easier to unfreeze and abandon it. Furthermore, in case of a sad initial mood, one shouldn't be particularly concerned whether the information to be encountered is particularly pleasant or unpleasant, for almost any information is likely to be more pleasant than one's current dejected mood.

Wegener, Petty, and Smith (1994) obtained supportive evidence for these predictions. They presented happy and sad subjects with similar messages framed as either pro- or counter-attitudinal. In accordance with the Wegener et al. hypothesis, happy subjects processed the message more when it was portrayed as pleasant (i.e., pro-attitudinal), but not when it was counter-attitudinal and hence potentially unpleasant. By contrast, the sad subjects, having nothing to lose as it were, extensively processed both the counter-attitudinal and the pro-attitudinal messages. The popular notion of escapism (e,g., of leaving one's own bleak world to vicariously experience, process, and/or empathize with the adventures of protagonists depicted in books or on film) seems consistent with the increase in empathy if one's own perspective relative to that of another was highly undesirable and hence incongruent with one's need for a specific closure.

☐ Interpersonal Communication

A fundamental presumption of communication theory is that in conveying messages to others, speakers take the listeners' perspective into account and refer their utterances to the social reality they both share. From this perspective, speakers tailor their messages according to their own and their listeners' shared beliefs and assumptions so that their communications reach the audience and are interpreted accurately.

A significant issue in this context is that different audiences may differ in the knowledge they share with the communicator. It is, therefore, necessary to pitch one's communications appropriately in order to take these differences into account. As Clark and Murphy (1982) noted, "in ordinary conversation we tailor what we say to the particular people we are talking to" (p. 287). They label this process as audience design and state that, "an essential part of (such) design … is the use of the speaker's and addressee's mutual knowledge, beliefs, and suppositions, or common ground" (p. 288). Indeed, the notion of common ground has been a mainstay of the communication literature, and even though its origins, development, and properties have been discussed in different ways (e.g., Danks, 1970; Fussell & Krauss, 1991; Horton & Keysar, 1996), its ubiquitous presence in interpersonal communication has been treated as a given.

The discussions of audience-design phenomena in the communication literature often have a functionalist flavor in deriving the existence of such effects from their role in making the communication process efficient. Yet not all communications are in fact efficient, and there may exist a corresponding variability in the success of imposing adequate audience designs on one's communications. After all, taking the perspective of another and determining what is and what is not part of a common ground may require fairly advanced reasoning skills involved in appreciating the potential differences in perspective between oneself and one's interlocutor in given communicative circumstances.

An important task for communication theory is, therefore, to specify conditions under which extensive efforts at audience design will be undertaken and to characterize the cognitive activities they may involve. Krauss and Fussell (1991) argued in this connection that assumptions about what others know may be thought of as tentative "hypotheses that participants continuously modify and reformulate on the basis of additional evidence" (p. 4), such as verbal and nonverbal feedback (see also Powell & O'Neal, 1976). The realization that an important aspect of communication entails a hypothesis-testing process suggests that the discovery of a valid common ground may not be taken for granted. As with other hypothesis-testing endeavors, the search for common ground may vary in depth and directionality, and ultimately in the degree to which it yields an accurate perception.

Intriguing questions concerning the hypothesis-testing process in audience design concern (1) its point of departure; the hypothesis about the other's perspective that first pops into mind, and (2) its depth or extent; the degree to which it deviates from the early hypotheses and adjusts them in light of additional processing of information. With regard to the first question, extant evidence indicates that the point of origin is often the communicator's own knowledge projected onto the listener (Fussell & Krauss, 1991; Horton & Keysar, 1996; Nickerson, Baddeley, & Freeman, 1987; Ross, Greene, & House, 1977). Indeed, Horton and Keysar (1996) found that while in the absence of time pressure, speakers did incorporate common ground into their communications, common ground was not used when the speaker was under time pressure. They concluded that this finding supported their monitoring and adjustment model, whereby a speaker's initial hypothesis in formulating an utterance is based on his or her own knowledge and on information that is salient to him or her. Given sufficient time, however, the individual will modify or adjust that hypothesis to incorporate the common ground shared with the listener. Of course, the presence or absence of subjectively sufficient time (time pressure) has constituted one of the major ways in which the need for (nonspecific) cognitive closure has been operationalized in past research (Kruglanski & Freund, 1983; Shah, Kruglanski, & Thompson, 1998). It is thus possible that a high level of this need may reduce the amount of effort communicators invest in their search for common ground. As a consequence, communications by high-need-for-closure individuals may be excessively biased in the direction of the communicator's own perspective, which might reduce their comprehensibility to the listeners. Richter and Kruglanski (1997) recently investigated this hypothesis using Fussel and Krauss's (1989) two-stage referential task paradigm.

In that particular paradigm, participants are provided with a set of abstract figures and are asked to write descriptions of those figures so that they themselves (the nonsocial condition) or another person (the social condition) can match the descriptions to the figures on a subsequent occasion. In our experiment, this task was performed by participants with high or low dispositional need for nonspecific closure (Webster & Kruglanski, 1994). In Fussell and Krauss's (1989) research, participants in the social condition exhibited attempts at creating common ground with their audience. They provided lengthier, as well as more verbal descriptions, and used more literal (less figurative) language in their communications, that is, language less idiosyncratically comprehensible to themselves but not to others. We expected to replicate this result and to find in addition that high- (versus low-) need-for-closure individuals will produce shorter and more figurative messages, a difference expected to be particularly pronounced in the social condition.

Participants, introductory psychology students at the University of Maryland, were scheduled to appear in the laboratory for two sessions, corresponding to two separate research phases. In the description phase, participants wrote descriptions of each of 30 figures after having received either social or nonsocial encoding instructions. In the identification phase, carried out 3 to 5 weeks later, participants attempted to match a series of 90 descriptions written by themselves and others to their respective 30 figures presented on a poster board.

The results confirmed our predictions. First, we strongly replicated Fussell and Krauss's (1989) findings that communications in the social condition were significantly lengthier as well as more literal (or less figurative) than those in the nonsocial condition. Of greater present interest, the need for closure variable produced the expected effects: Participants with high (versus low) need for closure used significantly fewer words in their descriptions, and produced significantly more figurative (or less literal) descriptions. Furthermore, the predicted interaction between encoding condition (social versus nonsocial) and need for closure was significant for message length, though not for literalness. The average number of words used by participants with low need for closure was more than double in the social versus the nonsocial condition. This difference was much less pronounced and nonsignificant for participants with a high need for closure.

Do these need-for-closure-driven differences matter to communicative efficacy? Apparently so. First, replicating again Fussell and Krauss's (1989) research, we found that in decoding descriptions by other people, the rate of successful matching was significantly higher if those descriptions were encoded in the social versus the nonsocial condition. More importantly from the present perspective, significantly more descriptions encoded by low-need for-closure communicators were correctly matched to the appropriate figures than descriptions encoded by high-need-for-closure communicators.

Specific closure effects. If our theoretical analysis is correct, needs for specific closure should also have significant impact on communicators' ability to impose effective audience designs on their messages. Specifically, the ability to impose such designs should depend on the relative pleasantness to the communicator of his/her own versus the interlocutor's perspective. If the communicator's perspective was rather subjectively pleasing, whereas the interlocutor's was rather undesirable (to the communicator), her/his audience design may be relatively poor. Marie Antoinette's famous alleged message to the hungry Parisians that in the absence of bread they should eat cakes represents a prototypical case of such failed communication based on the freezing on one's own pleasing perspective that all is basically well with the world, and the motivated reluctance to attune oneself to the audience's desperate conviction that things cannot go on in the business-as-usual manner. The case where one's own perspective is much more pleasing than that of one's interlocutor is, in fact, prototypical of severe conflicts of various types (on interpersonal, intergroup, or international levels) resulting in severe communication failures and misperceptions (cf. Jervis, 1976; Vertzberger, 1990) that may undermine the parties' capability to reach satisfactory resolution of their conflicts. The institution of third-party mediation (e.g., in marriage counseling) aims precisely at improving each party's ability to appreciate the other's perspective and hopefully increase their success in taking that perspective into account while designing their communications to the other party.

To the contrary, if the communicator's perspective was much less pleasing to him or her than the interlocutor's perspective, he or she may rather readily alter her or his perspective to that of the interlocutor and adjust her or his messages accordingly. Research on cognitive tuning (Zajonc, 1960) and the "communication game" (Higgins, McCann, & Fondacaro, 1982) indeed attest to communicators' tendencies to modify the communications to suit their audience's putative preferences. In this particular case, the communicator's initial perspective might be less pleasing or desirable to herself/himself than the audience's perspective, as adhering to the former might bring about a cool reaction from the audience. By the same token, adopting the audience's perspective is desirable or pleasing as its adoption promises a warm audience response that speakers typically desire.

It appears then that the seizing and freezing tendencies prompted by the need for cognitive closure are not restricted to intrapersonal effects on social perception and cognition, but impact such important interpersonal phenomena as empathy and communication. As may be expected, these tendencies may often have a detrimental effect on our capacity to interact with others: They may diminish our ability to empathize with their lot and to appreciate their unique vantage point, hence reducing our ability to coordinate our own activities so as to ensure mutually advantageous outcomes. Interpersonal negotiations research described in what follows furnishes further intriguing evidence for this proposition.

☐ Interpersonal Negotiations

De Dreu, Koole, and Oldersma (1998) recently proposed that the uncertainty, ambiguity, and lack of definite knowledge that typically surround negotiations should be particularly aversive to negotiators with high versus low need for nonspecific closure. Consequently, high-need-for-closure negotiators may seize and freeze on any information that promises to reduce uncertainty. After reaching closure early in the negotiations, individuals high in the need for closure may refrain from considering seriously additional, potentially relevant, information that might undermine their subjective certainty. By contrast, low-need-for-closure individuals should be bothered less by the uncertainty and hence remain open to further information and use it in contemplating their negotiation moves.

De Dreu et al. (1998) conducted three separate experiments to investigate these notions. The first experiment investigated the negotiators' tendency to seize and freeze on focal points (Lax & Sebenius, 1986; Shelling, 1960) such as an initial strategy of reaching an agreement (Neale & Bazerman, 1991) or a norm based on prior negotiation outcomes. Participants in Study 1 acted as sellers who negotiated a price with a buyer. Some participants were told that previous participants in the study attained outcomes around 3,000 Dutch Guilders (Dfl) constituting a low focal point. Other participants were given a high focal point via information that the prior norm was around 11,000 Dfl. Other participants were not given any information about a prior norm and hence were not provided with a focal point. Need for closure was assessed by means of a validated Dutch translation (Cratylus, 1995) of the original Need for Closure Scale (Webster & Kruglanski, 1994).

The negotiation task itself was presented to participants on computers. It was designed to represent the main characteristics of real-life negotiations by including multiple issues that differed in their utilities for the negotiators, providing them with information about their pay-offs only, and retaining the offer/counter-offer structure of many negotiations (Pruitt, 1981). Participants were informed that their outcomes could be affected in three ways: (1) they could be lowered by longer delivery time because of the need to store the merchandise in costly warehouses, (2) they could be lowered by discounts given to the buyers, and they could be influenced by (3) financing terms (e.g., cash, monthly payments, credit cards, etc.). Participants were shown an issue chart listing fifteen levels of possible agreements per issue with corresponding numbers representing the net profit value at each agreement level. In short, the participants faced a fairly complex and ambiguous negotiation situation. To increase their involvement in the study, they were informed that their final profits would be converted into lottery tickets for an attractive financial prize. The negotiations commenced with an offer from a buyer to which participants were prompted to make a counteroffer. This process continued for six rounds following which the participants filled out a brief questionnaire.

This study yielded several results of interest. First, prior to the negotiations, participants were asked what minimum amount of profit they would accept. This defined a limit the negotiators set for themselves (Northcraft & Neale, 1987; Yukl, 1974). As predicted, the focal points had stronger effects on limits for participants with high (versus low) need for closure. Thus, in the low-focal-point condition, negotiators with a high need for closure reported lower limits than negotiators with a low need for closure. By contrast, in the high-focal-point condition negotiators with a high need for closure reported higher limits than negotiators with a low need for closure. Finally, in the absence of a focal point there were no differences in limits as a function of the need for closure.

Whereas limits refer to prenegotiation effects, concessions refer to the actors' actual behavior during the course of the negotiations. Specifically, De Dreu et al. (1998) measured concessions, operationally defined as the difference between the level of agreement (i.e., the profit for themselves) participants asked for the three issues (delivery time, discount, financing terms) at Round 1 of the negotiations, and the level of agreement demanded in the last round (Round 6). It turned out that, overall, high-need-for-closure negotiators made smaller concessions than low-need for-closure negotiators. Furthermore, for high-need-for-closure participants, the high focal point led to smaller concessions than did the low focal point, whereas no similar differences due to focal point emerged for low-need-for-closure negotiators. Finally, high- (versus low-) need-for-closure participants reported significantly less systematic information processing during negotiations.

In their second study, De Dreu et al. (1998) examined the degree to which seizing and freezing on social stereotypes about the other party may affect the initial strategy formed by the negotiators. In one condition, participants believed that the other party was a business student, whereas in another condition that it was a theology major. Based on prior findings (De Dreu, Yzerbyt, & Leyens, 1995), it was assumed that the business student will be viewed as more competitive than the theology major and invite a higher reciprocal competitiveness from the participants. That is exactly what was found. Whereas participants with a low need for closure were not influenced by the other party's group membership, those with a high need for closure made significantly smaller concessions when their opponent majored in business, rather than in theology. Furthermore, concessions made to the business major were significantly smaller when the participants had high rather than low need for closure.

A critic might argue that the differences in concessions between persons high versus low in the need for closure were due to the inherently greater competitiveness of the former (versus the latter) participants. To investigate this possibility, De Dreu et al. (1998) conducted a third study examining the relation between need for closure and social value orientation toward cooperation, individualism, and competition (Deutsch, 1973). Social value orientation was assessed using the Kuhlman and Marshello (1975) decomposed game measure. Specifically, participants were presented with nine decomposed games in each of which they could choose from different distributions of outcomes to themselves and a hypothetical other person. Participants were given a choice among three alternatives, each representing one of the three social value orientations being investigated. This work suggested that social value orientation is not significantly related to the need for cognitive closure, arguing against the possibility that the differences in concessions observed in De Dreu et al.'s (1998) prior studies were in part due to differences in social value orientation (but see Golec & Federico, 2003 reviewed later). De Dreu et al.'s research also supports the notion that in negotiation contexts the need for closure evokes both the seizing and the freezing tendencies assumed by the present theory. The evidence for seizing relates to participants' tendency to anchor their initial limits in prior focal points, and the evidence for freezing relates to their subsequent tendency, manifested throughout the course of the negotiations, to offer smaller concessions as a function of prior cues (represented by focal points or stereotypes).

De Dreu and Koole (1997) also obtained evidence that situational variations in the need for closure may importantly impact negotiations. Specifically they lowered the need for closure via accountability instructions (cf. Tetlock, 1992) or via increasing the cost of invalid judgments and decisions; that is, by arousing a fear of invalidity (Kruglanski & Freund, 1983) and found that these manipulations significantly lowered participants' tendency to use the consensus implies correctness heuristic, as well as to behave more competitively and to reach an impasse more often when a majority suggested a competitive strategy.

In short, the need for closure seems to be highly relevant to the negotiation process. Neale and Bazerman (1991) have stressed the detrimental effects of the use of heuristics on negotiations, and Fisher and Ertel (1995) warned against the excessive focusing on one's own perspective (via its mental rehearsal) and the barriers to listening and understanding the other party's communications this may foster. The research by De Dreu and his associates (De Dreu et al., 1998; De Dreu & Koole, 1997) attests that such effects may be more likely under some conditions than others, specifically under conditions that may elevate the participants' need for nonspecific closure.

Specific closure effects. How might needs for specific closure affect negotiators' propensity to seize and freeze on focal points, stereotypes, or heuristics accessible early in the negotiation process? This should depend on the desirability to the negotiator of such cognitive cues. For instance, if the initial anchor represented considerable profit for the negotiator, hence constituting a highly desirable specific closure, her/his tendency to seize and freeze upon it should be greater than if the anchor represented a trivial profit. Similarly, if one felt strong dislike for the other party, one might be less likely to make concessions than if one felt a strong positive sentiment for that individual (e.g., in a dyadic situation such as a marriage). These ideas could be profitably explored in subsequent negotiation research manipulating the desirability of focal points or the valence of sentiments felt by the negotiating parties toward one another.

☐ Conflict Behavior

The very interpretation of a situation as conflictual may importantly determine the participants' subsequent moves in an interpersonal context (Bar-Tal, Kruglanski, & Klar, 1989; Kruglanski, Bar-Tal, & Klar, 1993). There is much evidence from real and simulated international and intergroup conflicts that in confrontational situations, where indecision might prove dangerous, intolerance for ambiguity increases (e.g., Singer, 1958; Streufert & Fromkin, 1969). In such situations, the need for closure may well arise and reach considerable proportions, particularly where alternative sources of this motivation, like fatigue, time pressure, etc., are also present and compound the effect. Labeling a situation as a conflict provides a clear-cut definition that dispels possible ambiguity. Such definition allows for well-defined responses and removes the need for further informational search, pushing the participants in a uniformly conflictual or competitive direction. As Rubin & Brown (1975) have noted in their classic review of bargaining and negotiation research "when expectations are unclear, competitive behavior is likely to ensue" (p. 140).

Similarly, there exists evidence that where the need for closure is lowered, the tendency toward competitiveness is reduced. This research has to do with the finding that increasing the incentives or stakes of bargaining increases cooperativeness (for a review see Rubin & Brown, 1975, pp. 136–145). As Rubin and Brown summarized it, "competitive behavior may be constrained by a reward structure which unambiguously increases the risk of loss associated with such behavior" (p. 144). That is, even if the competitive schema came first to mind, it might be abandoned if it was manifestly inferior in its consequences to the cooperative schema and if the participants were motivated and/or able enough to discover this fact.

Admittedly, the relation between need for closure and behavior in conflict situations is not simple or straightforward. Rather it should depend on what the most accessible course of action happened to be. Though the interpretation of the relationship as conflictual and the competitive mode of responding may often pop into mind quite readily, at other times cooperation or concession making may be the more accessible action schema; in such a case, increase in need for closure may lead to increased cooperativeness. Consistent with such an interpretation are the results of research on the relation between time pressure, known to induce the need for closure (cf. Kruglanski & Freund, 1983) and behavior in negotiation situations. Pruitt and Carnevale (1993) comment specifically on this issue as follows: "the basic effect of time pressure is to reduce the feasibility of inaction, and thus to heighten the urgency of taking action ... Concession making is one form such action can take, contending is another, hence, time pressure can produce both reactions" (p. 61).

Specific closure effects. The conflict schema may be desirable because of its congruence with needs for specific closure as well, for instance, if the opponent is seen as different from oneself in her or his basic moral values and commitments. In this vein, Finlay, Holsti, & Fagen (1967) attributed John Foster Dulles's beliefs about the existence of an insurmountable conflict with the Soviet Union to his Puritan ideology and commitment to Christian ethics. The Soviets' rejection of Christian principles, promotion of atheism, and the preaching of a new social order elevated the threat and danger that reinforced Dulles's conflictual interpretation of Soviet-American relations. Ronald Reagan's perception of the Soviet Union as an "evil empire" may have contributed, similarly, to his adherence to a conflict schema in thinking about relations with the U.S.S.R., and the religiously based rejection of the West by Islamic fundamentalists may well fuel their notion that the only way of dealing with its vestiges is via a holy war (i.e., an extreme form of competitiveness). The same appears true of George W. Bush's view of Saddam Hussein as evil incarnate.

The desirability (or undesirability) of specific closures may also relate to the specific meanings attached to cooperation or compromise in a confrontational situation. A compromise on tangible rewards may not carry any particular stigma, whereas compromise on symbolic values may be highly undesirable and carry negative connotations. Along these lines, Gallo (1968) argued that increasing the magnitude of tangible resources may often increase cooperativeness (possibly via increasing the fear of costly mistakes and, hence, lowering the need for nonspecific closure), whereas increasing the magnitude of symbolic resources may decrease cooperativeness (possibly by increasing the desirability of the specific closure that one is a staunch defender of lofty moral principles).

Research by Lee Ross and his colleagues (Ross, 1995; Stillinger, Epelbaum, Keltner, & Ross, 1990) indicates that compromise proposals for bilateral concessions as well as the concessions that have actually been offered are often rated more negatively when they have been proposed by the other party in the negotiations, versus being put forward by an apparently neutral third party or the representative of one's own side. Along these lines, Stillinger et al. (1990) measured student responses to university plans concerning financial divestment from South Africa, which fell short of the students' own demands for divestment. Stillinger et al. found that students' reactions to the plan were significantly more positive before the plan was actually proposed by the university than after this had occurred; that is, after it had become an object of a need for a specific closure to devalue it.

Research on negotiation by representatives (for a review, see Pruitt and Carnevale, 1993, pp. 56–58) is consistent with the notion that the desirability of toughness versus concession making may determine the negotiators' behavior in a bargaining situation. As may be expected, the negotiators are typically motivated to please their constituents. Often they seem to assume that a tough stance on their part will be viewed more favorably by those they were sent to represent than a conciliatory stance (Gruder, 1971; Walton & McKersie, 1965). Indeed, the research shows that representatives tend to be less conciliatory and take more time to reach an agreement than negotiators who bargain on their own behalf (Benton, 1972; Benton & Druckman, 1973, 1974; Druckman, Solomon, & Zechmeister, 1972). This seems to be the case where no specific information about the constituents' preferences is available. However, when the representatives believe that their constituents are more interested in reaching an agreement than in winning, they tend to be more conciliatory than negotiators without a constituency (Benton & Druckman, 1974; Tjosvold, 1977).

As the above discussion suggests, there seem to exist intriguing relations between needs for nonspecific and specific closure and individuals' behavior in interpersonal (or intergroup) conflict situations, well worthy of further systematic study.

☐ The Language of Interpersonal Discourse

If need for closure induces the tendency to seek permanent knowledge and avoid the recurrence of ambiguity, it should foster a bias toward general, trans-situationally stable knowledge. Accordingly, people under a heightened need for closure should prefer abstract descriptions and category labels over concrete, situationally specific depictions. Consistent with these assumptions, Mikulincer, Yinon, and Kabili (1991) found that persons with high (versus low) need for structure (an alternate term used to denote the need for closure) tended more to attribute failure to stable and global (hence, general and abstract) attributions as assessed by the Attributional Style Questionnaire (Seligman, Abramson, Semmel, & Von Baeyer, 1979). In the same research, high- (versus low-) need-for-structure individuals who worked on unsolvable problems were more likely to attribute failure to global causes and exhibited impaired performance on a subsequent task.

In a different paradigm, Boudreau, Baron, and Oliver (1992) asked participants to communicate their impressions of a target to an individual either more or less generally knowledgeable than themselves. Boudreau et al. assumed that the task of communicating to a knowledgeable other would increase concerns about judgmental validity and lower the need for closure, whereas communication to a less knowledgeable other would reduce concerns about validity, thus enhancing the need for closure. Consistent with this expectation, their results revealed that participants expecting to communicate their impressions to an unknowledgeable other increased the preponderance of global trait-labels in their descriptions, whereas participants expecting to communicate to a knowledgeable other used a lower proportion of global trait labels.

Assuming the existence of such an abstraction bias under heightened need for closure, how might it affect the use of language in interpersonal discourse, and what effects might it have on interpersonal rapport? Rubini and Kruglanski (1997) set out to investigate these issues in a question-and-answer paradigm. This particular paradigm simulates the situation wherein we acquire knowledge by formulating questions and directing them at others capable of providing informative answers. Recent work by Semin, Rubini, and Fiedler (1995) indicates that the abstractness level of questions influences the locus of causal origin for answers. Specifically, questions formulated with action verbs (e.g., to help, to write) cue the logical subject of a question as the causal origin of answers. Questions formulated with state verbs (e.g., to love or to like) cue the logical object of a question as the causal origin for answers. Thus, if asked such a simple and mundane question as, "Why do you own a dog?" (using an interpretative action verb) persons are prompted to respond by referring to themselves (the subject of the question) as the causal agent in the answer; for example, by stating "Because I enjoy the companionship that dogs provide." If one is asked "Why do you like dogs?" however, one is prompted to respond by referring to the object itself "Because dogs are good companions."

One interesting implication of this effect is that individuals might feel that they disclose more about themselves when asked a question formulated with action verbs as opposed to inactive verbs, or more generally speaking, questions formulated at a lower (versus higher) level of abstractness. As a consequence, respondents asked questions at a low level of abstractness might feel closer and friendlier toward the interviewer, which may elicit reciprocal friendliness on his/her part. By contrast, respondents asked questions at a higher level of abstractness may feel more distant and less friendly toward the interviewer, again inviting a response in kind.

Semin, Rubini, and Fiedler also found that the abstractness level of the questions tends to be matched by the abstractness of the answers. Thus, the more abstractly formulated questions tend to elicit the more abstract answers. Such a drift toward abstraction might increase the felt interpersonal distance and feelings of estrangement in and of itself, apart from any possible effects due to implicit causality. After all, abstractness connotes generality and deindividuation, hence it may well depersonalize the interaction and render it more distant and less friendly.

In their first experiment designed to investigate these issues, Rubini and Kruglanski (1997) had participants under high (versus low) need for closure (operationalized via ambient noise) rank questions out of a list in terms of their likelihood of using them in a real interview. The list included 32 questions, eight questions on each of four different topics. It was found that participants under noise (versus no noise) assigned higher ranks to questions characterized by a higher (versus lower) level of abstractness. In a follow-up study, questions selected by participants under high (versus low) need for closure were found to elicit more abstract answers from respondents, and ones focused more on the logical object (versus subject) of the question. Also, respondents reported feeling less friendliness toward the interviewer whose questions were more (versus less) abstract. Finally, in a third study the results of the previous two experiments were replicated in a free-interaction context. In that research, interviewers with high (versus low) need for closure asked more abstract questions, which in turn elicited more abstract answers and ones focused more on the logical object (versus subject) of the question, and elicited less friendliness from the interviewee. These results suggest that the permanence tendency induced by the need for nonspecific closure may affect the level of linguistic abstractness, and in so doing may imbue the nascent social relations among conversation partners.

Specific closure effects. The inclination toward (linguistic or conceptual) abstractness, and its interpersonal consequences should be affected by needs for specific (as well as nonspecific) closure. That should depend on whether, and to what degree, abstractness or concreteness was congruent with the desirable closure. Abstractness signifies that the characteristic in question transcends the specific situation and that it therefore implies generality, stability, or globality. If such a characteristic was desirable and pleasing, one might well want to perpetuate its applicability and hence manifest an abstraction bias. By contrast, if the characteristic in question was negative or undesirable, one might wish to minimize its implications and restrict them to the specific context by concretizing the way one thinks or talks about this particular feature.

Research on the linguistic intergroup bias (LIB) (Maass & Arcuri, 1992; Maass & Stahlberg, 1993; Maass, Salvi, Arcuri, & Semin, 1989, Maass, Milesi, Zabbini, & Stahlberg, 1995) is consistent with these notions. The LIB involves a tendency for individuals to describe positive in-group and negative out-group behaviors in relatively abstract terms, implying that the behavior is attributable internally to the actor's stable characteristics. Conversely, negative in-group and positive out-group behaviors are typically described in relatively concrete terms, implying situational specificity, and hence an external attribution of the behavior. One possible mechanism of the LIB could be motivational (Maass & Stahlberg, 1993) having to do with the fact that abstract descriptions of positive in-group behaviors and of negative out-group behaviors portray the former in favorable and the later in unfavorable terms. Similarly, concrete depictions of negative in-group behaviors minimize their significance as evidence for corresponding group characteristics, as do concrete depictions of positive out-group behaviors. In other words, those linguistic (and conceptual) tendencies serve to protect the perception that the in-group is superior to the out-group. I shall discuss the LIB more fully in a subsequent chapter that deals with the intergroup implications of the needs for closure.

☐ Summary

Research findings described in this chapter suggest that the needs for cognitive closure, whether of the specific or nonspecific variety, may importantly impact our interpersonal relations. To be intelligible, such relations require grounding in a common understanding (cf. Grice, 1975). The needs for closure may impact the arrival at such common understanding in various ways. The need for nonspecific closure may prompt the seizing and freezing on one's own perspective and bring about failures to take the other's perspective into account. A need for a specific closure may promote either freezing or unfreezing depending on the relative subjective desirabilities of one's own and the other's perspectives. As we have seen, the seizing and freezing on own perspective or initial notions may impact a wide range of interpersonal behaviors including empathy, communication, and interpersonal negotiations.

Seizing and freezing under a heightened need for closure may also foster a conflictual interpretation of one's relations with another because conflict represents a cut-and-dried, definite conception with clear behavioral implications. The tendency to adhere to a conflict schema may be further enhanced by needs for specific closure related to one's initial disparagement of, and condescension to, the other.

The permanence tendency affected by the needs for closure may impact our interpersonal relations by inducing a tendency to think and communicate to others in abstract terms and broad categories. A person treated as a member of an abstract category (gender, professional, ethnic, or age related for example) may feel that he or she is being pigeonholed rather than treated as a unique individual. This may induce a sense of interpersonal distance between people, reduce their readiness to self-disclosure, and forestall the development of intimacy and closeness.

Group Phenomena

The distal effects of epistemic motivations extend to a plethora of group processes. How do group members treat each other? How do they allocate their resources? How they treat a diversity of opinions in their midst? How strongly they adhere to group norms? What kind of leadership do they prefer, and how do they render group decisions? These are all phenomena to which the needs for nonspecific and specific closure are highly relevant. The present chapter discusses these issues in the context of pertinent empirical research.

☐ Task versus Socio-Emotional Orientation in Group Contexts

Groups are often assembled for a specific purpose or in the service of specific tasks they are entrusted to perform: Juries are expected to render verdicts, work teams are formed to create products, personnel committees to recruit new employees, and so on. But beyond the official task a group is charged with, a great many other goings-on may take place during a group's interaction. Members may chitchat, crack jokes, extend or withdraw emotional support from each other, express a variety of feelings, posture, and try to impress one another by engaging in extensive self-presentational maneuvers. Small-group researchers (e.g., Bales, 1950; Fiedler, 1967) distinguished between a task orientation, which includes those member behaviors that pertain to the task as such, and a social-emotional orientation, including behaviors that reflect members' interpersonal goals in the situation and their affective reactions to events occurring in the interaction context.

How might the need for closure affect those member orientations? Though members of a work team may perform a variety of interpersonal and emotional acts, the way they define to themselves the situation they are in, probably relates predominantly to the task the group has been assembled to perform. In other words, the task at hand is likely to constitute the single most accessible notion whereby group members may define their situation. Based on prior work (Ford & Kruglanski, 1995; Thompson, Naccarato, & Parker, 1994) described in Chapter 3, we expected that high-need-for-closure individuals will be particularly likely to seize on such an official, highly accessible, definition and adhere to its various dictates. Should this be true, high (versus low) need for closure members should be particularly likely to exhibit a preponderance of task-oriented responses relative to task-unrelated responses of a social-emotional nature.

De Grada, Kruglanski, Mannetti, & Pierro (1999) investigated this hypothesis with University of Rome ("La Sapienza") students as participants. We assembled 24 leaderless groups of four members each. Participants in each group were asked to role-play the managers of four corporate departments at a meeting designed to negotiate the division of a monetary prize among four meritorious workers representing their respective sectors. To that end, each manager was provided with his/her own candidate's resume. Two members of each group were preselected as high on the dispositional need for closure (assessed by the Italian translation [Pierro et al., 1995] of the scale developed by Webster & Kruglanski, 1994) and the remaining two as low on this need. After the first half-hour of group discussion, a time-pressure manipulation was carried out in 12 (i.e., half) of the groups. Video recordings of the ensuing discussions were subjected to Bales's (1950) interaction process analysis (IPA). The main dependent variables of interest, inferred by coding the recorded interaction according to the IPA, were the proportions of members' acts in four areas: (1) task-oriented questions, (2) task-oriented responses, (3) positive instances of socio-emotional acts, and (4) negative instances of social-emotional acts.

In the absence of time pressure, groups continued their discussion for another 36 minutes on the average, whereas groups exposed to time pressure quit after 20 minutes on the average. This difference was significant (p < .05) suggesting that our manipulation successfully imposed an appreciable degree of time pressure on the participants. More importantly, our predictions in regard to need-for-closure effects on group interaction were strongly supported. We predicted that a heightened need for closure (either due to time pressure or to a stable disposition) would enhance participants' task orientation and reduce their engagement in acts of a social-emotional nature because of the tendency to seize and freeze on the "official" definition of the situation in terms of the task at hand. That is precisely what happened. Participants under time pressure produced a higher proportion of task-oriented responses than participants not exposed to time pressure, as did participants with a high versus low need for closure. Participants under time pressure also produced a lower proportion of positive social-emotional acts than did participants not exposed to pressure, as did participants under high versus low dispositional need for closure. Very few behaviors were classifiable as task-oriented requests or negative social emotional acts. Neither time-pressure nor need for closure registered significant effects on those infrequent interactional dimensions.

Specific closure effects. Various needs for specific closure may also affect group members' tendency to emphasize the task at hand over various socio-emotional behaviors. For instance, if the task definition was pleasing to members, perhaps because they felt particularly confident or competent on the performance dimension represented by the task, they might well freeze on that particular definition and hence orient more toward the task, neglecting the socio-emotional aspects of the group interaction. On the other hand, if members felt rather incompetent or anxious with respect to the task, they might tend less to freeze on the official definition of the situation in terms of the task and orient more toward the socio-emotional aspects of the group interaction to the relative neglect of task execution. The work of Claude Steele and his colleagues (Steele, Spencer, & Aronson, 2002) on stereotype threat could be relevant to these phenomena. These investigators find that members of a stereotyped group (e.g., African Americans or women), may do poorly on academic tasks presumed to measure an ability on which their group is stereotyped as inferior as compared to their performance on an identical task portrayed as insensitive to the stereotyped performance differences. Relatively little is known at this time about the mechanisms mediating these intriguing phenomena, but from the present perspective it could be that where the performance dimension of the task is assumed to represent one on which an individual expects to do poorly, he or she may exhibit less of a task orientation and focus instead on her or his own socio-emotional needs evoked in this unpleasant circumstance. Indeed, Steele and his coworkers find increased anxiety under stereotype threat, attesting to the arousal of persons' emotional needs in this situation. If so, participants under a stereotype threat might spend more time on socio-emotional group interaction than they would in a similar situation not defined as threatening. These issues could be profitably studied in future research.

Beyond the seizing and freezing effects that may affect task versus socio-emotional orientation under heightened needs for specific or nonspecific closure, these motivations may affect group interaction via the permanence tendency and the quest for consensus and the stable social reality it implies. These phenomena are discussed next.

☐ Consensus Strivings under Need for Nonspecific Closure

In a 1998 cinematic hit, a pair of teenage siblings, Bud and Jennifer, are teletransported from the 1990s to the 1950s into a little town named Pleasantville (the movie's title). The town is depicted in black and white without as much as a patch of color. All of its residents behave in exactly the same serenely pleasant way, think the same serenely pleasant thoughts, and possess the exactly the same, extremely limited, knowledge imparted by the local school.

Every evening without fail, husbands return from work signaling their reentry with an enthusiastic "Honey, I am home!" cheer. They are immediately handed a martini prepared by a loving spouse, impeccably groomed and totally enthusiastic about her role as a housewife. A tasty (and highly caloric) dinner is churning on the stove, ready to be served as soon as the master of the house is prepared to sit at the table. And after dinner and coffee, what could be more pleasant than a strong cigarette smoked in the family room by the fire.

There are no books in Pleasantville. No, this isn't quite true. There are plenty of books (e.g., in the local library), but their pages are completely blank. Thus, there is no danger whatever of any new ideas upsetting the tranquility of the Pleasantville community. No danger, that is, until Bud and Jennifer arrive at the scene with their 1990s mentality. Their coming totally disturbs the peaceful lives of Pleasantville inhabitants and injects bright smudges of color into their formerly black-and-white existence. Slowly the town inhabitants are introduced to new ideas: the notion that there is a world out there beyond the Pleasantville city limits, that there is a sensuality to explore and enjoy, and a wealth of literature to be stirred by. These revelations send veritable shock waves through Pleasantville. While some of the residents embrace the novelties with curious anticipation, many are profoundly upset. They do not take kindly to the newly introduced "cool" and are shaken by the threat to their old way of life. Uncertainty and chaos ensue and the town's unity breaks down, leading to violent internal conflict involving window smashing, beating of the deviants (referred to as the "coloreds," and desperate attempts by the reactionary faction to restore things to the way they once were.

Though lighthearted and comic in tone, Pleasantville captures a fundamental truth about the interface of epistemic certainty and human sociality. Social uniformity is essential for the maintenance of epistemic certainty. You cannot have the latter without the former. Upset uniformity and certainty comes tumbling down. As Festinger (1950) has noted, social reality requires the homogeneity of opinions within a group. It follows, therefore, that the quest for permanence under a heightened need for nonspecific closure should fuel the desire for consensus.

There exists long-standing and varied evidence that this is so. On a broad level, varied sociological analyses suggest a link between the desire to remove uncertainty and collective behaviors in various shapes and forms. Blumer (1956), for example, asserted that, "Collective behavior ... is behavior formed or forged to meet undefined or unstructured situations" (cited in Smelser, 1962, pp. 8–9). Smelser's own (1962) classic work on social movements, from cases of panic, through the eruption of trends and fashions in various realms of life, to political bandwagons during presidential elections, views them as, by and large, a response to what he refers to as "structural strain" (p. 47), a principal kind of which is ambiguity that "at the psychological level (translates to) 'uncertainty'" (pp. 51–52).

Writing much later, Broadbent (1993, p. 14), in his analysis of the Japanese mentality, also noted the co-occurrence in Japan of worrisome uncertainty and high degrees of collectivism that pervade typical Japanese attitudes and behavior. As he put it: "Japanese business leaders, politicians and common people frame life in terms (of) insecurity ... Japanese companies want to buy up a good stock of real estate abroad as a form of insurance, because they don't know when an earthquake will hit Japan and destroy what they own at home." Hofstede's (1980) research on uncertainty avoidance in 44 nations is consistent with Broadbent's analysis. Controlling for age of respondents, Japan's uncertainty avoidance index (reflecting, presumably, the presence of aversive insecurity) is the highest (p. 14) of all the countries surveyed!

A response to the nagging sense of insecurity, according to Broadbent, is a profound dependence on one's group. "The snug embrace of long-term group membership feels good and provides good collective insurance against hard times. Pushing one's own advancement at the cost of another group member runs against the grain. Rather, tremendous effort goes into keeping everyone in the group feeling happy, included and peaceful, what the Japanese call 'wa' or harmony. Hence people live with a constant nervousness over how the group is going to evaluate one's performance ... The desire for cultural homogeneity leads to severe discrimination against those who deign to differ. Any foreigner is familiar with being called 'gaijin' (literally, outsider). But it doesn't let up even for those who have lived in Japan for generations. Japanese-Koreans who have been there for three generations fear to use the Korean style pronunciation of their names. Even a completely native group, Burakomin is still often treated with contempt" (Broadbent, 1993, p. 16).

Broadbent refers to the Japanese society as a "pressure cooker" and Miyamoto (1995), in a recent work calls it the "straitjacket society." Also of interest, and consistent with need for closure theory, is the apparent relative difficulty, which according to Broadbent, the Japanese have in appreciating perspectives different from their own. Such difficulty may well be expected if the Japanese as a group were characterized by a heightened need for closure. Along these lines, Broadbent comments on the Japanese apparent difficulty in grasping the U.S. perspective on World War II or on contemporary trade relations with the United States: "When thinking of World War II, many Japanese see only half of the story. They see their nation mainly as victim of atomic bomb attack, not as initiator of the Pacific war through invasion of Korea and China and attack on Pearl Harbor. This sense of victimization makes Japanese war actions 'understandable' to themselves … the U.S. trade demands are interpreted in similar light. Most Japanese have no real comprehension of the damage that Japanese economic penetration is doing to U.S. industry and the society at large. They lack the habit of extending their imagination into the shoes of the other. This frame of mind makes U.S. objections seem without justification and, once again, merely the senseless victimization of Japan" (p. 16).

Though the analyses by Broadbent or Miyamoto (1993) are suggestive, they are impressionistic and anecdotal rather than grounded in firm scientific findings. The question, therefore, is whether there exists more systematic evidence for the hypothesized relations between need for (nonspecific) closure and the kind of group-centered society described by these authors.

Need for nonspecific closure and consensus seeking. In research by Kruglanski, Webster, & Klem (1993) referred to earlier, participants, members of alleged two-member juries, were asked to what extent they wished to reach agreement with the other member, and to what extent they wished to do so quickly. These two items were highly correlated and hence were combined into a Need for Agreement Index by simple summation. Whether the need for closure was elevated by means of ambient noise or assessed via the Need for Closure Scale, those participants high on this motivation reported a significantly greater desire for agreement with their partner. This tendency was reflected in a significant noise or need for closure main effect, that is, it obtained irrespective of whether the participants were provided with a (fictitious) legal analysis allowing them to form a relatively firm personal opinion as to the appropriate verdict, or whether they were given no such legal counsel and hence were left with no more than a hunch in this matter. Mind you, the way participants under high (versus low) need for closure dealt with disagreement from the other jury member differed appreciably as a function of whether they did or did not possess a firm prior opinion. Those with a firm opinion were relatively recalcitrant and intransigent. They were refractory to arguments from the other juror and refused to change their minds as a consequence of the discussion. If they desired consensus, as they apparently did, they probably hoped to attain it by the *change other* strategy identified by Festinger (1950); that is, by exerting influence attempts geared at altering their partner's views to coincide more closely with their own. Markedly different was the behavior of participants absent a firm prior opinion. These individuals were quite persuadable in fact, and exhibited considerable opinion shifts in the direction of the other juror's arguments. One might say that their strategy of attaining consensus was via Festinger's *change self* option; that is, by altering their own views to bring it into closer correspondence with those of the other.

But Festinger and Schachter (1951) were quick to identify a third way of securing consensus within a group: Rejection of opinion deviates and redefinition of the group's boundaries so that only the consensual members remain included within them. Following up on implications of this logic, Donna Webster and I (Kruglanski & Webster, 1991) carried out several experimental studies designed to see whether rejection of deviates is indeed intensified under a heightened need for (a nonspecific) closure.

In the first study, groups of Tel-Aviv (boy and girl) Scouts were presented with a decision regarding the location of their annual two-week "working camp." Two choices were presented, one a well established, veteran, kibbutz settlement in the middle of the land (Naan) equipped with swimming pools, lush lawns, television sets, and tennis courts; the other, a new, fledgling settlement in the Judean desert (Ktorah) with hardly any amenities at the time (1983), not even in-house bathrooms. Despite what to some might appear as the obvious choice, the Israeli scouts were an idealistic bunch and they overwhelmingly preferred the struggling pioneer settlement over its lush alternative. Within each group of scouts we, therefore, solicited the help of one of the members occupying a median sociometric standing in the group and asked her or him to argue either for the consensual choice (the conformist condition) or for the unpopular one (the deviant condition).

Need for closure was manipulated via time pressure. Specifically, the confederate expressed the (dissenting or conforming) viewpoint at one of three times: in the objectively early condition, he/she did so near the start of the discussion; in the objectively late condition near the expected deadline, and in the subjectively early condition at the same temporal point as in the objectively late condition but, as the deadline was postponed in this condition, with the same time remaining to the new deadline as in the objectively early condition. Manipulation checks suggested, as expected, that need for closure was proportionate to the discussion time presumed to remain at the point when the confederate's view was expressed.

The main dependent variable was the magnitude of evaluative shifts toward the confederate following the discussion. No significant differences in evaluative shifts as a function of timing emerged in regard to the conformist. A very different pattern of reactions greeted the deviant, however! These reactions became progressively more negative with increasing proximity to the deadline. Specifically, whereas no significant evaluative shifts toward the deviant occurred in the objectively early condition, substantial shifts were registered in both the subjectively early and objectively late conditions, the latter being significantly more pronounced than the former.

We replicated these findings in an additional experiment conducted at the University of Maryland (Kruglanski & Webster, 1991, Study 2), which operationalized the need for closure in terms of ambient noise. Groups of University of Maryland students in favor of drug testing for athletes (as was the majority of the student body at that time) were asked to reach consensus on a case involving compulsory drug testing. Two confederates participated in the group discussions and rotated the enactment of two roles: One confederate enacted the role of a conformist and argued the majority viewpoint in favor of testing; the other enacted the deviant role and argued the minority viewpoint against testing.

If working in a noisy environment raises the need for closure by making information processing more costly, greater rejection of the deviate should occur in the noisy (versus the quiet) conditions. This prediction was confirmed, as ratings of the deviant were significantly lower in the noise versus the no-noise condition. To examine the alternative possibility that greater rejection of the deviate occurred under noise due to a noise-induced irritation rather than due to the need for closure, another study was conducted that replicated Study 2, but included an additional experimental variation. Specifically, in some conditions, participants were given the option of reaching closure by formally excluding the deviate from the decision-making process. These participants were allowed to form their decision by a majority rule rather than by consensus. Results indicated that rejection of the deviate occurred only in the noise/consensus rule condition where the deviant frustrated the other group members' desire for collective closure. No comparable rejection occurred in the noise/majority rule condition, presumably because collective closure was satisfied via the allowable majority rule. Consistent with this interpretation, in an additional study a conformist who vocally endorsed the consensual view was evaluated more positively, in fact, under the noisy versus the quiet conditions. Thus, it seems that noise-induced need for closure may instill a striving for consensus manifest in the rejection of opinion deviants as well as in the adulation of conformists.

Experiencing pressures to uniformity. Whereas rejection of deviates is generally interpreted as a consequence of uniformity pressures within a group (Festinger, 1950; Schachter, 1951), it would be desirable to have more direct evidence that such pressures are indeed exerted and experienced by group members under a heightened need for closure. Research by De Grada et al. (1999, Study 2) set out to look for such evidence. As in the previous study by De Grada et al. (1999, Study 1) described earlier, members of four-person groups role-played the managers of four corporate departments negotiating the division of a monetary prize among meritorious candidates. We investigated 10 such groups. Five were composed of members high on the dispositional need for closure (as assessed by the Italian version of the Need for Closure Scale (Webster & Kruglanski, 1994) and five, of members low on this need. The discussion, lasting 46 minutes on the average, was videotaped and its participants answered several questions about their experiences during the session. These questions were designed to tap the perception of conformity pressures by group members and were based on a modified version of the Conformity Pressure Questionnaire developed by Kroon, van Kreveld, & Rabbie (1992). This questionnaire included the following:

In order to avoid a long discussion, I often did not insist on defending my interests.
I was annoyed when somebody expressed ideas in contrast with those of all the others.
Even when I totally disagreed with the others, I often did not stand up to defend my views.
In order to reach a conclusion, the group was reluctant to accept new ideas.
The group manifested hostility toward those who kept on defending their own interest even when we were about to reach a conclusion.
In order to allow us to finish in time, I sometimes kept dissenting points of view to myself.
In order to reach a unanimous decision quickly, I put the group's interest before mine.
In order to reach a conclusion, we did not take into account opinions in contrast with those expressed by the majority.
We always listened carefully to anyone who advanced new ideas, even though these were in contrast with others' views.

Divergent ideas have been discouraged by the group.
I always defended my opinion even when the others disagreed.

Based on these items it was found that, as predicted, members of the high-need-for-closure groups reported greater perceived pressure to conformity than those of the low-need-for-closure groups.

A question arises as to whether the reported conformity pressures reflect accurately what has transpired during the group discussion as opposed to reflecting a reporting bias on part of the high-need-for-closure individuals independent of what actually transpired. To answer this question, two independent observers blind to the composition of the various groups viewed the video recorded group discussions and responded to several relevant questions about group behavior. These were:

In order to avoid hindering the progress of the discussion, the group forced members to accept the opinions of the majority against their individual will.

In order to avoid a long discussion, the group exerted strong pressure to uniformity.

The group was annoyed when somebody expressed ideas in contrast with those of all the others.

Divergent ideas have been discouraged by the group.

The group always listened carefully to anyone who advanced new ideas even though these were in contrast with others' view.

In order to reach a conclusion, the group did not take into account opinions in contrast with those expressed by the majority.

The group discouraged those who kept on defending their own interest even when the group was about to arrive at a conclusion.

The group was reluctant to accept new ideas.

Group members advancing divergent ideas have been often interrupted by others.

Often the group ignored opinions that might be an obstacle to reaching a conclusion.

The group pressured participants to conform to group norms.

Relevant to our analysis, the observers rated the perceived pressures to conformity in the high-need-for-closure groups as significantly greater than that in the low-need-for-closure groups. It appears that groups composed of high- (versus low-) need-for-closure individuals do exert greater conformity pressures on their members and that such pressures are both experienced by the members and are visible to outside observers.

Focus on shared versus unshared information. One consequence of striving for consensus under a heightened need for cognitive closure could be the members' tendency to focus on information they all share, to the relative exclusion of unique information possessed by some members only and not others. The tendency of groups to predominantly discuss such shared information has been discovered by Stasser in a series of studies (Stasser & Titus, 1985, 1987; Stasser & Stewart, 1992). Recently, however, Webster (1993) tested the further notion that this tendency to focus on shared information is magnified by the need for closure. Specifically, she reasoned that under a heightened need for closure, persons may focus on shared information because of their strong desire for consensus and because shared information provides a common knowledge base on which consensus can be built. Webster manipulated the need for closure via the ingestion of alcohol, based on the assumption that alcohol increases the effortfulness of information processing, which, in turn, should increase the need for closure.

Participants in groups of three members each ingested either pure orange juice (in the placebo condition), orange juice mixed with a low dose of alcohol (.5 ml ethanol/KG of body weight), or one mixed with a moderate dose of alcohol (.7 ml ethanol/KG of body weight). The alcohol was vodka, and in the placebo condition vodka was spread around the rim of the glass to lend it a characteristic alcoholic scent. Orthogonally to the alcohol manipulation, Webster (1993) varied the participants' accountability: high-accountability participants were expected to have to explain to the experimenter why did their group reach the decision it did. The high-accountability participants were also told that each such explanation would be tape recorded for purposes of further analysis; the low accountability participants had no such expectation.

All participants were informed that they would discuss three candidates for a student political office on campus. For that purpose, each participant was provided with background reading materials consisting of statements made by each of the three candidates regarding several campus-relevant issues such as parking fees, dormitory policies, class sizes, registration policies, and campus security. The candidate profiles contained 12 items of information. These included a certain number of positive, negative, and neutral items of information as determined by ratings made by an independent sample of university students. The profile for Candidate A contained 4 positive, 4 negative, and 4 neutral items; that for Candidate B, 2 positive, 6 negative, and 4 neutral items; and that for Candidate C, 6 positive, 4 neutral, and 2 negative items. Overall, 18 items of information were shared by group members, meaning they were included in each member's reading materials, while 18 were unshared, meaning they were included in only one of the member's reading materials. As can be calculated from the above description, the actual items of information that were shared versus unshared were selected to bias each group member's prediscussion preference in favor of Candidate A. Nonetheless, because the three members of each group received differing amounts of information, the total body of information received by all members of each group favored Candidate C.

Webster's results provided strong support for her predictions. First, in the no-accountability condition, the need for closure, as assessed by the appropriate manipulation checks, differed monotonically as a function of the amount of alcohol contained in the drink. These manipulation checks included participants' confidence in their group's collective choice, their desire to reach agreement with the other members of their group, and their desire to do so quickly. These measures were highly inter-correlated and hence they were combined into an overall need-for-closure index. On that measure, participants in the moderate-dosage condition manifested a higher need for closure than participants in the low-dosage condition, who in turn manifested a higher need for closure than participants in the placebo condition. By contrast, in the accountability condition, the need-for-closure index did not demonstrate any significant differences as a function of alcohol ingestion. It appears then that accountability pressures, or the fear of invalidity they may induce, reduced the motivation for closure to such a considerable extent so as to override any differences in this motivation that alcohol may have produced.

Tracking the need for closure differences, Webster found that in the no-accountability condition, the tendency to bring up unique information varied inversely with the amount of alcohol ingested, but the differences due to alcohol entirely disappeared in the accountability condition. These results were mimicked, in turn, by the proportion of groups who reached the correct solution (i.e., who properly selected C as the best qualified candidate): In the no-accountability condition, the tendency to select C varied inversely and in a linear fashion with the amount of alcohol ingested, whereas no significant differences as a function of alcohol emerged in the accountability condition.

Finally, but not least importantly, the alcohol-induced differences in the tendency to discuss unique information, and to select the correct candidate appeared to be mediated by the need for closure as assessed by the index of this motivation described above (Baron & Kenny, 1986). It may be concluded, therefore, that the focus on shared information and the tendency to exclude unshared information during group discussion is at least in part determined by members' need for cognitive closure, presumably due to their strong desire in this motivational state to establish group consensus.

Creativity of individuals and groups under heightened need for closure. The findings that individuals under high need for closure tend to generate less hypotheses (Mayseless & Kruglanski, 1987), that they strive for consensus (Kruglanski & Webster, 1991; Kruglanski, Webster, & Klem, 1993), and that they exert uniformity pressures when in groups (DeGrada et al. 1999) suggest that these individuals may not be particularly creative. Several lines of evidence converge to confirm this is the case. Rocchi (1998) used a mental imagery task (Finke & Slayton, 1988) in which participants were required to combine several "impoverished stimuli" such as letters and geometric figures, into a synthesized image, the creativity of which was subsequently assessed by independent observers. One of Rocchi's studies used an American sample (of University of Maryland students), whereas the second used an Italian sample (students at the University of Verona). Both studies obtained a significant negative relation between participants' need for closure as assessed by the Webster and Kruglanski (1994) scale and creativity.

Using a very different procedure based on the work of Ward and his colleagues (Ward, Patterson, Sifonis, Dodds, & Saunders, 2002), Ip, Chen, & Chiu (2003) had American and Hong Kong Chinese participants list birds, entertainments, occupations, fruits, and diseases that first came to their minds. An output precedence score was computed for each exemplar in a category reflecting the degree to which the exemplar was commonly mentioned (and hence was highly accessible) in the respective cultural (Chinese or American) sample. To the extent that creativity is conceived of as coming up with unconventional, culturally inaccessible exemplars, output precedence may be considered to reflect the absence of creativity. Conceptually replicating the results of Rocchi (1998), Ip et al. (2003) found the need for cognitive closure to be significantly and positively correlated to output precedence in both the Chinese and the American samples.

Two experimental studies conducted by Chirumbolo, Mannetti, Pierro, Areni, and Kruglanski (2003) tested the creativity exhibited by groups under high (versus low) need for cognitive closure. In the first of these, the need for closure was manipulated via environmental noise (see also Kruglanski & Webster, 1991; Kruglanski, Webster, & Klem, 1993), and groups of three members each engaged in a brainstorming task. It was found that groups under noise displayed lesser ideational fluency (i.e., produced a lesser number of ideas) than groups in a quiet environment. This relation was mediated by a motivational, need for closure, index composed of items inquiring into participants' experienced difficulty of the task and their reluctance to expend effort on its execution. In the second study by Chirumbolo et al. (2003), participants in groups of four created advertising slogans for a given product. Some of the groups were composed of individuals with high dispositional need for closure, whereas other groups were composed of low-need-for-closure individuals. Results indicated that ideational fluency, degree of elaboration, and creativity, as rated by independent judges, was lower in high (versus low) need for closure groups. Considered collectively, these results suggest that need for closure driven tendencies to restrict the number of hypotheses generated and to produce conventional ideas (reflecting perceived consensus) tends to lower the degree of creativity in interacting groups.

Inequality of participation. Beyond uniformity pressures, need for closure may impact group interaction in another, intriguing, way. Groups consisting of high- (versus low-) need-for-closure individuals may manifest a less evenly distributed interaction pattern and greater dominance of the discussion by some individuals over others. This prediction also follows from the quest for opinion uniformity that high-need-for-closure members are expected to exhibit. Uniformity may obtain more readily where one (or only a few) opinion(s) govern the discussion than where a heterogeneity of opinions is offered that impedes consensus. Accordingly, groups composed of high-need-for-closure members may exhibit more autocratic (or less democratic) patterns of participation and decision making than those composed of low-need-for-closure members.

De Grada et al. (1999, Study 2) used the sociolinguistic index of speech dominance to assess the emergence of an autocratic discussion pattern. Specifically, they looked at the number of instances in which members seized the discussion floor and maintained it despite interruption attempts by others. The question was whether groups composed of high- (versus low-) need-for-closure members would exhibit a greater asymmetry in the seizing and/or maintaining of speaking turns during group discussion.

The group discussions were transcribed following the notational system routinely employed in conversational analyses and developed originally by Jefferson (1985, for a thorough review of the system and its development, see Psathas & Anderson, 1990, and Dabbs & Ruback, 1987). Each group's transcript was used to calculate two indices of conversational floor control: the number of speaking turns successfully taken (referred to as turns obtained) and the number of such turns successfully maintained despite others' interruptions (turns maintained). To normalize the frequency distribution, a square-root transformation was applied to both indices. The index of asymmetry was computed for each group by dividing the standard deviation by the average frequency of (1) obtained turns and (2) maintained turns. The logic of this index was as follows. The standard deviation in each group reflects asymmetry or variability in the degree to which the group members obtained or maintained their speaking turns, but the different groups may also vary in the overall intensity with which their members attempted to control the floor. To correct for this factor, we divided the standard deviations by the average frequency of obtaining or maintaining turns within a given group. The resulting measure is known statistically as the coefficient of variation (cf. Armitage, 1971; Vogt, 1993) and is commonly used to compare standard deviations derived from different distributions. Whereas no significant difference emerged in regard to the asymmetry of obtained turns, it did manifest itself with maintained turns. As expected, the asymmetry of maintained turns was higher in the high-need-for-closure groups than in the low-need-for-closure groups. It appears then that members' high need for closure encourages a conversational pattern wherein some of the members manifest greater dominance of the discourse (or a more extensive "floor control") than do others.

These results were replicated in an additional study (Pierro et al., 2003) using an identical procedure and method of analysis. Specifically, we tested 12 four-person groups composed of students at the University of Rome "La Sapienza," six of which consisted of members high on the need for closure, and six of members low on the need for closure. The results indicted, again, that the asymmetry of both the obtained and the maintained turns, this time, was greater in groups composed of high-need-for-closure individuals.

In the successive phase of this study, Pierro et al. (2003) analyzed the degree to which the emergent group leader tended to exhibit autocratic characteristics and whether this varied as a function of members' need for closure. Independent observers who viewed the video recordings of the group interaction rated each of the four participants on the degree to which he/she appeared to be authoritarian, assertive, dogmatic, and egocentric. These ratings were highly intercorrelated and were, therefore, combined into a single scale by simple averaging. Pierro et al. (2003) then correlated scores on this autocracy index with the numbers of obtained as well as maintained speaking turns. It was found that the correlation between autocracy and floor control was significantly higher for groups composed of high-need-for-closure members than for groups composed of low-need-for-closure members. Finally, Pierro et al. (2003) found that the tendency to control the floor is perceived (by the group members as well as by independent observers) as a demonstration of influence and leadership in the group, all of which combines to suggest that high (versus low) need for closure groups indeed foster the emergence of more autocratic leaders.

In their final study, Pierro et al. (2003) manipulated the need for closure via time pressure and measured the tendency toward centralization in a group via Interaction Process Analysis (Bales, 1950). It was found that groups under time pressure (versus no pressure) exhibited significantly greater asymmetry between members in their degree of centrality (assessed via the number of acts emitted as well as acts received). Again then, it appears that groups whose members are under high need for closure exhibit a greater degree of centralization and hierarchical differentiation between members in their degree of influence than do groups whose members are under a lower degree of this need.

Participation in individual versus group sports. An unobvious implication of the notion that high-need-for-closure individuals prefer autocratic versus democratic leadership because the latter retards the arrival at clear-cut judgments and decisions, relates to people's personal preferences for individual versus group sports. In individual sports, such as tennis, wrestling, or gymnastics, the participant decides by him- or herself on the appropriate response affording quick closure, whereas in a group sport such as basketball or football, the response depends on the judgments of several individuals often creating considerable ambiguity as to what will transpire. Indeed, Giovannini and Savoia (2002) report research finding that individuals with high need for closure tend to participate more in individual sports and less in group sports than individuals low in the need for closure group.

☐ Need for Closure and Groupthink

Analysis presented in this and previous chapters suggests that under a heightened need for (nonspecific) cognitive closure, a group's decision-making style may be characterized by consensus seeking, rejection of opinion deviates, incomplete information search, incomplete survey of the available alternatives, and overconfidence. These characteristics fit remarkably well the group decision-making style characterized as groupthink in Irwin Janis's well-known 1972 work.

Janis defined groupthink "as a mode of thinking that people engage in when they are deeply involved in a cohesive in-group, when the members' striving for unanimity override their motivation to realistically appraise alternative courses of action" (Janis, 1972, p. 9). Janis illustrated the groupthink phenomenon via several striking examples of faulty political decision making including (1) the poor preparedness policies of the U.S. Navy at Pearl Harbor in December 1941, (2) the problematic decision by the Eisenhower administration to pursue the defeated North Korean army on its home territory, (3) the Bay of Pigs invasion decided on by President Kennedy and his advisors, and (4) the series of decisions by the Johnson administration to continue and escalate the Vietnam War. A revision of the original volume published ten years later (Janis, 1982) included another striking case study of groupthink, the Watergate cover-up operation by President Nixon and his advisors.

Whereas the need for cognitive closure may not be the exclusive determinant of the groupthink syndrome, it does seem to constitute a factor that relates to many of its facets both as regards its presumed antecedent conditions and its special characteristics. First, the likelihood of groupthink is seen to increase when decision makers are under stress, occasioned, for example, by the complexity and impenetrability of the issues the group is grappling with. From the present perspective, these are precisely the conditions under which the need for closure is likely to arise because of the difficulty of information processing and the laboriousness of deliberations that they entail. Second, the putative characteristics of groupthink are those one could expect under the need for closure. In fact, Janis identified closed mindedness, including collective rationalizations and stereotyped images of out-groups, as one of the three major characteristics of groupthink. The other two also strongly resemble the phenomena that need for closure was known to induce. They are pressures to uniformity (including direct pressure on dissenters), and an overestimation of the in-group, both of which are the likely consequences of the desire for consensus and for firm social reality that the permanency tendency under heightened need for cognitive closure may be expected to foster.

Whereas the notion of groupthink is typically invoked in reference to disastrous decisions made by governmental bodies, our analysis suggests that the need for closure plays a central role in all decisions, for without it, the group's deliberations could continue endlessly. Hart's (1994) comprehensive work on the groupthink syndrome is consistent with such an interpretation. As he put it, "Concurrence-seeking as such is a necessary element within each collective decision process (especially when unanimity is called for). At a certain point in the deliberative process, discussions need to be concluded and actions taken. In this respect, there is not so much difference with processes of individual decision making, where decision makers start 'bolstering' their preferred alternatives. However, concurrence-seeking becomes excessive when it takes place too early and in too restrictive a way" (p. 11).

Specific closure effects. How might consensus-seeking phenomena in groups be affected by needs for specific closure? Briefly, if the forming consensus was of the kind a member considered desirable, the greater this member's need for the specific closure represented by the consensus, the greater her or his tendency to promote it. This might be accomplished by exerting uniformity pressures on the other members, an emphasis on shared (versus unique) information affording a quicker arrival at consensus, or indeed the support for an autocratic leadership perceived as likely to foster such consensus quickly and efficiently. In real world situations, for example, military dictatorships or other forms of totalitarianism (in Nazi Germany or the Communist Soviet Union, for example) are often supported on the basis of the desirability of the consensus they are expected to forge, such as advancement of some humanistic (as in the case of Communism) or nationalistic (as in the case of Nazism) ideals, provision of law and order for the citizens, etc. Specific closure effects on consensus seeking have not yet received the research attention they deserve, and their full exploration remains a task for future investigations.

□ Norm Stability

In addition to inducing consensus-seeking tendencies, the pressures toward epistemic permanence and freezing on extant knowledge structures fostered by a heightened need for closure may induce in members the disposition toward conservatism, traditionalism, and the preservation of group norms.

The relation between need for closure and the tendency to preserve group norms was also the subject of a recent experimental work by Livi (2001). Participants were given information about a (fictitious) new voice-activated computer software and were asked to answer, in a group format, a number of questions allegedly posed by a marketing firm, including the age of potential users, optimal number of TV commercials, and optimal advertising budget for effective marketing of the product. Livi utilized a generational procedure modeled after Jacobs and Campbell (1961). Each generation was composed of three members. In the first generation, two of these were confederates who agreed on rather low values (as determined by a pretest) with respect to all three issues being discussed (i.e., on relatively low age of potential users, low optimal number of TV commercials, and low optimal advertising budget) thus influencing the third member who was a naïve participant.

After having stated their opinions, one of the confederates left the group and was replaced by a naïve participant. After the second cycle, the second confederate was replaced, and after the third cycle, the original naïve participant was replaced, and so forth for the total of eight generational cycles. Half of the groups were placed under a high need for closure by means of a great deal of ambient noise (presumably generated by a faulty air conditioner). The remaining half of the groups did not experience noise. In support of the present theory, Livi (2002) found that over the several generational cycles investigated, norms were considerably more stable in groups under noise versus no noise. These findings were replicated in Livi's (2002) second study wherein dispositional differences in need for closure were substituted for ambient noise.

Specific closure effects. The needs for specific closure should also be relevant to the phenomenon of norm stability, but this should depend on the attractiveness of the norm. Simply, norms congruent with the

individuals' dominant desires should be stable whereas those incongruent with such desires, should be unstable. I know of no specific research,
however, that directly investigated these possibilities.

☐ Summary

Members' need for nonspecific closure appears to play a significant
role in a broad range of group phenomena. It may focus members'
attention on the group task at hand and lower their tendency to
engage in activities outside the officially prescribed realm. Such tendency to stick with the explicit agenda seems to reduce members'
inclination to display various forms of sociability or to perform personal and affective functions for one another. As far as the task-
oriented behaviors are concerned, groups constituted of high- (versus low) need-for-closure members may apply considerable pressure
toward uniformity upon members. Such pressures may include discouragement of views that deviate from the group consensus and
the derogation and exclusion of members who express them. They
may also include discouragement of the sharing of unique information possessed locally by some members of the group and not others,
and the tendency to focus the group discussion on commonly shared
information. In general, then, need for closure effects on group interaction closely resemble the syndrome of groupthink identified by
Janis (1972) in political decision-making processes.

Members' need for nonspecific closure may also impact the emergent
leadership and decision-making structure in a group. Specifically, groups
high on such a need were shown to encourage the emergence of centralis-
tic or hierarchical structures with a considerable differentiation in
members' degree of prestige, centrality, and dominance over the group
activities. Groups whose members are high on the need for closure have
been shown to exhibit conservative tendencies and a considerable degree
of norm stability as compared with groups whose membership is low in
the need for closure. Finally, needs for specific closure may affect both
task (versus socio-emotional) orientation of the group members and their
tendency to strive for consensus in the group context, both as a function
of the perceived desirability of the group task and of the emerging
consensus. As of now, little systematic evidence exists on those latter
effects, and their empirical probing must await further investigations.

Need for Closure Impact on Inter- Group Processes

Among the many functions that groups serve for individuals, few are more fundamental than the sense of *social reality* group membership affords (cf. Festinger, 1950; Hardin & Higgins, 1996). At work, home, or play—our actions, thoughts, and feelings are guided by standards and purposes shared with fellow participants in specific collectives. Terms such as success or failure, insult or complement, treason or patriotism, sin or virtue are nearly meaningless outside a consensually validated belief system unique to a given community of people at a given time and a given place. Participation in some form of group life (of one's nation, profession, religion, or culture) lends coherence to what otherwise would have been an unimaginable jumble of stimuli and events, and bestows a sense of purpose on one's very existence (cf. Greenberg, Simon, Pysczyn-ski, Solomon, & Chatel, 1992). It provides the needed permanence and stability wherein the time-course of one's activities may be charted and progress to ward one's chosen objectives may be gauged.

However, fundamental social reality may be to people in general, it might be more important to some people than to others. Not all persons crave stability to the same degree, nor is everyone lost to the same degree without order, coherence, or a sense of purpose. And the same person may desire these qualities to different degrees in different situations. Such (interpersonal and situational) fluctuations in the appeal of coherence and stability may correspondingly imbue people's attitudes toward groups they belong to (i.e., in-groups), and toward ones to which they don't (i.e., out-groups). The relevance of the need for closure construct to these phenomena is striking. The increased desire for consensus and for stable knowledge under heightened need for closure may lend one's group special value as a source of closure. Janis (1972), for example, counted an overestimation of the in-group and stereotyped images of out-groups among the quintessential characteristics of the groupthink syndrome, which closely parallels need for closure effects.

To take a recent example, the rise of ethnic conflicts in the Balkans during the 1990s, following the disintegration of the former Yugoslavia, may be explained in part by the uncertainty and instability that prevailed in those circumstances, and the heightened need for cognitive closure and epistemic permanence that this may engender. It is instructive to consider from this perspective Samuel Huntington's (1997) analysis of the resurgence of religion in the second half of the twentieth century the world over. As he put it: "The most obvious, most salient, and most powerful cause of the global religious resurgence is ... the process of social, economic, and cultural modernization that swept across the world in the second half of the twentieth century. Long-standing sources of identity and systems of authority are disrupted. People move from the countryside into the city, become separated from their roots, and take new jobs or no job. They interact with large numbers of strangers and are exposed to new sets of relationships. They need new sources of identity, new forms of stable community, and new sets of moral precepts to provide them with a sense of meaning and purpose. Religion, both mainstream and fundamentalist, meets these needs" (p. 97).

In brief, the upheaval, turmoil, and increased mobility that increasingly characterize modern life may create a surrealistic experience of rootlessness; the sort of mental chaos that evokes yearnings for stable anchorage in fundamental meanings that might lend direction to one's existence. In other words, the frantic pace of modernism may have evoked in numerous individuals a heightened need for closure, fostering the embracement of clear-cut social realities (contained in ethnic or religious identities), the increased attraction to in-groups whose members share in the same realities, and a rejection of out-groups whose discrepant realities threaten one's own sense of the world. In various ways, these phenomena have been examined in the research literature on groups and intergroup relations.

Social psychological analyses of the in-group bias. Dating from Sumner's (1906) seminal work on ethnocentrism, overidentification with one's in-group, has been regarded as a fundamental social psychological phenomenon, at the root of numerous pernicious intergroup conflicts in the world at large. A striking feature of the in-group bias is its pervasiveness. Though its magnitude may vary across cultural settings (Bond, 1988, its presence appears universal or nearly so (Smith & Bond, 1993; Stephan & Stephan, 1996). Furthermore, in-group favoritism has been observed not only in real-world social groups boasting enduring history and profound significance for their members (e.g., the various ethnic, national, or religious groups), but also in the ephemeral and relatively insignificant groups created artificially in the experimental laboratory. In fact, the mere experience of inclusion in one group and exclusion from another often seems sufficient to instigate an in-group bias, however transient and seemingly unimportant the groups involved (Allen & Wilder, 1975; Tajfel, Billig, Bundy, & Flament, 1971).

In a recent analysis, Hogg & Abrams (1993) specifically stressed the epistemic functions of in-groups, and proposed that uncertainty reduction might constitute an important motivational basis underlying in-group favoritism. From Hogg and Abrams's perspective, people are generally inclined to reduce uncertainty or ambiguity and they do so through agreement on essential matters with in-group members. Viewed in these terms, the in-group bias may reflect a fundamental human desire to acquire and maintain epistemic certainty in one's attitudes, beliefs, and experiences gratifiable through the social validation of one's cognitions by like-minded others. To the individual member, the in-group represents a source of unambiguous social knowledge—a highly valued psychological commodity. If so, it is easy to see why members may considerably appreciate the in-group, identify with it, and be generally biased in its favor. It should also be the case, therefore, that where one's desire for epistemic certainty is heightened, appreciation of one's in-group should rise. Recently, we (Shah, Kruglanski, & Thompson, 1998) investigated this possibility systematically in a number of laboratory studies.

Need for closure and the in-group bias. Our first study examined three separate samples of University of Maryland students. We investigated the relation between need for closure assessed via the need-for-closure scale (Webster & Kruglanski, 1994) and the affect toward one's own and other ethnic groups (samples 1 and 2), as well as feelings of collective self-esteem (Luhtanen & Crocker, 1991) (sample 3).

Participants first identified themselves as European American, Hispanic American, Asian American, or African American. Then they filled out the need-for-closure scale, and following some filler questionnaires, completed a series of four "feeling thermometers" designed to measure their affect toward the four ethnic groups comprising our sample. We operationalized the construct of *in-group favorability* as participants' positivity of affect toward their own ethnic group, and that of *out-group favorability* as the average of positive affect ratings of the remaining three

ethnic groups. These data revealed that need for closure was (1) significantly and positively related to the positivity of affect with regard to the
in-group, and (2) significantly and negatively related to the positivity of
affect with regard to their out-groups. The second sample replicated both
findings, controlling additionally for participants' self-esteem, which in
this study was not significantly correlated with need for closure or with
the affect ratings of own and other groups.

Luthanen and Crocker have shown that individuals high in chronic
collective self-esteem demonstrate greater bias toward experimentally
formed in-groups than do individuals low in collective self-esteem. If
heightened need for closure magnifies the degree of in-group favoritism,
it may also enhance the level of collective self-esteem for the group's
members. Consistent with this prediction, in our third sample the need
for cognitive closure and collective self-esteem were significantly and
positively correlated.

Though of considerable interest, the results of our first study are
somewhat limited because of their correlational nature. Our conceptual
analysis suggests that a heightened need for closure should augment the
in-group bias by increasing the subjective value of the social reality (or
consensus) provided by the in-group. However, our results are compatible also with the opposite causal direction, whereby a strong identification with the in-group produces a heightened need for closure. It may not
be too far-fetched to assume, in other words, that a strong liking for the
in-group lends particular appeal to the social reality such a group
defines. This may lead to an uncritical acceptance of such a reality, and to
a generalized liking for clear-cut realities, resulting in a strong need for
cognitive closure.

To explore the causal role of the need for closure in the in-group bias,
in the second study we manipulated it experimentally and explored the
effects this has on one's identification with one's in-group, one's attitudes
toward an out-group, and one's acceptance of influence from in-group
versus out-group members. Participants in this study were led to believe
that together with a teammate they would be competing against a rival
team of two participants on a reading-comprehension task. Participants
received two alleged self-descriptions; one written by their own teammate and the other by a member of the competing team, ostensibly to
provide them with some information about the other participants. Each
participant received the same two descriptions. One was said to belong
to the participant's teammate, the other to a member of the competing
team. Each self-description contained five attributes, which according to
the alleged author, best described his or her own personality. It also contained the author's three "best strategies" for retaining written informa-

tion, presumably prepared with the forthcoming reading-comprehension task in mind.

The situational manipulation of the need for closure was accomplished via time pressure. In the high-need-for-closure condition, participants were told that because we wished them to answer the questions as quickly as possible, a time limit was imposed for providing their responses. If they exceeded that limit (the exact extent of which was left unspecified), they would have to answer an additional set of questions as a penalty. In the low-need-for-closure condition, participants were told that because we wanted them to answer the questions as carefully as possible, a *minimum* time requirement (again left unspecified) was imposed on their responses; that is, they were expected to take their time and not rush into responding too quickly. The main dependent variables in this study included rated liking of one's teammate and member of the other team, as well as rated similarity to oneself of these two individuals. Furthermore, participants were asked to list the retention strategies that they themselves would use in trying to do well on the reading comprehension task. Our interest in this case was in the extent to which the participants' lists would include the suggestions of their teammate to greater or lesser extent than those of the competing team member.

The findings lent strong support to the notions that the need for closure may induce in-group favoritism and out-group derogation. Participants whose need for closure was elevated by time pressure expressed greater liking for their teammate and lesser liking for member of the other team than participants not exposed to time pressure. The former (versus the latter) participants also perceived themselves as more similar to the in-group member and less similar to the out-group member. Finally, participants under time pressure (versus no pressure) incorporated into their set of retention strategies a greater proportion of their teammate's than the competing team member's suggestions. All of these findings were strongly replicated in a third study, where the need for closure was assessed via the Webster and Kruglanski (1994) scale rather than being manipulated with time pressure.

The two studies just described allay the potential concerns one might have in regard to the first study in this series. First, in study 2, the need for closure was experimentally manipulated and participants were assigned randomly to conditions. Second, in both studies 2 and 3, the experimental situation was new and measurement of the dependent variables came *after* the need for closure was manipulated and/or assessed—hence it is unlikely to have affected the degree of such a need. It thus seems that a causal direction predicted by our theory is justified whereby a heightened need for closure augments both in-group favoritism and out-group derogation.

Homogeneity effects of in-groups and out-groups. If the reason for enhanced in-group bias under heightened need for closure has to do with the in-group's epistemic status as a social reality provider, rather than, say, with the positive stereotype of the in-group and a negative one of the out-group that are seized and frozen upon, the *epistemic characteristics* of groups should affect their appeal to members under need for closure. An important such characteristic may be the degree of a group's perceived homogeneity. Homogeneity may broach a high likelihood of consensus without which group beliefs may be insufficiently consistent and internally coherent to furnish a solid sense of the way things "really" are. A diverse group membership is likely to disagree internally on various matters; its attitudes and beliefs are likely to echo its compositional differences, shattering the common thread of understanding at heart of the shared reality experience (Hardin and Higgins, 1996). By contrast, a homogeneous group composed of largely similar members may agree on the same basic premises and fundamental assumptions. Accordingly, it may quickly reach consensus on attitudes and opinions that such premises imply. In other words, homogeneity implies a high likelihood that consensus will serve as "evidence" for a given attitude or opinion, and allow it to be upheld with confidence. Where epistemic confidence is at a premium, one should find particularly appealing groups whose membership is homogeneous rather than characterized by diversity.

There is, however, one boundary condition for these effects. If the greater appeal to high-need-for-closure persons of homogeneous versus heterogeneous groups is due to their potential for provision of a stable social reality, then it should profoundly matter whether the group membership is similar to or dissimilar from oneself. Only a self-similar group would constitute an adequate source of social reality, and hence only a self-similar group would gain advantage from its homogeneity as a reality provider. A self-dissimilar group, on the other hand, might be expected to differ from oneself on important attitudes and opinions. This may fundamentally undermine its reality provision potential, leaving little room for additional effects due to its perceived homogeneity.

We conducted four studies to investigate these notions (Kruglanski, Shah, Pierro, & Mannetti, 2002). In the first two, a pair of field experiments conducted in Italy by Antonio Pierro and Lucia Mannetti, we looked at in-group and out-group homogeneity without considering the potential moderator of homogeneity effects by the groups' perceived self-similarity. The remaining two studies were conducted in the United States and incorporated the full-fledged design inspired by the present analysis, including the need for closure, in-group and out-group homogeneity, and these groups' self-similarity. The first two studies attested that the relation between the need for nonspecific closure and in-group favoritism/out-group derogation phenomena is moderated by these groups' perceived homogeneity. Fans of rival soccer clubs based in Rome, Italy—"La Roma" and "La Lazio"—rated the fans of these clubs on a variety of personal characteristics and reported their liking of the fans of each club. We found that need for closure was positively related to in-group favoritism/out-group derogation, but the relation between the need for closure and in-group favoritism was stronger when the in-group was perceived as homogenous in the personality features of its members, and the relation between need for closure and out-group derogation was weaker when the out-group was perceived as homogenous. These findings were replicated in another study conducted in Naples, Italy, using as in- and out-groups southern Italians (the in-group) and northern Italians (the out-group), respectively.

Finally, in two experimental studies conducted in the United States (at the University of Wisconsin and at the University of Maryland), we replicated the finding that the relationships between need for closure and in-group favoritism/out-group derogation are moderated by the perceived homogeneity of the in-group and the out-group; we investigated additionally the role that perceived similarity to oneself of the groups involved is pertinent to these phenomena. In one of these studies we manipulated the need for closure using a time-pressure manipulation. Participants, University of Wisconsin (at Madison) undergraduates, rated how similar they were to typical University of Wisconsin students. They also rated how similar University of Wisconsin students were to each other and how similar University of Michigan students (the out-group) were to each other. Participants then indicated the degree to which they had warm and cold feelings toward students at each university, and how positively and negatively they were disposed toward students at each school.

In our fourth study in this series, the need for closure was again measured as a dispositional variable (via Webster & Kruglanski's 1994 Need for Closure Scale). They were then given two responses to an alleged survey question (about their perception of average U.S. students' attitudes). These responses were said to be provided either by two University of Maryland students (the in-group) or by two George Washington University students (a local out-group), who either agreed among themselves (signifying homogeneity of perceptions) or disagreed (signifying heterogeneity). After having seen these responses, participants rated how much they thought they would like these particular George Washington students, and how much they would like these particular University of Maryland students. They also rated the degree to which the two University of Maryland (George Washington University) students were similar to each other, and how similar they were to the participant.

The results of these two last experiments were highly similar. Replicating the prior two studies in this series, we found that the higher the members' need for closure, the greater their liking of the homogeneous versus the heterogeneous in-groups, and the lesser their dislike for homogeneous versus heterogeneous out-groups. Of greatest interest, the preference of high- (versus low-) need-for-closure individuals for homogeneous (versus heterogeneous) in-groups held only when the in-group was perceived as relatively similar to oneself.

These findings support our analysis regarding the epistemic function of the in-group as a provider of a social reality for its members. As we have seen, this lends the in-group a particular value and imbues it with particular appeal to members high on the need for closure (and, by way of contrast, to a greater derogation by those in the out-group) for whom a firm sense of social reality is particularly important. Consistent with the present analysis, these relations appear to obtain only when the in-group fulfills its epistemic function satisfactorily; that is, where the characteristics or opinions of its members are sufficiently homogeneous so as to afford a member a coherent sense of social reality, assuming this reality is similar enough to her or his own attitudes and beliefs to be of use.

Specific closure effects. Of course, an in-group can be valuable for its members because it provides them with a specific (not just any kind of) social reality. A group may lend its members a sense of optimism, self-worth, and self-assurance. All those are specifically desirable closures that group memberships may afford. For example, a member of a militia group or a white-supremacist organization may feel good about partaking of a social reality that extols her/his virtues and boosts her/his self esteem. In fact, national, ethnic, or religious groups often highlight the value of their group membership (by commemorating the group's past achievements, celebrating the group's traditions, and worshiping the group's eminent forebears), implying that by dint of belonging, the individual gains status and esteem, and may thus "bask in reflected glory" (Cialdini, Borden, Thorne, Walker, Freeman, & Sloan, 1976). The upshot is that individuals may join and adulate in-groups that afford them a desirable sense of social identity, and may disparage out-groups that denigrate those in-groups.

The foregoing perspective complements, in a sense, the Social Identity theory (Tajfel & Turner, 1986) whereby group membership represents an important component of social identity, and hence constitutes a significant source of self-esteem. According to the latter notion, group membership is a given, and the individual's tendencies toward in-group favoritism represent attempts at esteem enhancement. In that regard, the social identity theory is particularly well suited to *ascribed group memberships*, for example, the ethnic, gender, or age-group memberships into which one is born and that are nearly immutable. By contrast, the notion that an individual joins groups that provide them a desirable social identity is more suited to cases of *achieved group membership* (e.g., a club that one might join, a political party, or an elite academic institution).

☐ Linguistic Intergroup Bias

Research referred to earlier (Boudreau, Baron, & Oliver, 1992; Mikulincer, Yinon, & Kabili, 1991; Rubini & Kruglanski, 1996;) has shown that under a heightened need for closure, individuals are likely to exhibit an *abstractness bias* (they might be drawn to general labels or trait terms in thinking or talking about others). Such allure of the abstract is compatible to the *permanence tendency* assumed to arise under need for closure, and to reflect the quest for stable knowledge consistent across situations as well as with the eschewal of narrow, situationally specific knowledge. But as we also know (cf. Kruglanski, Webster, & Klem, 1993; Webster & Kruglanski, 1998; De Grada, Kruglanski, Mannetti & Pierro, 1999), persons under a heightened need for closure are also likely to exhibit a *consensus bias* (to be attracted to consensual knowledge shared by significant others in their community). Again, this is compatible with the permanence tendency as it reflects a quest for knowledge that is stable across persons, and is hence unlikely to be challenged or undermined by important social referents. As we have seen, this may assume the form of increased in-group favoritism under a heightened need for closure (Shah, Kruglanski, & Thompson, 1998).

An intriguing question to ask at this point is how might the abstractness and consensus biases (both born of the need for closure!), interact? This question, precisely, was addressed in research by Webster, Kruglanski, & Pattison (1997) on the relation between need for closure and the linguistic intergroup bias (LIB). The LIB, discovered by the Italian social psychologists Anne Maass and Luciano Arcuri (Maass & Arcuri, 1992) refers to the tendency by group members to describe positive in-group and negative out-group behaviors in relatively abstract terms (implying that the behaviors in question represent relatively stable characteristics of the actor), and to describe negative in-group and positive out-group behaviors in relatively concrete terms (implying that the behaviors represent relatively transient, situationally specific occurrences that must not be expected to recur with any frequency).

The underlying mechanism of the LIB could be both expectancy based and motivational in nature (Maass & Stahlberg, 1993). Thus, because the stereotype of the in-group is typically positive and that of the out-group is often negative, positive behaviors of the in-group and negative ones of the out-group are easily assimilated to the stereotype and hence are described in general terms. By the same logic, negative in-group and positive out-group behaviors are inconsistent with their respective stereotypes, and hence should be alternatively ascribed to the situation.

A motivational basis of the LIB might reflect in-group favoritism. Specifically, abstract descriptions of the positive in-group behaviors and the negative out-group behaviors serve to portray the former favorably and the latter unfavorably. Similarly, concrete descriptions of negative in-group behaviors minimize their significance as evidence for an unwanted ascription of stable negative characteristics to the in-group or of stable positive characteristics to the out-group. In this sense, abstract or concrete descriptions may serve one's motivational interests in regard to one's in-group or an out-group with which it is in conflict or in competition.

But how might the linguistic intergroup bias be impacted by the need for closure? Somewhat complexly, it seems. Need-for-closure-based *abstraction* and *consensus* tendencies (the latter giving rise to in-group favoritism), should work in concert in regard to positive in-group and negative out-group behaviors. Both tendencies should contribute to enhanced abstraction level of linguistic descriptions. These tendencies should clash, however, when it comes to negative in-group and positive out-group behaviors: The general abstraction tendency should be at odds with the preference for concrete descriptors implied by in-group favoritism. Thus, differences in descriptive abstractness due to the need for closure should be reduced or eliminated in the case of negative in-group and positive out-group behaviors.

To test these ideas, Webster, Kruglanski, & Pattison (1997) conducted two separate experiments. In the first of these, participants previously classified as high or low in dispositional need for closure (Webster & Kruglanski, 1999) took part in an experiment presented as an investigation of impression formation. The in-group and out-group status of a target person was operationally defined in terms of her/his endorsement of the pro-choice versus the pro-life position on abortion—an issue that continues to divide the American public and one that was particularly hot in the fall and winter of 1995—the time during which the Webster et al. (1997) studies were carried out. An in-group status of the target was assumed to exist when the participant and the alleged target held the same position on abortion, and an out-group status when their positions on abortion differed.

As part of the alleged impression-formation task, the target disclosed two behavioral items of information about himself/herself, and the participants' task was to describe these behaviors in their own terms. One of these behaviors was positive and involved the lending of money to a friend in need. The second behavior was negative and involved persuading a friend to cheat.

The results of this experiment lent support to our hypothesis. Specifically, individuals with a high (versus low) dispositional need for closure adopted a significantly higher level of abstraction when describing positive in-group and negative out-group behaviors. Such need-for-closure differences were rendered insignificant for negative in-group as well as for positive out-group behaviors.

A second experiment by Webster et al. (1997) adopted the same methodological paradigm except that the need for closure, rather than being assessed via a scale, was now manipulated via ambient noise (a noisy computer printer) introduced in half the experimental sessions. As in our prior studies of this kind (e.g., Kruglanski & Webster, 1991; Kruglanski, Webster and Klem, 1993; Rubini & Kruglanski, 1997), we assumed that high ambient noise elevated the individuals' need for cognitive closure because it made information processing difficult. Indeed, appropriate manipulation checks administered by Webster et al. (1997), attested that participants' need for closure in this situation varied as a function of the noise manipulation. Furthermore, the results strongly replicated those of the previous study. Participants' descriptions were more abstract under high (versus low) need for closure when they pertained to positive in-group or negative out-group behaviors, but not when they pertained to negative in-group or positive out-group behaviors.

These findings support the notion that the permanence tendency fostered by the need for closure, even though it produces a general tendency toward abstractness, also produces a tendency toward in-group favoritism that at times may conflict with the tendency toward abstractness. The latter may be the case where in-group favoritism demands concrete rather than abstract depictions—that is, when describing negative behaviors of the in-group-members or positive ones of the out-group members.

Specific closure effects. Of course, one could favor one's group for reasons other than the social reality it provides (e.g., because of the prestige, congeniality, or instrumentality it affords its members [cf. Back, 1951]). Similarly, one could disfavor the out-group for a variety of reasons. If such specific closure needs were sufficiently high in magnitude, they too could produce the linguistic intergroup bias leading to the depiction of negative in-group behaviors and positive out-group behaviors as situationally specific.

Need for Closure in Real- World Contexts

As we go about daily affairs, we form a variety of knowledge types needed to guide our decisions and activities in diverse spheres of endeavor, and in forming our knowledge, we typically turn to various social sources whose judgments we trust. Reciprocally, we may serve often as authoritative sources for others with whom we communicate. Thus, knowledge formation processes form an integral part of nearly anything we do, both on our own and with others. And the state of closed-mindedness, insofar as it is enters into all knowledge formation activities, therefore insinuates itself into most aspects of our dealings with the (social and nonsocial) world.

The foregoing chapters illustrate the ubiquity of closed-mindedness phenomena and the pervasive role that the need for cognitive closure (in its specific and nonspecific forms) plays in human affairs. As we have seen, the social psychological significance of the need for closure cuts across different levels of analysis, including the intrapersonal, inter-personal, group, and intergroup levels at which social psychological phenomena may transpire. To a considerable extent, the evidence for need-for-closure effects reviewed thus far comes from controlled experimental studies conducted with college undergraduates as partici-pants, and with relatively mild experimental manipulations in circumscribed and sheltered contexts of university laboratories. It is of interest, therefore, to ask what evidence there is for need-for-closure effects in real-world contexts, and/or with more involving manipulations of the variables of interest. The present chapter is devoted to a review of such evidence.

☐ Freezing on Prior Notions and Reactions to Close- Call Counterfactuals

Research by Tetlock (1998) examined how political experts (diplomatic and military historians, international-relations and area-study specialists) react when their forecasts of international events are confirmed or disconfirmed. Such forecasts are usually derived from explanatory schemata in which terms the experts use impose meaning on the historical events. As an example, Tetlock describes what he calls the *neorealist balancing schema* whereby, "when one state threatens to become too powerful and capable of dominating the entire international system, other states, rational self-preserving actors as they are posited to be—coalesce against it, thereby preserving the balance of power."

In one of his studies, Tetlock investigated experts' reactions to close-call counterfactuals implying that past events implied by these experts explanatory schemata were not really inevitable and could have readily taken an alternative course. Thus, the experts' beliefs in the nonrealist balancing schema were assessed. These experts were then questioned about the likelihood of the pertinent counterfactuals, suggesting that no necessary balancing of power exists; for example, statements implying that Germany's failure to achieve hegemony in Europe in one of the two world wars was by no means foreordained ('If Germany had proceeded with its invasion of France on August 2, 1914, but had respected the neutrality of Belgium and Luxemburg, Britain would have remained neutral and France would have fallen in a few months'). Other explanatory schemata tapped in Tetlock's study included the *macro causes of war schema* (e.g., implying that "War is most likely when the state of military technology leads decision makers to believe that the side that strikes first will possess a decisive advantage"), the *essentialist view of Soviet Union schema* (e.g., "Primary blame for the terrible crimes of the Stalinist period should rest with the Soviet Communist Party, not with any one person"), and the *efficacy of nuclear deterrence schema* (e.g., "Nuclear weapons compelled the American and Soviet governments to act with great restraint during the Cold War"). Each of these schemas was presented to participants along with its corresponding counterfactuals.

Tetlock (1998) found that experts who strongly (versus less strongly) endorsed a given schema were particularly likely to reject the specific counterfactuals inconsistent with the schema-based explanation of past events, but *only* if they were high on a combined measure of need for closure and cognitive complexity (Tetlock, 1988). For instance, high closure/ low complexity experts who strongly (versus less strongly) subscribed to the neorealist balancing schema rejected close-call counterfactuals whereby given a slightly different turn of events, Germany could have won either of the two world wars. High closure/low complexity experts who believed in nuclear deterrence were dismissive of counterfactuals that implied that a nuclear war could have easily erupted between the United States and the U.S.S.R. High closure/low complexity experts who held an essentialist view of the Soviet Union rejected counterfactuals that the Cold War might have been avoided if only either or both superpowers had different leaders. Finally, high closure/low complexity experts who subscribed to macro causes for World War I had little patience with counterfactuals asserting that its outbreak could have been readily prevented if singular events had only taken a different course (e.g., "If the carriage driver of Archduke Ferdinand had not taken a fateful wrong turn that gave the Serbian assassins a remarkable second chance to carry out their previously botched assassination plot, war would not have broken out in August 1914").

Whereas Tetlock's (1998) first study examined experts' reactions to counterfactual questioning of their favored explanations of past events, his second study looked directly at the forecasting of future events. Based on expert forecasts collected over twelve years, Tetlock examined the subset of predictions that subsequent historical events have clearly proven correct or incorrect. These predictions were classifiable into three domains: the future governance of the Soviet Union as seen by experts in 1988, the future of South Africa as seen by experts in 1989, and the future of Canada as seen by experts in 1992. Tetlock hypothesized and found that high closure/low complexity experts were less likely than their low closure/high simplicity counterparts to concede that they erred where the events controverted their predictions. Instead, they defended their basic assumptions in various ways, thus supporting the counterfactual propositions whereby they were "almost right" if only some local conditions took on the expected values. For example, high closure/low complexity experts who predicted that hard-line communism would make a comeback in the Soviet Union endorsed statements like "the hard-liners almost succeeded in their coup attempt against Gorbachev." Those who predicted that Quebec would secede from Canada endorsed statements like "The Quebecois separatists almost won the referendum that would have torn apart Canada," etc.

These findings are consistent with the view that the cognitive style partially defined by the need for nonspecific closure and low cognitive complexity (possibly itself the result of the need for closure) may lead individuals to defensively freeze on their prior conceptions. This research is particularly valuable in demonstrating how epistemic freezing might affect the treatment of hypothetical possibilities or close-call counterfactuals that support or undermine one's prior notions. It is also valuable in demonstrating need-for-closure effects in the highly involving real-world context of political forecasting. Unlike participants in a typical social psychological experiment, whose involvement and prior knowledge of the attitude topics studied is often quite limited, the experts in Tetlock's research had considerable factual and theoretical knowledge to draw on in reacting to the counterfactual statements relevant to their forecasts and explanations. Yet the closure/complexity factor was found to be a powerful determinant of those reactions attesting to its psychological significance in realistic settings.

☐ Political Conservatism

Recent reviews by Jost, Glaser, Kruglanski, and Sulloway (2003 a, b) find consistent evidence for a correlation between individual differences in the need for closure and various measures of conservatism. Thus, Webster & Kruglanski (1994) obtained a significant correlation between need for closure and authoritarianism. Similarly, Jost, Kruglanski, & Simon (1999) found a positive correlation between the need for closure and a single-item measure of self-reported liberalism-conservatism. A study conducted by Kemmelmeier (1997) in Germany found that as one moves in a steady monotonic fashion from left-wing to right-wing party membership, one's need-for-closure score increases accordingly. Democratic Socialists score lower on the need-for-closure scale than do members of the Green Party, who score lower yet than members of the Social-Democratic Party, scoring lower than members of the Free Democratic Party, who score lower than members of the right-wing Christian Democratic Party.

Jost et al. (1999) found a positive correlation between the need for closure and the tendency to support the death penalty, presumably because capital punishment implies a resolution that is unambiguous, permanent, and final. Thus, an empirical connection was found between the need for closure and specific ideological opinions. Research conducted in Poland by Golec (2001, 2002a, b) supports the hypotheses that (1) the need for closure is associated with the preservation of the status quo (whether left-wing or right-wing), and (2) persons who are high on the need for closure tend to prefer right-wing ideologies over left-wing ideologies (especially when they are relatively high on political expertise). Thus, in two studies with Polish citizens and students at various colleges and universities, Golec (2001, 2002a, b) found that need-for-closure scores were correlated positively with cultural (religious and nationalist conservatism), but they were correlated negatively with economic conservatism, presumably because of Poland's traditionally socialist economy.

Similar findings emerged from an investigation by Kossowska & Van Hiel (2003), who studied the relation between the need for closure and conservatism in Polish and Flemish samples composed of heterogeneous groups of adults. Kossowska and Van Hiel's results replicated in both samples the positive relation between the need for closure and general conservative beliefs, left-right self-placement, and political party preferences. The second study, which distinguished between cultural and economic conservatism, found that both were positively related to the need for closure in the Flemish sample, but that the economic conservatism was negatively related to the need for closure in the Polish sample, consistent with Golec's findings.

The Greenberg and Jonas critique. The negative relation found in the Polish samples between the need for closure and economic conservatism (e.g., as characterized by espousal of a free market economy) relates to Greenberg and Jonas's (2003) critique of the Jost et al. (2003a) findings of a positive relation between need for closure and political conservatism (i.e., right-wing thinking). Like others before them (Eysenck, 1954; Shils, 1954; Rokeach, 1960), Greenberg and Jonas (2003) argued that left-wingers are also capable of the kind of rigidity and traditionalism associated with the need for closure, and other personality characteristics found to be correlated with conservatism (Jost et al., 2003). Greenberg and Jonas (2003) cite examples of rigid left-wing regimes, such as the former Soviet Union, Cuba, or Communist China, to conclude that "rigid, extreme, and dogmatic adherence is characteristic of all types of extreme political ideologies, left-wing as well as right wing" (p. 379). These authors also note that such an arch-conservative politician as Ronald Reagan ran for president on a platform of change, and that conservatives "are also currently on the march for change in ... Great Britain, the Netherlands, and France ... [and that] two of history's most horrifying conservative movements, Hitler's Nazism and Mussolini's fascism, gained power specifically because their leaders promised change" (p. 377).

And yet the data speak for themselves and they do so unequivocally. As Jost et al. (2003b) point out, evidence from no less than 12 countries, 88 samples, and 22,818 individual cases stubbornly reveal positive correlations between the various psychological characteristics associated with rigidity and dogmatism (such as the need for cognitive closure) and political conservatism, ranging in magnitude from .20 to .50. This hardly denies the possibility of negative correlations between the need for closure and conservatism (cf. Golec, 2001, 2002a, b; Kossowska & Van Hiel, 2003). In fact, nonspecific need for closure should foment the adherence to any accessible ideology (Kruglanski & Webster, 1996), which could be a left-wing, right-wing, religious, or nationalistic ideology to mention just a few ideological prototypes. That does not mean, however, that all ideologies are equal as far as the need for closure is concerned. Because left-wing ideologies espouse egalitarianism, democracy, and openness to new ideas, their contents are incompatible with need-for-closure-based psychological strivings for stability and inequality (i.e., an epistemic hierarchy, where everyone is "entitled to the boss' opinion"). Thus, whereas nonspecific need for closure may foster the adherence to any accessible ideological contents, the specific contents do matter (as the empirical data show) because they can be more or less appealing or motivationally desirable to individuals with a high need for closure. In this particular circumstance, the nonspecific need for closure exhibits the property of a need for a specific closure because beyond its tendency to promote the seizing and freezing on any accessible closure, it also exhibits a selective preference for some closures (those promising stability and inequality) over others.

As for the Greenberg and Jonas (2003) argument that right-wingers sometimes do advocate change, it is important to note that such change is often in the service of preserving the status quo or the restoration of some prior idealized state of affairs. As Huntington (1957) put it, "To preserve the fundamental elements of society, it may be necessary to acquiesce in change on secondary issues" (p. 455). Edmund Burke (1789/1982, p. 9), the patron saint of conservative intellectuals similarly asserted that, "A state without the means of some change is without the means of its conservation. Without such means it might even risk the loss of that part of the constitution which it wished most religiously to preserve." Finally, "most of Ronald Reagan's 'changes' as president of the United States were in the name of restoring traditional American values, including individualism, religion, capitalism, family values, and law and order" (Jost et al. 2003b, p. 383).

Public debate over the psychology of conservatism. The Jost et al. (2003a, b) papers on political conservatism as motivated by social cognition evoked a heated public reaction, primarily from conservative commentators, publicists, and scores of upset e-mail writers who misinterpreted those articles as a condemnation of conservatism. In response, Kruglanski and Jost (2003) noted that unlike previous psychological analyses of conservatism and liberalism (e.g., by Adorno et al., 1950; Jaentsch, 1938, and others), which pathologized the tendencies to support particular political views, our present analysis related such tendencies to the operation of general psychological variables, such as the need for closure, which may influence most of the people some of the time, that is, under specific situational circumstances (see, e.g., Kruglanski & Webster, 1996).

Moreover, Kruglanski and Jost (2003) stressed the functional value of the need for closure in the formation of judgments and beliefs on all kinds of topics. Finally, as they put it, "Our 'trade-off' model of human psychology assumes that any trait or motivation has potential advantages and disadvantages, depending on the situation. A heightened sensitivity to threat and uncertainty is by no means maladaptive in all contexts. Even closed-mindedness may be useful, provided one is 'closed-minded' about appropriate values and accurate opinions; a reluctance to abandon one's prior convictions in favor of new fads can be a good thing" (Kruglanski & Jost, 2003, p. 22).

☐ Attitudes toward Political Conflicts

The negative correlation, referred to earlier, between the need for closure and economic conservatism in Polish samples (Golec, 2001, 2002a, b; Kossowska & Van Hiel, 2003, Study 2) reveals a psychological tension between two incompatible tendencies stemming from the need for closure: the nonspecific tendency to seize and freeze on any accessible ideology, and the specific tendency to reject an ideology whose contents are antithetical and undesirable from the need-for-closure perspective. Several recent studies illustrate such tensions in reference to individuals' attitudes toward current political conflicts. In this vein, Golec and Federico (2003) argued that the need for closure, in motivating a preference for simplistic, easy to reach interpretations, may prompt individuals to frame conflicts in one-sided, black-and-white fashion, wherein their party is right and the opponent wrong. In turn, such interpretations might encourage an approach to perceived conflict characterized by competitiveness and aggression. Of course, need for closure is hardly the sole determinant of one's conflict-related interpretations. Other determinants of such interpretations are possible and likely, in particular the "conflict-schemata" (Bar-Tal, Kruglanski, & Klar, 1989; Kruglanski, Bar-Tal, & Klar, 1993) reflecting the prevalent conflict-related attitudes of one's central reference groups. Insofar as the need for closure motivates the adherence to highly accessible interpretations—it might encourage a strong support for one's accessible conflict-schemata as well. For some individuals in some situations, a *direct* need-for-closure effect on conflict-related interpretations, and a mediated effect channeled via adherence to accessible schemata, might be compatible and work in the same direction. For high-need-for-closure individuals, this would happen if their conflict schemata, in and of themselves, construed conflict in competitive, zero-sum-type terms. Under those conditions, high-need-for-closure individuals should be much more competitive and aggressive in regard to conflict than their low-need-for-closure counterparts. Imagine, however, a situation wherein the accessible conflict schema is cooperative. This would create a dilemma for high-need-for-closure individuals as to the appropriate conflict response. Their need for closure as such should propel them toward a competitive solution, and their adherence to the accessible conflict schema, to a cooperative solution. The low-need-for-closure individuals might also confront a dilemma. Their motivational makeup may push them toward a cooperative solution, but their feeble tendency to adhere to accessible schemata may prevent them from embracing such solution with exceeding vigor. Consequently, no clear-cut prediction is possible regarding need-for-closure-based differences in responses to conflict, where the accessible conflict schema is of the cooperative variety.

In their first study, Golec and Federico (2003) examined American foreign policy officials at the height of the Cold War. To do so, they used a specialized 1966 survey of American foreign service officers (Mennis, 1971). The interviewed individuals were all employees of either the U.S. Department of Defense or the U.S. Department of State at the time, and hence they can be considered to represent elite political actors with decision-making powers on behalf of the United States in the international arena. This study considered two independent variables: (1) a proxy measure of the need for cognitive closure, consisting of 15 "rigidity" items from the original survey that mapped onto the content domains of the Need for Closure scale (Webster & Kruglanski, 1994), and (2) respondents' conflict schemas assessed via items from the original survey, which asked for their endorsement of a view of social conflicts in black-and-white, right-and-wrong terms, and for the degree of their espousal of a competitive approach to conflict resolution. The two major dependent variables were opposition/support to (1) arms control agreements and (2) the 1963 Test Ban treaty. The results of this research were consistent with the authors' hypotheses. Specifically, there obtained evidence for direct need-for-closure effects on hawkishness (i.e., lesser support on the part of high- [versus low-] need-for-closure individuals for arms control agreements and the 1963 Test Ban treaty). Furthermore, this effect was qualified by an interaction such that the need-for-closure effects on hawkishness were significantly stronger for respondents with a competitive conflict schema than for those with a cooperative conflict schema.

In their second study, Golec and Federico (2003) investigated activists and functionaries of two contemporary political parties in Poland, the Union of Liberty, characterized by a cooperative approach to political conflicts (i.e., a cooperative conflict schema), and the League of Polish Families, characterized by a competitive approach to conflicts (i.e., a competitive conflict schema). Need for closure was assessed this time via a Polish translation of Webster and Kruglanski's (1994) Need for Closure scale. The attitude issue under study, hot at the time this research was carried out, concerned the possibility of Poland joining the European Union. The cooperative approach in this case meant a welcoming of such a possibility, and a competitive approach—its rejection. Conceptually replicating their first study, Golec and Federico (2003) obtained a direct need-for-closure effect here as well, such that the higher this need the greater the rejection of Poland's integration into Europe. However, this effect was qualified by the predicted interaction, such that its strength was significant for members of the (competitive) League of Polish Families party and insignificant for the (cooperative) Union of Liberty members.

A third study (Federico & Golec, 2003) was carried out in the fall of 2002, a time during which the possibility of a military action against Iraq was an active topic of discussion in the United States and elsewhere. It investigated the attitudes of American undergraduates toward the U.S. engaging in such actions. The authors looked at need-for-closure effects on hawkish attitudes toward military action as they might be moderated by political ideology espoused by the respondents. Two ideologies were investigated, both representing a form of identification with one's country: *nationalism,* an aggressive stance premised on the superiority of the national in-group, and *patriotism,* representing a neutral, nonaggressive love of the national group (Feshbach, 1994; Viroli, 1995). The findings of this study indicated that the relation between need for closure and support for a military action against Iraq was significant and positive at high levels of nationalism, but not at low levels of nationalism. In contrast, the relationship between need for closure and support for military action at different levels of patriotism indicated a trend in the opposite direction. The need for closure was significantly associated with hawkishness only at low levels of patriotism and not at high levels of patriotism. Thus, it appears that the relationship between the need for closure and aggressive international attitudes may be stronger at high levels of national identification only when the form of identification is associated with a conflict schema that calls for hostility toward one's adversaries.

Mortality Salience Effects and Need for Closure Although death is one of the few certainties of life, the thought of it may induce considerable uncertainty. Death, by definition, is essentially foreign to our experience as living beings, and hence its very concept is subjectively unfathomable, incomprehensible, and anxiety evoking. In a sense, the notion of death brings together the ultimate in uncertainty with the supreme in "badness" (representing to many the worse that could happen). Such association may lend uncertainty an air of utmost negativity, and hence instilling the tendency to avoid it or evoking a high need for nonspecific closure. Recent research within the framework of the terror management theory (Greenberg, Solomon, & Pysczynski, 1986; Solomon, Greenberg, & Pyszczynski, 1991; Pysczynski, Solomon, & Greenberg, 2003) lends strong support to this possibility.

   Mortality salience mimicks need-for-closure effects. Recall the hypothesis of Shah et al. (1998) that the quest for consensual knowledge and a firm social reality intensified by the need for closure leads to increased ingroup bias because the in-group is the major reality provider for its members. Terror management theory similarly treats the consensual validation of beliefs (hence, the affirmation of one's social reality) as a central tenet in its analysis. Consistent with this notion, research has revealed that mortality salience enhances ingroup identification (e.g., Harmon-Jones, Greenberg, Solomon, & Simon, 1996) and enhances the "false consensus" effect (Pyszczynski, Wicklund, Floresku, Koch, Greenberg, & Solomon, 1996). A related domain wherein need-for-closure effects have been found with mortality salience manipulations was the evaluation of similar and dissimilar others. According to need-for-closure theory, the intensified quest for a firm social reality under a heightened need for closure should enhance the positive evaluation of similar others and the negative evaluation of dissimilar others. Indeed, in research described earlier, Kruglanski and Webster (1991), it was found that the experimental elevation of the need for closure led to increased rejection of a confederate when he expressed an opinion different from that of the participants, and increased liking of the same confederate when he expressed (and vocally argued for) an opinion in accord with that of the participants. Similarly, Doherty (1998) found that participants motivated to reach closure professed a more negative attitude toward a woman who deviated from cultural norms than did participants motivated to avoid closure. Analogously, terror management theory posits that people who are reminded about their mortality are likely to cling to their cultural world-view more strongly than people who are not so reminded. Rosenblatt, Greenberg, Solomon, Pyszczynski, and Lyon (1989), for example, demonstrated that moral transgressions were more heavily penalized when participants (both professional judges and students) were reminded about their mortality.

   Convergence of need for closure and mortality-salience effects can also be found in the domain of stereotyping. As discussed earlier, according to need for closure theory, because stereotypes allow the individual to perceive the world in a stable and orderly manner, they should be used more often by individuals under high versus low need for closure. Indeed, Dijksterhuis, Van Knippenberg, Kruglanski, and Schaper (1996) found that high-need-for-closure participants exhibited more stereotypically biased memories of persons and events than did low-need-for-closure participants. Experimentally heightened need for closure was found to have similar effects (Dijksterhuis et al. 1996). Analogously, in the domain of terror management theory, Schimel, Simon, Greenberg, Pysczynski, Solomon, Waxmonsky, and Arndt (1999) argued that stereotypes constitute an important component of a cultural world-view, which provides a sense of order, stability, and permanence. Consistent with this line of reasoning, Schimel et al. found that mortality salience led participants to prefer people who behaved in a stereotype-consistent manner, and to dislike those who behaved in a stereotype-inconsistent manner.

More direct evidence that mortality salience may increase the need for closure comes from two recent studies by Dechesne and his colleagues. Dechesne and Pyszczynski (2002) had participants in an experiment read an article about the near-death experience. Half the participants were informed that such experiences provide evidence for the existence of afterlife, and the other half were informed that they can be explained by a physiological reaction to extreme stress. Subsequently, half the participants were induced to contemplate their feelings and thoughts about their own death, whereas the remaining participants contemplated their feelings and thoughts associated with dental pain. Finally, participants were asked to indicate their belief in the afterlife. Consistent with what one might expect if mortality salience induced the need for cognitive closure, participants seized and froze upon the explanation provided them. As compared to their counterparts in the dental pain condition, participants exposed to the mortality salience manipulation exhibited a greater belief in the theory offered them irrespective of its contents; that is, they believed more in the afterlife theory or in the physiological-reaction theory, in accordance with the explanation they had been provided.

In another study, Dechesne and Wigboldus (2001) argued that (1) mortality salience enhances the need to adopt and use cognitive schemata in order to establish a sense of order, predictability, and stability, and (2) this effect should be nonspecific in nature (i.e., it should apply to any sort of schema, not just culturally shared and meaningful schemata). As in the prior study, half the participants were exposed to the mortality salience manipulation, and the remaining half were induced to contemplate dental pain. All participants were then asked to recognize, as quickly and accurately as possible, repetitive patterns of A and B letters presented on a computer screen. Participants recognized the existing patterns significantly more quickly under the mortality salience manipulation than under the dental pain manipulation, consistent with the notion that mortality-salience-induced need for closure prompted the participants to diligently seize on the information given in order to develop coherent knowledge.

If an important aspect of mortality salience is the (aversive) uncertainty that it introduces, persons who are habitually loathe of uncertainty,(individuals with a high need for closure as a personality characteristic) should be particularly fearful and upset when confronted with the prospect of their own mortality. Research by Dechesne, Jannsen, and Van Knippenberg (2001) is consistent with this notion. In one study participants were asked to write down, in one sentence, the thoughts and feelings that came to their minds when thinking about death. The covariation of need for closure with the amount of distress participants expressed about death was striking! Typical answers of low-need-for-closure individuals indicated acceptance (e.g., "it's something that has to come anyway; it's not something to be afraid of"), while some even expressed curiosity about death (e.g., "I am curious what will happen afterwards"). In contrast, virtually all high-need-for-closure participants evidenced considerable distress in reference to the idea of their own demise, a typical answer being simply "I do not want to die."

In another study, Dechesne, Jannsen, and Van Knippenberg (2001) found that low-need-for-closure participants spent almost twice the amount of time in answering questions about their death than did high-need-for-closure participants. Moreover, when compared to answering questions about watching television, high-need-for-closure participants spent significantly less time on their answers to questions about death. In contrast, low-need-for-closure participants spent significantly more time answering questions about death than answering questions about watching television. These findings imply that high-need-for-closure individuals attempt to avoid the uncertainties associated with death, and that they seek the cozy comfort of culture and convention when faced with the prospect of their own mortality, whereas low-need-for-closure individuals may actually be intrigued by the uncertainties that the notion of death may evoke (see also Dechesne & Kruglanski, in press).

☐ Applications of a Closed Mindedness Analysis to Specific Events: The Challenger Disaster, the Yom Kippur Surprise, and Immigrants' Acculturation

The real-world relevance of the need for closure, however, relates not only to the arousal conditions (such as mortality salience) or the attitudes or judgments it may encourage, but also to the actions or inactions that many such judgments may foster. In what follows, I analyze need for closure in terms of two actual events wherein freezing on an erroneous preconception happened to have brought about disastrous consequences of a broad social significance: The deadly explosion in 1986 involving the space ship Challenger, and the surprise attack on Israel perpetrated by Egypt and Syria in October of 1973, which started what is generally known as the Yom Kippur war.

Admittedly, the following analyses are not based on detailed quantitative analysis of participants' psychological responses in controlled settings. The evidence for their plausibility rests, therefore, on qualitative knowledge of the circumstances in which the target events took place gleaned from public records and documents in case of the Challenger disaster, and additionally abetted by extensive interview data in case of the Yom Kippur event (Bar-Yosef & Kruglanski, 2003). Thus, the following applications of need-for-closure theory resemble historical reconstructions of past events in light of extant theoretical knowledge and the currently known facts. The way I see it, this type of endeavor constitutes a desirable use of social psychological knowledge that enables our input as a discipline into general dialogues about societal issues of considerable importance to the public at large (Kruglanski, 1994, 2001).

☐ Freezethink and the Challenger Disaster

The United States' space program, while often the object of wonderment and admiration, is occasionally derailed from its course by profound disasters. The latest such catastrophe, as of this writing, was the disintegration upon its return to Earth orbit of the shuttle Columbia. Little is known at the present time of the exact circumstances and possible causes of this terrible mishap in which several astronauts lost their lives, and an extensive probe is currently under way. Incomparably more information is available about the preceding space tragedy 16 years earlier: the explosion that destroyed the Challenger shuttle minutes after its launch, again killing all the astronauts aboard. There is a sense in which the Challenger disaster was as much a failure of *decision making* as of *technology*. The determination to launch was made under so much psychological pressure that normal procedures of the National Aeronautics and Space Administration (NASA) were circumvented and the objections of experts either overruled or kept from key decision makers. The pressures on NASA were intense and varied. They included the desire to secure Congressional funding through displays of cost effectiveness and productivity (15 shuttle flights in the year 1986 and 24 by 1988), the intense public interest in the flight, the heavily advertised Teacher in Space program, and the wish to demonstrate the capabilities of NASA technology. All of these created a powerful psychological "pressure cooker" in which NASA decision makers fixated on a set of ideas and became largely impervious to contrary facts that were readily available.

The psychological situation in which NASA decision makers found themselves likely involved a combination of the needs for specific and nonspecific closure. As concerns the need for a specific closure, in the Challenger case a lift-off decision was clearly more desirable than a decision to delay. A "go" decision meant that the flight schedule could be kept, that the public would not be disappointed, and that the shuttle program would score another major achievement. Also, any mention of possible system failure would have meant the need to spend more money, a conclusion NASA found distasteful in light of its commitment to cost effectiveness and economy. In addition to the need for a specific closure, the motivations of NASA decision makers very likely contained a substantial dose of the need for a nonspecific closure occasioned by the time pressure and the impending deadline of the lift-off. Insofar as their prior judgment was to proceed with the launch, the heightened need for nonspecific closure may have augmented their freezing on that decision as the deadline drew near. Thus, even though engineers at Morton-Thiokol (the company that manufactured the solid rocket boosters) were concerned about the presence of cold spots on a booster rocket, such information somehow did not register with the responsible officials, undoubtedly in part because of their motivation to freeze on the positive decision.

It is of interest that different players in the Challenger drama had different attitudes toward the launch, which may well have stemmed from their different motivational concerns. For instance, the engineers at Morton-Thiokol experienced little time pressure to make a decision (hence little nonspecific need for closure) and little concern about the decision's political and economic implications for NASA. On the other hand, they probably experienced the greatest fear of invalidity (known often to lower the need for nonspecific closure), lest the product they developed be found at fault. Significantly, they were the ones who most strongly objected to the launch.

Top management at Morton-Thiokol had a different set of motivations. Highly dependent on NASA for a contract bringing an estimated $400 million a year, Morton-Thiokol brass could readily identify with their client's concerns. Robert Lund, vice president for engineering at Thiokol, testified that he initially opposed the launch, but changed his position "after being told to take off his engineering hat and put on one representing management." In short, it was not the failure of indicators that may have led to the Challenger disaster, but the failure to pay attention and properly interpret the indicators. This, in turn, might have been profoundly affected by the epistemic motivations for specific and non-specific closure experienced by major players in the decision-making process as to whether or not to proceed with the fateful launch.

☐ Need for Closure and the Yom Kippur Surprise

The ubiquity of closed mindedness phenomena encompasses all kinds of fateful judgments and decisions, including those in the technological realm illustrated by the Challenger story, but also those in the military domain where stakes in terms of human lives are particularly high. A telling case where decision makers' closed mindedness may have played a critical role is the misperception by the Israelis of the likelihood of a combined Egyptian-Syrian attack in October 1973 on the Jewish Day of Atonement, or Yom Kippur. Along with the German attack against the U.S.S.R. in June 1941 (Operation Barbarossa), and the Japanese attack six months later on Pearl Harbor, the coordinated Egyptian-Syrian attack of Yom Kippur is considered a classic example of a successful surprise attack and a costly intelligence failure. What is particularly striking about all three cases is that the surprise took place despite ample available evidence concerning the ability and the intention of the initiator to launch an attack. Nonetheless, in all three cases the intelligence agencies involved failed to provide a timely and accurate warning.

In case of the Yom Kippur attack, despite extensive Egyptian and Syrian attempts to prevent Israel from gaining information about their plan to go to war, the Israelis had detailed intelligence information regarding both (for discussion and specific references see Bar Yosef and Kruglanski, 2003). Most academic experts on the Yom Kippur war, and the governmental commission appointed to investigate it, concluded that in the days preceding the attack, the research division of military intelligence had plenty of warning signs that the attack was imminent. Consequently, consensus among researchers is that the failure was the outcome of human nature and errors. Thus far, however, no analysis attempted to penetrate the "black box" wherein the interpretation of the incoming information took place. And none linked specific dysfunctional behavior by specific officers to a specific result: The creation of an intelligence picture that did not properly reflect the available information, and the biased process whereby such information was assessed by relevant intelligence analysts. It is quite possible that a high need for closure on the part of major figures in the Israeli intelligence establishment significantly contributed to such a process.

Two major figures in the Yom Kippur war drama especially stand out in this regard, the chief director of military intelligence, Major-General Eli Zeira, and the primary estimator for Egyptian affairs Lieutenant-Colonel Yona Bandman. Specifically, based on their general demeanor and management style, both can be characterized as persons with a generally high need for cognitive closure. That particular feature of their character might well have contributed to their tendency to freeze on an early conception that an attack by Egyptian and Syrian armies was highly unlikely. But what evidence is there to suggest that Zeira and Bandman actually were characterized by a high need for closure? And what evidence is there to suggest that their conduct on eve of the Yom Kippur war reflects a need-for-closure-based freezing process? Let us consider both in turn.

Individuals with a high need for closure are known (1) for their authoritarian style (cf. Webster & Kruglanski, 1994; Jost, Glaser, Kruglanski, & Sulloway, 2003 a, b), and (2) for their tendency to be intolerant of others whose opinions contradict their own (Kruglanski & Webster, 1991). These characteristics fit remarkably the personality descriptions of Zeira and Bandman. Both exhibited a highly authoritarian and decisive management style. Both lacked the patience for long and open discussions and regarded them as "bullshit." Zeira was heard at least once as saying that those officers who estimated in spring 1973 that a war was likely, should not expect promotion. His high status, autocratic manner, and low tolerance of dissenting opinions may well have suppressed disagreeing voices and contributed to a sense that his estimates rested on a wider base of consensus than actually was the case.

Though less influential than Zeira, Bandman also used to express either verbally or in body language, his lack of inclination to listen to the opinions of others. He was also known for his rejection of any attempt to change a single word, even a comma, in any document of which he was an author (Bar Yosef & Kruglanski, 2003). Neither Bandman nor Zeira were ready to provide consumers with estimates other than their own.

Consequently, policy makers were not aware of the fact that different members of the Israeli Intelligence organization had contradicting assessments as to Egyptian and Syrian war intentions.

Common wisdom has it that the duty of the intelligence officer is to provide consumers with the most precise intelligence picture possible, regardless of its complexity. If the available information suggests an intricate and ambiguous picture, then he or she should describe it to the policy makers as such. Zeira and Bandman thought differently. As Zeira explained to some Knesset (Israeli Parliament) members a few months before the war:

"The chief of Staff has to make decisions and his decisions should be clear. The best support that the Director of Military Intelligence (DMI) can provide him with—if this is objectively possible is to provide him with an estimate as clear and as sharp as possible. It is true that the clearer and sharper the estimate is, then if it is a mistake, it is a clear and sharp mistake—but this is the risk of the DMI" (Agranat, 1975).

The emphasis on clarity and coherence in Zeira's and Bandman's conception of their professional duties is consistent with their portrayal as high in the need for cognitive closure. Also consistent with that need was their tendency to avoid or suppress information at odds with their own assessment. The most critical instance in which Zeira behaved this way took place 20 hours before the war broke out, when he decided to delay the dissemination of information about Soviet knowledge that Egypt and Syria intended to launch a war. Here again, a combination of Zeira's over-confidence, his unique perception of his professional duties (with an overriding emphasis on clarity), and dogmatic beliefs concerning Arab war intentions (all indications of a high need for cognitive closure), may have withheld critical knowledge from Israeli decision makers, which ultimately ushered in the notorious Yom Kippur "surprise."

In the early hours of Yom Kippur, after receiving an excellent warning from the Mossad, the chief of staff finally ordered the IDF to prepare for war that would start around sunset. By now, Zeira's belief in the validity of his conception was badly shaken. And yet even at that time, when every piece of information clamored "war," he was reluctant to abandon it totally. He continued casting doubt whether there will be a war, emphasized that Sadat did not need it politically, and speculated that if the Egyptians initiated hostilities they would nevertheless avoid crossing the canal because such a move was beyond their military capabilities. Bandman was thinking along similar lines. In a rather unprecedented manner he refused to sign a new document assessing that war was likely, and he prepared a new intelligence review that estimated the likelihood of war as low (cf. Bar Yosef & Kruglanski, 2003).

To summarize then, at least in case of the surprise attack that launched the Yom Kippur war, the mystery of a surprise despite ample premonitory signs presaging what is about to happen, is explicable in terms of a psychological variable, an apparently high need for cognitive closure of critically important figures in the Israeli intelligence establishment who controlled, to a considerable degree, the interpretations available to relevant military and governmental decision makers.

☐ Immigrants' Assimilation to the Host Culture

The examples of the Yom Kippur surprise and of the Challenger disaster highlight the potentially disastrous real-world outcomes that a heightened need for (nonspecific) closure may bring about. But we must not forget that this particular need serves a quintessential epistemic function without which no judgment formation is possible. Whether a given judgment to which formation of the need for closure may have contributed is desirable or undesirable should depend on the criteria for desirability or undesirability. This notion is illustrated by our recent research on immigrants' assimilation (Kosic, Kruglanski, Pierro, & Mannetti, in press). Whether one deems it desirable that immigrants quickly assimilate to the culture of their host country and become integrated with its native population (representing the melting pot ideal of immigration) or, to the contrary, retain their culture of origin and hence contribute to cultural diversity in their land of arrival (representing the multiculturalism ideal of immigration), a heightened need for closure could contribute to either of these divergent outcomes under the appropriate circumstances.

Those circumstances have to do with the kind of social reality that the immigrant encounters upon her or his arrival in the new land. When she or he is surrounded by co-ethnics, possibly including family and longstanding friends who may have arrived in the same group or when he or she is welcomed to an extant community of compatriots who arrived on prior waves of immigration, there is a coherent social reality in place representing to a large extent the familiar values, norms, and worldviews of the immigrant's culture of origin. If, as the present theory suggests, individuals' quest for social reality increases with their need for closure, the higher such need the stronger the immigrants' tendency should be to adhere to their community of co-ethnics, and hence the lesser their readiness to assimilate into the host culture, which constitutes a distinct social reality quite unlike what the immigrant may have been used to thus far.

A very different psychological situation may exist when, upon arrival, the newcomer is relatively isolated from her or his co-ethnics, and for whom the only social reality to be found (the only game in town, as it were) is the novel (for the immigrant) culture of the country of arrival represented by its members, whom our immigrant may meet at the workplace and perhaps befriend in social circumstances. The same social reality echoed by the host country's media of communication to which the immigrant is inevitably exposed is one that he or she encounters while negotiating her or his way through the numerous mundane encounters that make up everyday existence. Because they crave social reality, and because in such circumstances the only social reality that is clear and present is represented by the culture of the host country, high-need-for-closure individuals may tend to embrace it more quickly and intensely than their low-need-for-closure counterparts. In other words, if upon arrival the immigrants are isolated from their co-ethnics, their tendency to assimilate to the host culture should rise proportionately to their need for closure.

We (Kosic, Kruglanski, Pierro, & Mannetti, 2003) recently executed three studies designed to put these notions to empirical test. Participants in the first study were Croat immigrants to Italy residing there between 10 months and 10 years. They responded to a Croatian translation of our Need for Closure scale (Kruglanski & Webster, 1994; Mannetti et al., 2002), as well as a Sociocultural Adaptation Scale (Kosic, 1998; Berry & Kim, 1988) and an Acculturation Strategies Scale (Kosic, 1998; Dona & Berry, 1994). They also responded to three items inquiring (a) whether they joined family, relatives, or friends in the host country ("yes" versus "no"), (b) with whom they came into Italy (response alternatives being "with family or friends" *versus* "alone"); (c) with what reference group they had social relationships during their first three months of residence in Italy. These items were appropriately combined into an overall index of the "reference group at entry." Consistent with our analysis above, we found that for immigrants whose reference group at entry consisted predominantly of their co-ethnics, the higher their need for (nonspecific) closure, the lesser their assimilation into the Italian culture as attested by both our scales (which loaded highly on the same general factor). By contrast, for immigrants whose reference group at entry significantly included Italians, the higher their need for closure, the more extensive and thorough their assimilation into the Italian culture.

We conceptually replicated this study with two samples of Polish immigrants to Italy. Participants in the first sample responded to the (Polish translation of) the Need for Closure scale (Webster & Kruglanski, 1994), the Acculturation Strategies and Socio Cultural Adaptation Scales used in our previous study, and a scale of Italian Cultural Knowledge (including questions about the names of the regions of Italy, the colors of the Italian flag, and the name of the president of Italy). As in the Croat sample, participants also responded to the three items tapping the composition of their reference group at entry. We found, again, that for Poles who tended initially to interact with other Poles, the higher their need for closure, the more they tended to maintain their culture of origin, had limited relations with Italians, and exhibited a limited cultural knowledge of Italy. By contrast, for Poles who initially found Italian partners to interact with, the higher their need for closure, the less they tended to maintain their culture of origin, the more extensive their relations with Italians, and the better their Italian cultural knowledge.

Finally, in a third study we investigated another sample of Polish immigrants using this time a vignette methodology (Van Oudenhoven, Prins, & Buunk, 1998) in which the protagonist exhibits one of the four acculturation identified by Berry (1990, 1997) namely, assimilation, integration, marginalization, and separation. We found that for Polish immigrants who, within the first three months upon arrival, found predominantly other Poles to interact with, the higher their need for closure, the greater their identification and empathy for the protagonist who opted for the acculturation strategy of *separation*. By contrast, for immigrants who during that period found predominantly Italian interaction partners, the higher their need for closure, the greater their identification and empathy with the protagonist who opted for the acculturation strategy of *assimilation*. In summary then, depending on the circumstances, the need for closure could facilitate or impede immigrants' assimilation into the host culture. Whether one or the other of these modes is considered "better" or "more appropriate," the need for closure as such remains value neutral with regard to this issue.

☐ Epilogue: Need for Closure and the Psychology of "Good" Judgments

As the above suggests, the problematic issue is not a heightened need for closure per se, but rather its combination with information or knowledge considered inappropriate from some perspective (e.g., the social reality of the culture of origin to a supporter of assimilation) which is then frozen to the exclusion of alternative information (e.g., reflecting the realities of the host country). To the contrary, the combination of need for closure and highly appropriate information (from some perspective) should yield superior outcomes, because, in absence of such a need, the individual might stray from the "correct" way of reasoning and be (inappropriately) open to inferior and potentially misleading information. To take an analogy from the world of sport, as many well-trained athletes know, one must not ponder one's next move too extensively, lest it become slow and cumbersome. Their high level of training effectively ensures the correctness of their initial inclination. Seizing and freezing upon it is therefore adaptive, whereas considering alternative possibilities (prompted by a high *need to avoid closure*, for example) could be detrimental to performance. Similarly, the expert with a superior background knowledge in a domain (e.g., an expert plumber, auto mechanic, or cardiologist) may probably be served better by freezing on her expertise than by seriously (and open-mindedly) pondering various possibilities brought up by interested lay-persons and other nonexperts (e.g., trainees, clients, or patients). In short, the need for closure may mediate good judgmental outcomes if one's initial knowledge is correct, and it might mediate poor outcomes if one's initial knowledge is, erroneous. Of course it is often difficult to know in advance whether one's initial knowledge is, in fact, good or poor in reference to some criterion. How can one maximize the likelihood of good judgmental outcomes under these circumstances?

There are two general policy options that one could pursue. One is to mechanize the judgmental process by identifying in advance the potentially relevant information sources in a given context and evaluating their likely quality. Such evaluations would then be given the appropriate weight in the final judgment in proportion to their predetermined quality. An algorithm to that effect could be administered by a computer, which effectively removes all contextually present motivational concerns (including those stemming from the need for closure) from the judgmental process. Such mechanistic information integration (Meehl, 1956) does not guarantee a good judgmental outcome (no judgmental scheme can accomplish that), but at least it ensures consistency of the judgment with stable background knowledge and shields it against the influence of momentary psychological states of motivational and affective nature.

The second option, where potential information sources cannot be readily identified, is to ensure that the need for closure of the decision-making entity (the individual decision maker or the group) is at an optimal level. One way of accomplishing this is through judicious personnel selection and assignment. Thus, one can select for a decision-making body individuals with an intermediate degree of the need for closure (as assessed by the pertinent individual difference measure, for example). Alternatively, one could include in a group a mix of individuals varying widely on their need for closure, to stimulate lively discussion and examination of the issue (prompted by individuals with a low need for closure) that ultimately will end up with a definite conclusion (prompted by high-need-for-closure individuals). Finally, one could deliberately steer the judgmental process clear of situational circumstances that may foster an excessively high or an inappropriately low need for cognitive closure. Thus, one may want to avoid making important decisions under time pressure, stress, cognitive load, fatigue, or alcoholic intoxication. On the other hand, one may also want to avoid conditions where the fear of invalidity, accountability pressures, and/or the fear of commitment leave one perennially buried in a judgmental limbo, a state of "paralysis by analysis" wherein one's ability to see things clearly is compromised by an obsessive concentration on minute details, the proverbial trees obscuring the vision of the forest.

In a certain sense, the crux of the matter in maladaptive closed mindedness is the failure to consider rival alternatives to one's initial conception. One avenue of countering premature closure is to systematically generate such alternatives. This is not a novel suggestion. It appeared previously in several forms including the proposal of appointing a member or a group of members of the overall decision-making body to serve as the "devil's advocate"(Janis, 1982), and the kindred idea of "multiple advocacy" (George, 1980). The latter calls for instituting opposing teams of analysts deliberately instructed to interpret the available data in contrasting manners, one team a priori attempting to forge an optimistic assessment and the other trying their best to interpret the same data in a pessimistic or alarming manner. Although the policy makers would still need to decide between the two interpretations, this procedure will ensure that both are given an equal opportunity to be carefully thought through and formulated on the basis of the available information. These solutions can be effective if implemented in an appropriately cautious manner. Primarily, it is essential that both teams be equally motivated to produce compelling interpretations, and that neither perform its job in a routine, ritualized manner. Experience gained in the Research Division of the Israeli intelligence since the mid-1970s, when the function of the devil's advocate was institutionalized, suggests that if the alternative point of view is argued with less than complete seriousness, it can be readily dismissed, hence only adding strength to belief in the original conception (Kam, 1988).

As a different possibility, intelligence analysts could be made aware (in the appropriate workshops and crash courses) of their own psychological vulnerabilities to premature closure. Specifically, they would be made aware of the role of motivation in judgment formation and be trained to recognize the specific motivations likely to be operative in given decision-making contexts, and to appropriately correct for their potential biasing effects. Such meta-cognitive awareness might reduce, at least to some degree, analysts' inclination to believe that their assessment is driven exclusively by the facts, and to increase their openness to alternative interpretative possibilities.

To be sure, none of the foregoing possibilities can guarantee the goodness of the judgmental outcome ultimately reached. All they can accomplish is to ensure that the judgmental process is not short circuited by inappropriate degrees of the need for cognitive closure on part of the decision makers. In that sense then, taking the need for closure into consideration may allow decision makers to do their very best in the light of what is scientifically known about the psychology of judgment.

☐ Summary

The need for cognitive closure (of the nonspecific or specific variety) represents a ubiquitous aspect of human functioning affecting all our judgments and decisions and insinuating itself into our dealings with the social and nonsocial world at the intrapersonal, interpersonal, group, and intergroup levels of analysis. Both its antecedents and its consequences range from the mundane to the profound. Its antecedents may involve on one hand such everyday conditions as noise, time pressure, or fatigue, and on the other, the uniquely human awareness of our own mortality. Its consequences may involve at one end such minute cognitive phenomena as the tendency to assimilate one's judgments to primed constructs, and at the other such momentous decisions as those responsible for the launching of space shuttles or neglecting to adequately prepare for an enemy assault.

Though the need for closure may often bring about disastrous consequences and should be carefully guarded against in those circumstances, it is essentially involved in all human judgments and decisions, and hence its effects must be considered value free in principle. Thus, if the initial knowledge at an individual's disposal is good, veridical, effective, or adaptive by some criteria, seizing and freezing on such knowledge should have desirable consequences *by definition*. For instance, need for closure could promote the preservation of one's original culture as well as the assimilation into other cultures, all depending on initial conditions. If cultural preservation is at a premium, attaining it might involve combining the need for nonspecific closure with a high concentration of co-ethnics serving to make salient the social reality of the culture in question. If, however, cultural assimilation is deemed more desirable, the way of bringing it about may entail combining the need for closure with novel cultural surroundings (or novel social realities) and a relative isolation from co-ethnics. In this sense then, the need for cognitive closure may be considered value neutral, a motivation "for all seasons," as it were, serving to facilitate such judgments, whatever their nature, whose attainment brings about epistemic security most promptly and stably.

References

Abelson, R. P. (1959). Models of resolution of belief dilemmas. *Journal of Conflict Resolution, 3*, 343–352.

Abelson, R. P. (1968). Psychological implication. In R. P. Abelson, E. Aronson, W. J. McGuire, T. M. Newcomb, M. J. Rosenberg, & P. H. Tannenbaum (Eds.). *Theories of cognitive consistency: A source book.* Chicago: Rand McNally.

Adorno, T. W., Frenkel-Brunswik, E., Levinson, D. J., & Sanford, R. N. (1950). *The authoritarian personality.* New York: Harper.

Agranat Commission. (1975). *The report of the Agranat commission.* Tel Aviv: Am Oved.

Allen, V. L., & Wilder, D. A. (1975). Categorization, belief, similarity, and intergroup discrimination. *Journal of Personality and Social Psychology, 32(6),* 971–977.

Altemeyer, B. (1981). *Right-wing authoritarianism.* Manitoba: University of Manitoba Press.

Altemeyer, B. (1988). *Enemies of freedom: Understanding right-wing authoritarianism.* San Francisco: Josey-Bass Publishers.

Altemeyer, R. A. (1996). *The authoritarian specter.* Cambridge, MA: Harvard University Press.

Armitage, P. (1971). *Statistical methods in medical research.* Oxford: Blackwell.

Asch, S. E. (1946) Forming impressions of personality. *Journal of Abnormal and Social Psychology, 41,* 258–290.

Atkinson, J. W. (1958). *Motives in fantasy, action, and society: A method of assessment and study.* Princeton, NJ: Van Nostrand.

Back, K.W. (1951). Influence through social communication. *Journal of Abnormal and Social Psychology, 46,* 9–23.

Bales, R. F. (1950). *Interaction process analysis, a method for the study of small groups.* Reading, MA: Addison-Wesley.

Bandura, A. (1977). *Social learning theory.* Englewood Cliffs, NJ : Prentice-Hall.

Bar-Hillel, M. (1973). On the subjective probability of compound events, *Organizational Behavior and Human Performance, 9,* 396–406.

Bar-Joseph, U., & Kruglanski, A. W. (2003). Intelligence failure and need for cognitive closure: On the psychology of the Yom Kippur surprise. *Political Psychology, 24,* 75–99.

Baron, R. M., & Kenny, D. A., (1986). The moderator/mediator variable distinction in social psychological research: conceptual, strategic, and statistical considerations. *Journal of Personality and Social Psychology, 51 (6),* 1173–1182.

Bar-Tal, D., Kruglanski, A. W., & Klar, Y. (1989). Conflict termination: An epistemological analysis of international cases. *Political Psychology, 10,* 233–255.

Batson, C. D., O'Quin, K., Fultz, J., Vanderplas, M., & Isen, A. M. (1983). Influence of self reported distress and empathy on egotistic versus altruistic motivation to help. *Journal of Personality and Social Psychology, 45,* 706–718.

Bennett, N., Herold, D., & Ashford, S. (1990). The effects of tolerance for ambiguity on feed-back-seeking behavior. *Journal of Occupational Psychology, 63,* 343–348.

Benton, A. A. (1972). Accountability and negotiations between group representatives. *Proceedings of the Eightieth Annual Conference of the American Psychological Association,* pp. 227–228. Washington, D. C.

Benton, A A., & Druckman, D. (1973). Salient solutions and the bargaining behavior of rep-resentatives and nonrepresentatives. *International Journal of Group Tensions, 3,* 28–39.

Benton, A. A., & Druckman, D. (1974). Constituents' bargaining orientation and intergroup negotiations. *Journal of Applied Social Psychology, 4,* 141–150.

Berry, J. W. (1990). Psychology of acculturation. In J. Berman (Ed.), *Cross-cultural perspec-tives. Nebraska Symposium on Motivation* (pp. 201–234). Lincoln: University of Nebraska Press.

Berry, J. W. (1997). Immigration, acculturation, and adaptation. *Applied Psychology: An Inter-national Review, 46,* 5–68.

Berry, J. W., & Kim, U. (1988). Acculturation and mental health. In P. R. Dassen, J. W. Berry, & N. Sartorius (Eds.), *Health and cross-cultural psychology: Towards applications* (pp. 207–236).

Bhushan, L. (1970). Leadership preference as a function of authoritarianism and intolerance of ambiguity. *Psychologia, 13,* 217–222.

Bless, H., Clore, G. L., & Schwarz, N. (1996). Mood and the use of scripts: does happy mood really lead to mindlessness? *Journal of Personality and Social Psychology, 71(4),* 665–679.

Block, J., & Block, J. (1950). Intolerance of ambiguity and ethnocentrism. *Journal of Personal-ity, 19,* 303–311.

Blumer, H. (1956). Sociological analyses and the "variable." *American Sociological Review, 21,* 683–690.

Bond, M. H. (1988). Finding universal dimensions of individual variation in multicultural studies of values: the Rokeach and Chinese value surveys. *Journal of Personality and Social Psychology, 55 (6),* 1009–1015.

Boudreau, L. A., Baron, R., & Oliver, P. V. (1992). Effects of expected communication target expertise and timing of set on trait use in person description. *Personality and Social Psy-chology Bulletin, 18,* 447–452.

Brehm, P. (1966). *A theory of psychological reactance.* New York: Academic Press.

Broadbent, J. (1993). The "melting pot" vs. "the pressure cooker": cultural misunderstand-ings in the U.S.-Japan trade relations, *Law and Politics, 4,* 14–17.

Brown, R. (1965). *Social psychology.* Free Press: New York.

Budner, S. (1962). Intolerance of ambiguity as a personality variable. *Journal of Personality. 30,* 29–59.

Burke, E. (1982). Reflections on the revolution in France. In R. Kirk (Ed.). *The portable conser-vative reader* (pp. 2–40). New York: Penguin Books. (Original work published 1789)

Chaiken, S., Liberman, A., & Eagly, A. H. (1989). Heuristic and systematic processing within and beyond the persuasion context. In J. S. Uleman and J. A. Bargh (Eds.), *Unintended thought* (pp. 212–252). New York: Guilford Press.

Chapman, M. (1988). *Constructive evolution: origins and development of Piaget's thought.* Cam-bridge: Cambridge University Press.

Cheng, C., Bond, M. H., & Chan, S. C. (1995). The perception of ideal best friends by Chi-nese adolescents. *International Journal of Psychology, 30,* 91–108.

Cherry, F., & Byrne, D. (1977). Authoritarianism. In T. Blass (Ed.). *Personality variables in social behavior,* p. 109–133. Hillsdale, NJ: Erlbaum.

Chirumbolo, A., Mannetti, L., Pierro, A., Areni, A., & Kruglanski, A. W. (2003). *Motivated closed mindedness and creativity in small groups.* Unpublished manuscript. University of Rome "La Sapienza."

Chiu, C. Y., Hong, Ying-yi, Menon, T., & Morris, M. W. (1999). *Motivated cultural cognitions: A process-oriented approach to culture and causal explanation.* Unpublished manuscript. Stanford University.

Christie, R., & Jahoda, M. (Eds.) (1964). *Studies in the scope and method of "The authoritarian personality."* New York: Free Press.

Cialdini, R. B., Borden, R. J., Thorne, A., Walker, M. R., Freeman, S., & Sloan, L. R. (1976). Basking in reflected glory: three field studies. *Journal of Personality and Social Psychology, 34,* 366–375.

Clark, H. H., & Murphy, G. L. (1982). Audience design in meaning and reference. In J. F. LeNy & W. Kintsch (Eds.), *Language and comprehension* (pp. 287–299). New York: North Holland.

Cooper, J., & Fazio, R. H. (1984). A new look at dissonance theory. In L. Berkowitz (Ed.). *Advances in experimental social psychology, 17,* pp. 229–266. San Diego, CA: Academic Press.

Costa, P. T., Jr., & McCrae, R. R. (1978). Objective personality assessment. In M. Storandt, I. C. Siegler, & M. F. Elias (Eds.), *The clinical psychology of aging,* pp. 119–143. New York: Plenum Press.

Costa, P. T., Jr., & McCrae, R. R. (1992). *The Revised NEO Personality Inventory (NEO-PI-R) and NEO Five-factor Inventory (NEO-FFI) professional manual.* Odessa, FL: Psychological Assessment Resources.

Cratylus (1995). De Nederlandse Need for Closure Schaal (The Netherlands Need for Closure Scale). *Nederlandse Tijdschrift Voor de Psychologie, 50,* 231–232.

Dabbs, J. M., & Ruback, R. B. (1987). Dimensions of group process: Amount and structure of vocal interaction. In L. Berkowitz (Ed.) *Advances in experimental social psychology* (vol. 20, pp. 123–169). San Diego, CA: Academic Press.

Danks, J. H. (1970). Encoding of novel figures for communication and memory. *Cognitive psychology, 1,* 179–191.

Davis, M. H. (1983). Measuring individual differences in empathy: evidence for a multidimensional approach. *Journal of Personality and Social Psychology, 44,* 113–126.

Dechesne, M., Greenberg, J., Arndt, J., & Schimel, J. (2000). Terror management and the vicissitudes of sports fan affiliation: The effects of mortality salience on optimism and fan identification. *European Journal of Social Psychology, 30,* 813–835.

Dechesne, M., Janssen, J., & Van Knippenberg, A. (2000). Derogation and distancing as terror management strategies: The moderating role of need for closure and permeability of group boundaries. *Journal of Personality and Social Psychology, 79,* 923–932.

Dechesne, M., & Kruglanski, A. W. (in press). Terror's epistemic consequences: Existential threat and the quest for certainty and closure. In J. Greenberg, S. Koole, & T. Pyszczynski (Eds.). *Handbook of Experimental Existential Psychology.* New York: Guilford.

Dechesne, M., & Pyszczynski, T. (2002). *The effect of evidence of literal immortality and mortality salience on immortality belief.* Unpublished manuscript, University of Nijmegen.

Dechesne, M., & Wigboldus, D. (2001). [Terror management in a minimal worldview paradigm.] Unpublished data, University of Nijmegen.

De Dreu, C. K. W., & Koole, S. L. (1997). [Motivated use of heuristics in negotiation.] Unpublished data. University of Amsterdam.

De Dreu, C. K. W., & Van Lange, P. A. M. (1995). Impact of social value orientation on negotiator cognition and behavior. *Personality and Social Psychology Bulletin, 21,* 1177–1188.

De Dreu, C. K. W., Koole, S. L., & Oldersma, F. L. (1999). On the seizing and freezing of negotiator inferences: Need for cognitive closure moderates the use of heuristics in negotiation. *Personality and Social Psychology Bulletin, 25,* 348–362.

De Dreu, C. K. W., Yzerbyt, V. Y., & Leyens, J-Ph. (1995). Dilution of stereotype-based cooperation in mixed-motive interdependence. *Journal of Experimental Social Psychology, 31,* 575–593.

De Grada, E., Kruglanski, A. W., Mannetti, L., & Pierro, A., (1999). Motivated cognition and group interaction: Need for closure affects the contents and processes of collective negotiations. *Journal of Experimental Social Psychology, 35,* 346–365.

De Grada, E., Kruglanski, A. W., Mannetti, L., Pierro, A., & Webster, D.M. (1996). Un'analisi stutturale comparative delle versioni USA e italiana della scala di "Bisogno di chiusura cognitive" di Webster and Kruglanski (A comparative structural analysis of the U.S. and Italian versions of the "Need for Cognitive Closure" Scale of Webster and Kruglanski). *Testing, Psicometria, Metodologia, 3,* 5–18.

Deutsch, M. (1973). *The resolution of conflict: Constructive and destructive.* New Haven: Yale University Press.

Dijksterhuis, A., Van Knippenberg, A., Kruglanski, A. W., & Schaper, C. (1996). Motivated social cognition: Need for closure effects on memory and judgment. *Journal of Experimental Social Psychology, 32,* 254–270.

Ditto, P. H., & Griffin J. (1993). The value of uniqueness: Self-evaluation and the percieved prevalence of valanced characteristics. *Journal of Social Behavior and Personality, 8 (2),* 221–240.

Ditto, P. H., & Lopez, D. F. (1992). Motivated skepticism: Use of differential decision criteria for preferred and nonpreferred conclusions. *Journal of Personality and Social Psychology, 63,* 568–584.

Ditto, P. H., Scepansky, J. A., Munro, G. D., Apanovitch, A. M., & Lockhart, L. K. (1998). Motivated sensitivity to preference—inconsistent information. *Journal of Personality and Social Psychology, 75,* 53–69.

Doherty, K. (1998). A mind of her own: Effects of need for closure and gender on reactions to nonconformity. *Sex Roles, 38,* 801–819.

Dona, G., & Berry, J. (1994). Acculturation attitudes and acculturative stress of Central American refugees. *International Journal of Psychology, 29,* 57–70.

Druckman, D., Solomon, D., & Zechmeister, K. (1972). Effects of representative role obligations on the process of children's distribution of resources. *Sociometry, 35,* 489–501.

Dunning, D. (1999). A newer look: Motivated social cognition and the schematic representation of social concepts. *Psychological Inquiry, 10 (1),* 1–11.

Eckhardt, W. (1991). Authoritarianism. *Political Psychology, 12(1),* 97–124.

Eckhardt, W., and Lentz, T .F. (1971). Factors of war/peace attitudes. *Peace Research Review, 1(5),* 1–102.

Ellis, S., & Kruglanski, A. W. (1992). Self as epistemic authority: Effects on experiential and instructional learning. *Social Cognition, 10,* 357–375.

Erb, H. P., Kruglanski, A. W., Chun, W. Y., Pierro, A., Mannetti, L., & Spiegel, S. (2003). Searching for commonalities in human judgement: The parametric unimodel and its dual mode alternatives. *European Review of Social Psychology, 14,* 1–47.

Erber, R., & Fiske, S. T. (1984). Outcome dependency and attention to inconsistent information. *Journal of Personality and Social Psychology, 47,* 709–726.

Eysenck, H. (1954). *The psychology of politics.* London: Routledge and Kegan Paul.

Eysenck, H. J., & Eysenck, S. B. G. (1969). *Personality structure and measurement.* San Diego, CA: R. R. Knapp.

Eysenck, H., and Wilson, G. D. (1978). *The psychological basis of ideology,* Lancaster, England: MTP Press.

Feather, N. (1969). Preference for information in relation to consistency, novelty, intolerance of ambiguity and dogmatism. *Australian Journal of Psychology, 31,* 235–249.

Federico, C. M., & Golec, A. (2003). *The relationship between need for closure and support for military action against Iraq: Moderating effects of national attachment.* Unpublished manuscript. University of Minnesota, Twin Cities.

Fein, S., & Spencer, S. J. (1997). Prejudice as self image maintenance: Affirming the self through derogating others. *Journal of Personality and Social Psychology, 73,* 31–44.

Feshbach, S. (1994). Nationalism, patriotism, and aggression: A classification of functional differences. In L. Huesmann (Ed.), *Aggressive behavior: Current perspectives* (pp. 275–291). New York: Putnam.

Festinger, L. (1954). A theory of social comparison processes. *Human Relations, 7,* 117–140.

Festinger, L. (1957). *A theory of cognitive dissonance.* Stanford, CA: Stanford University Press.

Festinger, L. (1950). Informal social communication. *Psychological Review, 57,* 271–282.

Festinger, L., & Schachter, S.G. (1951). Deviation, rejection and communication. *Journal of Abnormal Social Psychology, 46,* 190–207.

Fiedler, F. E. (1967). *A theory of leadership effectiveness.* New York: McGraw-Hill.

Finke, R., & Slayton, K. (1988). Explorations of creative visual synthesis in mental imagery. *Memory and Cognition, 16*, 252–257.

Finlay, D. J., Holsti, O. R., & Fagen, R. R. (1967). *Enemies in Politics*, Chicago: Rand McNally.

Fisher, R., and Ertel, D. (1995). *Getting ready to negotiate*. New York: Penguin Books.

Flavell, J. H. (1963). *The developmental psychology of Jean Piaget*. Princeton, NJ: Van Nostrand.

Frenkel-Brunswik, E. (1948a). Tolerance of ambiguity as a personality variable. (Abstract). *American Psychologist, 3*, 268.

Frenkel-Brunswik, E. (1948b). Intolerance of ambiguity as an emotional perceptual personality variable. *Journal of Personality, 18*, 108–143.

Frenkel-Brunswik, E. (1949). Tolerance towards ambiguity as a personality variable. *American Psychologist, 3*, 268.

Frenkel-Brunswik, E. (1951). Personality theory and perception. In R. Blake & G. Ramsey (Eds.), *Perception: An approach to personality*. New York: Oxford University Press.

Freud, S. (1912–1913) 1955. *Totem and taboo*. In J. Strachey (Ed.) *The standard edition of the complete psychological works of Sigmund Freud*, vol. 13, London: Hogarth Press.

Frone, M. (1990). Intolerance of ambiguity as a moderator of the occupational role stress-strain relationship. *Journal of Organizational Behavior, 11*, 309–320.

Fu, J. H. Y., Lee, V. S. L., Chiu, C. Y., Morris, M. W., & Hong, Y. Y. (2003). [Culture and reward allocation.] Unpublished data. Nanyang Technological University.

Fu, J. H. Y., Morris, M. W., Lee, S. L., Chiu, C. Y., & Hong, Y. Y. (2003). *Why do individuals display culturally typical conflict resolution choices? Need for cognitive closure*. Unpublished manuscript, Nanyang Technological University.

Furnham, A., & Gunter, B. (1993). *Corporate assessment*. London: Routledge.

Furnham, A., & Ribchester, T. (1995). Tolerance of ambiguity: A review of the concept, its measurement and applications. *Current Psychology: Developmental, Learning, Personality, Social, 14*(3), 179–200.

Fussell, S. R., & Krauss, R. N. (1989). The effects of intended audience design on message production and comprehension: Reference in a common ground framework. *Journal of Experimental Social Psychology, 25*, 203–219.

Fussell, S. R., & Krauss, R. N. (1991). Accuracy and bias in estimates of others' knowledge. *European Journal of Social Psychology, 21*, 445–454.

Gallo, P. S., Jr. (1968). *Prisoners of our own dilemma?* Paper presented at the meeting of the Western Psychological Association. San Diego, CA, April 1968.

George, A. L. (1980). *Presidential decision making in foreign policy: The effective use of information and advice*. Boulder, CO: Westview Press.

Gilbert, D. T., Pelham, B. W., & Krull, D. S. (1988). On cognitive busyness: when person perceivers meet persons perceived. *Jounal of Personality and Social Psychology, 54*, 733–740.

Giovannini, D., & Savoia, L. (2002). *Psicologia dello sport*. Roma: Caroci.

Golec, A. (2001). *Need for cognitive closure and political conservatism: Studies on the nature of the relationship*. Paper presented at the annual meeting of the International Society of Political Psychology, July 2001, Cuernavaca, Mexico.

Golec, A. (2002a). *Zaangazowanie polityczne a zwiazek potrzeby domkniecia poznawczego I konserwatyzmu politycznego*. (Political engagement and the relation between the need for closure and political conservatism) *Czasopismo Psychologiczne 2*, 43–60.

Golec, A. (2002b). Need for cognitive closure and political conservatisms: Studies on the nature of the relationship. *Polish Psychological Bulletin, 4*, 5–13.

Golec, A., & Federico, C. M. (2003). *Understanding responses to political conflict: Interactive effects of the need for closure and salient conflict schemas*. Unpublished manuscript. Institute of Psychology. Polish Academy of Sciences.

Greenberg, J., & Jonas, E. (2003). Political motives and political orientation—The left, the right, and the rigid: Comment on Jost et al. (2003). *Psychological Bulletin, 129*, 3376–3382.

Greenberg, J., Pyszczynski, T., Solomon, S., Rosenblatt, A., Veeder, M., Kirkland, S., & Lyon, D. (1990). Evidence for terror management theory II: The effects of mortality salience in reactions to those who threaten or bolster the cultural world view. *Journal of Personality and Social Psychology, 58*, 308–318.

Greenberg, J., Simon, L., Pyszczynski, T., & Solomon, S. (1992). Terror management and tolerance: Does mortality salience always intensify negative reactions to others who threaten one's worldview? *Journal of Personality and Social Psychology, 63* (2), 212–220.

Greenberg, J., Pyszczynski, T., & Solomon, S. (1986). The causes and consequences of a need for self-esteem: A terror management theory. In R. F. Baumeister (Ed.). *Public self and private self*, pp. 189–212. New York: Springer-Verlag.

Grice, G. P. (1975). Logic and conversation. In P. Cole and J. L. Morgan (Eds.). *Syntax and semantics. Vol. 3: Speech Acts.* New York: Academic Press.

Gruder, C. L. (1971). Relationship with opponent and partner in mixed-motive bargaining. *Journal of Conflict Resolution, 15*, 403–416.

Hanson, D. J. (1975). Authoritarianism as a variable in political research. *Il Politico, 15*, 700–705.

Hardin, C. T., & Higgins, E. T. (1996). Shared reality: How social verification makes the subjective objective. In R. M., Sorrentino, & E. T. Higgins (Eds.) *Handbook of motivation and cognition. Vol. 3. The interpersonal context*, pp. 28–84. New York: Guilford Press.

Harmon Jones, E., Greenberg, J., Solomon, S., & Simon, L. (1996). The effects of mortality salience on intergroup bias between minimal groups. *European Journal of Social Psychology, 26*, 677–681.

Hart, P. T. (1994). *Groupthink in government: A study of small groups and policy failure.* Baltimore, MD: Johns Hopkins University Press.

Heider, F. (1958). *The psychology of interpersonal relations.* New York: Wiley.

Heilman, M. E., Block, C. J., & Martel, R. F. (1995). Sex stereotypes: Do they influence perceptions of managers? *Journal of Social Behavior and Personality, 10*, 237–252.

Higgins, E. T. (1987). Self-discrepancy: A theory relating self and affect. *Psychological Review, 94*, 319–340.

Higgins, E. T. (1996). Knowledge activation: Accessibility, applicability and salience. In E. T. Higgins & A. W. Kruglanski (Eds.), *Social psychology: A handbook of basic principles* (pp. 133–168). New York: Guilford Press.

Higgins, E. T. (1997). Beyond pleasure and pain. *American Psychologist, 52*, 1280–1300.

Higgins, E. T., King, G. A., & Marin, G. H. (1982). Individual construct accessibility and subjective impressions and recall. *Journal of Personality and Social Psychology, 43*, 35–47.

Higgins, E. T., McCann, C. D.. & Fondacaro, R. (1982). The "communication game": Goal directed encoding and cognitive consequences. *Social cognition, 1*, 21–37.

Higgins, E. T., Rholes, W. S., & Jones, C. R. (1977). Category accessibility and impression formation. *Journal of Experimental Social Psychology, 13*, 141–154.

Hofstede, G. (1980). *Culture's consequences.* Beverly Hills, CA: Sage.

Hogg, M.A., & Abrams, D. (1993). Towards a single-process uncertainty reduction model of social motivation in groups. In Hogg and Dominic (Eds.). *Group motivation: Social psychological perspectives.* Hertfordshire: Harvester Wheatsheaf.

Holland, J. L., Johnston, J. A., Hughey, K. F., & Asama, N. F. (1991). Some explorations of a theory of careers: VII. A replication and some possible extensions. *Journal of Career Development, 18*, 91–100.

Horton, W. S,. and Keysar, B. (1996). When do speakers take into account common ground? *Cognition, 59*, 91–17.

Houghton, D. C., & Kardes, F. R. (1998). *Marketing Letters, 9*(3), 313–320.

Hsee, C. K. (1995). Elastic justification: How tempting but task–irrelevant factors influence decisions. *Organizational Behavior and Human Decision Processes, 62,* 330–337.

Huntington, S. (1957). Conservatism as an ideology. *American Political Science Review, 51*, 454–473.

Huntington, S. P. (1997). *The clash of civilizations: Remaking of world order.* New York: Touchstone.

Ip., G., Chen, J., & Chiu, C. Y. (2003). [Culture, motivation and categorical accessibility.] Unpublished data. University of Illinois, Champaign-Urbana.

Jaentsch, E. *Der gegentypus.* Leipzig. Barth.

Jacobs, R. C., & Campbell, D. T. (1961). The perpetuation of an arbitrary tradition through several generations of a laboratory microculture. *Journal of Abnormal and Social Psychology, 62*, 649–658.

Jamieson, D. W., & Zanna, M. P. (1989). Need for structure in attitude formation and expression. In A. R. Pratkanis, S. J. Breckler, & A. G. Greenwald (Eds.). *Attitude structure and function*, pp. 383–406. Hillsdale, NJ: Lawrence Erlbaum Associates.

Janis, I. L. (1972). *Victims of groupthink.* Boston: Houghton Mifflin.

Janis, I. L. (1982). *Groupthink*. Boston: Houghton Mifflin, 2nd rev. ed.
Jefferson, G. (1985). On the interactional unpacking of a "gloss." *Language and Society, 14,* 435–466.
Jervis, R. (1976). *Perception and misperception in international politics.* Princeton, NJ: Princeton University Press.
Jones, E. E. (1979). The rocky road from act to disposition. *American Psychologist, 34,* 107–117.
Jones, E. E., & Gerard, H. B. (1967). *Foundations of social psychology.* New York: Wiley.
Jones, E. E., & Harris, V. A. (1967). The attribution of attitudes. *Journal of Experimental Social Psychology, 3,* 1–24, 693–708.
Jost, J. T., Glaser, J., & Kruglanski, A. W., & Sulloway, F. J. (2003a). Political conservatism as motivated social cognition. *Psychological Bulletin, 129,* 339–375.
Jost, J. T., Glaser, J., Kruglanski, A. W., & Sulloway, F. J. (2003b). Exceptions that prove the rule: Using a theory of motivated·social cognition to account for ideological incongruities and political anomalies: A reply to Greenberg and Jonas (2003). *Psychological Bulletin, 129,* 383–393.
Jost, J. T., Kruglanski, A. W., & Simon, L. (1999). Effects of epistemic motivation on conservatism, intolerance, and other system-justifying attitudes. In L. I. Thompson, J. M. Levine, & D. M. Messick (Eds.), *Shared cognition in organizations: The management of knowledge* (pp. 91–116). Mahwah, NJ: Lawrence Erlbaum Associates..
Kagan, J. (1972). Motives and development. *Journal of Personality and Social Psychology, 22*(1), 51–66.
Kahneman, D., Slovic, P., & Tversky, A. (Eds.) (1982). *Judgment under uncertainty: Heuristics and biases.* Cambridge, England: Cambridge University Press.
Kahneman, D. & Tversky, A. (1996). On the reality of cognitive illusions. *Psychological Review, 103,* 583–591.
Kam, E. (1988). *Surprise attack: The victim's perspective.* Cambridge: Harvard University Press.
Keenan, J., & McBain, G. (1979). Effects of Type A behavior, intolerance of ambiguity, stress and work-related outcomes and locus of control on the relationship between roles. *Journal of Occupational Psychology, 52,* 277–285.
Kelley, H. H. (1967). Attribution theory in social psychology. In D. Levine (Ed.), Nebraska Symposium on Motivation, 15, 192–238. Lincoln: University of Nebraska Press.
Kemmelmeier, M. (1997). Need for closure and political orientation among German university students. *Journal of Social Psychology, 137* (6), 787–789.
Kohlberg, L. (1964). Development of moral character and ideology. In M. L. Hoffman & L. W. Hoffman (Eds.), *Review of Child Development Research, Vol. 1* (pp. 383–431). New York: Russell Sage.
Kosic, A., Kruglanski, A. W., Pierro, A., & Mannetti, L. (2004). Social cognition of immigrants' acculturation: Effects of the need for closure and the reference group at entry. *Journal of Personality and Social Psychology, 86* (6), 1–18.
Kosic, A. (1998). Adattamento degli immigzati in relazione al loro bisogno di chiuscora cognitiva e alle loro strategie di coping. [Immigrants' adaptation in relation to their need for closure and their coping strategies]. Unpublished Ph.D thesis. University of Rome "La Sapienza".
Kossowska, M,. & Van Hiel, A. (2003). The relationship between need for closure and conservative beliefs in Western and Eastern Europe. *Political Psychology, 24,* 501–518.
Krauss, R. M., & Fussell, S. R. (1991). Perspective taking in communication: Representations of others' knowledge in reference. *Social Cognition, 9,* 2–24.
Kreitler, S., Maguen, T., & Kreitler, H. (1975). The three faces of intolerance of ambiguity. *Archiv fur Psychologie, 127,* 238–250.
Kroon, M. B. R., van Kreveld, D., & Rabbie, J. M. (1992). Groups versus individual decision making. *Small Group Research, 23,* 427–458.
Kruglanski, A.W. (1975). The endogenous-exogenous partition in attribution theory. *Psychological Review, 82,* 387–406.
Kruglanski, A. W. (1981). The epistemic approach in cognitive therapy. *International Journal of Psychology, 16,* 275–297.

Kruglanski, A. W. (1989). *Lay epistemics and human knowledge: Cognitive and motivational bases*. New York: Plenum.

Kruglanski, A. W. (1994). The social-cognitive bases of scientific knowledge. In William Shadish and Steve Fuller (Eds.), *The Social Psychology of Science*. New York: Guilford Press.

Kruglanski, A. W. (1999). Motivation, cognition, and reality: Three memos for the next generation of research. *Psychological Inquiry, 10*, 54–58.

Kruglanski, A. W. (2001). That "vision thing": The state of theory in social and personality psychology at the edge of the new millennium. *Journal of Personality and Social Psychology, 80*, 871–875.

Kruglanski, A. W., & Ajzen, I. (1983). Bias and error in human judgment. *European Journal of Psychology, 13*, 1–44.

Kruglanski, A. W., & Freund, T. (1983). The freezing and unfreezing of lay inferences: Effects on impressional primacy, ethnic stereotyping and numerical anchoring. *Journal of Experimental Social Psychology, 19*, 448–468.

Kruglanski, A. W., & Jost, J. T. (2003). Political opinion, not pathology. (2003, August 28) *Washington Post*, p. 22.

Kruglanski, A. W., & Klar, Y. (1987). A view from a bridge: Synthesizing the consistency and attribution paradigms from a lay epistemic perspective. *European Journal of Social Psychology, 17*, 211–241.

Kruglanski, A. W., Shah, J. Y. Pierro, A., & Mannetti, L. (2002). When similarity breeds content: Need for closure and the allure of homogeneous and self-resembling groups. *Journal of Personality and Social Psychology, 83*, (3), 648–662.

Kruglanski, A. W. & Webster, D. M. (1991). Group members' reactions to opinion deviates and conformists at varying degrees of proximity to decision deadline and of environmental noise. *Journal of Personality and Social Psychology, 61*, 212–225.

Kruglanski, A. W., Webster, D. M., Klem, A. (1993). Motivated resistance and openness to persuasion in the presence or absence of prior information. *Journal of Personality and Social Psychology, 65* (5), 861–876.

Kruglanski, A.W. & Webster, D.M.(1996). Motivated closing of the mind: "Seizing and Freezing." *Psychological Review, 103* (2), 263–283.

Kruglanski, A. W., and Thompson, E. P. (1999)(a). Persuasion by a single route: A view from the unimodel. *Psychological Inquiry, 10* (2), 83–110.

Kruglanski, A. W., & Thompson, E. P. (1999)(b). The illusory second mode, or the cue *is* the message. *Psychological Inquiry, 10* (2), 182–193.

Kruglanski, A.W., Shah, J.Y., Pierro, A., Mannetti, L. (2002). When similarity breeds content: need for closure and the allure of homogenous and self-resembling groups. *Journal of personality and Social psychology, 83* (3), 643–662.

Kruglanski, A. W., Bar-Tal, D., & Klar, Y. (1993). A social cognitive theory of conflict. In K.S. Larsen (Ed.). *Conflict and social psychology* (pp. 45–56). London: Sage.

Kruglanski, A. W., Atash, M. N., DeGrada, E., Mannetti, L., & Webster, D. M. (1997). Psychological theory testing versus psychometric nay-saying: Comment on Neuberg et al.' s (1997) critique of the Need for Closure Scale. *Journal of Personality and Social Psychology, 73*, 1005–1016.

Kuhlman, D. M., & Marshello, A. (1975). Individual differences in game motivation as moderators of preprogrammed strategic effects in prisoner's dilemma. *Journal of Personality and Social Psychology, 32*, 922–931.

Kunda, Z. (1990). The case for motivated reasoning. *Psychological Bulletin, 108*, 480–498.

Kunda, Z., & Sinclair, L. (1999). Motivated reasoning with stereotypes: Activation, application and inhibition. *Psychological Inquiry, 10*, 12–22.

Laitin, D. D. (1977). *Politics, language and thought*. Chicago: Chicago University Press.

Lalwani, A. K., Shavitt, S., Johnson, T., & Zhang, J. (2003). *What is the relation between culture and socially desirable responding*. Unpublished manuscript. University of Illinois.

Lam, S. F., Lau, I. Y. M., Chiu, C. Y., Hong, Y. Y., & Peng, S. Q. (1999). Differential emphases on modernity and Confucian value in social categorization. The case of Hong Kong adolescents in political transition. *International Journal of Intercultural Relations, 23 (2)*, 237–256.

Landau, J. (1995). The relationship of race and gender to managers' ratings of promotion potential. *Journal of Organizational Behavior, 16,* 391–400.

Lax, D., and Sebenius, J. (1986). *The manager as negotiator: Cooperating for competitive gain.* New York: Free Press.

Lentz, T. F. (1929). Character research and human happiness. *Association forum, 10*(2), 1–8.

Lentz, T. F. (1930). Utilizing opinion for character measurement. *Journal of Social Psychology, 1,* 536–542.

Lentz, T. F. (1935). *C-R opinionaire and manual.* St. Louis, MO: Character Research Association (now the Lentz Peace Research Laboratory).

Le Resche, D. (1992). Comparison of the American mediation process with a Korean American harmony restoration process [Special issue]. Diversity: Some implications for mediation. *Mediation Quarterly, 9*(4), 323–339.

Leventhal, H., Jacobs, R., & Kurdirka, N. (1964). Authoritarianism, ideology, and political candidate choice. *Journal of Abnormal Social Psychology, 69,* 539–549.

Levine, D. N. (1977). Review of sociological ambivalence and other essays by Robert K. Merton. *American Journal of Sociology, 83,* 1277–1279.

Levine, D. N. (1985). *The flight from ambiguity: Essays in social and cultural theory.* Chicago, IL.: University of Chicago Press.

Levinson, D. J., & Huffman, P. (1955). Traditional family ideology and its relation to personality. *Journal of Personality, 23,* 251–273.

Livi, S. (2001). Il bisogna di chiuscora cognitiva e la transmissione delle norme nei piccoli gruppi. (The need for cognitive closure and norm-transmission in small groups). Unpublished Ph.D thesis, University of Rome " La Sapienza".

Loehlin, J. C. (1992). *Genes and environment in personality development.* Newbury Park, CA: Sage.

Luchins, A. S. & Luchins, E. H. (1950). New experimental attempts at preventing mechanization in problem solving. *Journal of General Psychology, 42,* 279–297.

Luhtanen, R., & Crocker, J. (1991). Self-esteem and intergroup comparisons: Toward a theory of collective self-esteem. In Suls, J., Wills, T. A. (Eds.), *Social comparison: Contemporary theory and research.* Hillsdale, NJ: Lawrence Erlbaum Associates, Inc.

Maass, A., & Arcuri, L. (1992). The role of language in the persistence of stereotypes. In G. Semin and K. Fiedler (Eds.), *Language, interaction and social cognition* (pp. 129–143). Newbury Park, CA: Sage.

Maass, A., & Stahlberg, D. (1993). *The linguistic intergroup bias: The role of differential expectancies and in-group protective motivation.* Paper presented at the conference of EAESP, Lisbon, September.

Maass, A., Milesi, A., Zabbini, S., & Stahlberg, D. (1995). The linguistic intergroup bias: Differential expectancies or in-group protection? *Journal of Personality and Social Psychology, 68,* 116–126.

Maass, A., Salvi, D., Arcuri, L., & Semin, G. (1989). Language use in intergroup contexts: The linguistic intergroup bias. *Journal of Personality and Social Psychology, 57,* 981–993.

Markus, H., & Kitayama, S. (1991). Culture and the self: Implications for cognition, emotion, and motivation. *Psychological Review, 98,* 224–253.

Mayseless, O., & Kruglanski, A. K. (1987). What makes you so sure?: Effects of epistemic motivations in judgmental confidence. *Organizational Behavior and Human Decision Processes, 39,* 162–183.

McCrae, R. R. (1996). Social consequences of experiential openness. *Psychological Bulletin, 120* (3), 323–337.

McCrae, R. R., & Costa, P. T., Jr. (1997). Conceptions and correlates of openness to experience. In R. Hogan, J. A. Johnson, and S. R. Briggs (Eds.), *Handbook of personality psychology.* New York: Academic Press.

Meehl, P. E. (1956). Wanted: A good cook book. *American Psychologist, 11,* 263–272.

McCrae, R. R. (1996). Social consequences of experiential openness. *Psychological Bulletin, 120*(3), 323–337.

Mennis, B. (1971). *American foreign policy officials: Who they are and they believe regarding international politics.* Columbus, OH: The Ohio State University Press.

Menon, T., Morris, M. W., Chiu, C., & Hong, Y. (1998). *Culture and attributions to individuals versus groups: North Americans attributte to personal dispositions; East Asians attribute to the dispositions of social collectives.* Unpublished manuscript. Stanford University.

Merton, R. K., (1963) with Elinor Barber (1963)/1976. *Sociological ambivalence and other essays.* New York: Free Press.

Mikulincer, M., Yinon, A., & Kabili, D. (1991). Epistemic needs and learned helplessness. *European Journal of Personality*, 5, 249–258.

Miyamoto, M. (1995). *Straitjacket society: An insider's irreverant view of bureaucratic Japan.* Tokyo: Kodansha International.

Moskowitz, G. B. (1993). Person organization with a memory set: Are spontaneous trait inferences personality characteristics or behaviour labels? *European Journal of Personality*, 7 (3), 195–208.

Murray, S. L. (1999). The quest for conviction? Motivated cognition in romantic relationships. *Psychological Inquiry*, 10, 23–34.

Murray, S. L., & Holmes, J. G. (1993). Seeing virtues in faults: Negativity and the transformation of interpersonal narratives in close relationships. *Journal of Personality and Social Psychology*, 65, 707–722.

Murray, S. L., & Holmes, J. G. (1997). A leap of faith? Positive illusions in romantic relationships. *Personality and Social Psychological Bulletin*, 23, 586–604.

Neale, M. A., and Bazerman, M. H. (1991). *Rationality and cognition in negotiation.* New York: Free Press.

Neuberg, S. L., & Newsom, J. T. (1993). Personal need for structure: Individual differences in the desire for simple structure. *Journal of Personality and Social Psychology*, 65, 113–131.

Neuberg, S., Judice, T. N., & West, S. G. (1997). What the Need for Closure Scale measures and what it does not measure: Toward differentiating among related epistemic motives. *Journal of Personality and Social Psychology*, 72, 1396–1412.

Nickerson, R. S., Baddeley, A., & Freeman, B. (1987). Are people's estimates of what other people know influenced by what themselves know? *Acta Psychologica*, 64, 245–259.

Nisbett, R., & Ross, L., (1980). *Human inference: Strategies and shortcomings of social judgement.* Englewood Cliffs, NJ: Prentice-Hall.

Northcraft, G. B., & Neale, M. A. (1987). Experts, amateurs, and real estate: An anchoring and adjustment perspective on property pricing decisions. *Organizational Behavior and Human Decision Processes*, 39, 84–97.

O'Connor, P. (1952). Ethnocentrism, 'intolerance of ambiguity', and abstract reasoning ability. *Journal of Abnormal and Social Psychology*, 47, 526–530.

Osgood, C. E., and Tannenbaum, P. H. (1955). The principle of congruity in the prediction of attitude change. *Psychological Review*, 62, 42–55.

Paulhus, D. L. (1998). *The balanced inventory of desirable responding.* BIDR Version 7. Toronto/Buffalo: Multi-Health Systems.

Petty, R. E., and Cacioppo, J. T. (1986). The elaboration likelihood model of persuasion. In L. Berkowitz (Ed.), *Advances in experimental social psychology* (vol., 19, pp. 123–205). San Diego, CA: Academic Press.

Piaget, J. (1975). *The construction of the real in the child.* Rio de Janeiro: Zahar.

Piaget, J. (1985). *Equilibration of cognitive structures.* Chicago: University of Chicago Press.

Pierro, A., Mannetti, L., DeGrada, El, Livi, S., & Kruglanski, A. W. (2003) Autocracy Bias in informal groups under need for closure. *Personality and Social Psychology Bulletin*, 29, 405–417.

Pierro, A., Mannetti, l., Converso, D., Garsia, V., Miglietta, A., Ravenna, M., & Rubini, M. (1995). *Caratteristiche strutturali della versione italiana della scale di bisogno di chiusura cognitiva (di Webster and Kruglanski)* [Structural characteristics of the Italian version of the Need for Cognitive Closure Scale (of Webster and Kruglanski)]. *Testing, Psicometria, Metodologia*, 2, 125–141.

Powell, R. S., & O'Neal, E. C. (1976). Communication feedback and duration as determinants of accuracy, confidence, and differentiation in interpersonal perception. *Journal of Personality and Social Psychology*, 34, 746–756.

Pruitt, D. G. (1981). *Negotiation behavior.* New York: Academic Press.

Pruitt, D. G., & Carnevale, P. J. (1993). *Negotiation in social conflict.* Pacific Grove, CA: Brooks/Cole Publishing Company.

Psathas, G., & Anderson, T. (1990). The 'practices' of transcription in conversation analysis. *Semiotica, 78* (1/2), 75–99.

Pyszczynski, T., Solomon, S., & Greenberg, J. (2003). In the wake of September 11: The psychology of terror. Washington D.C.: American Psychological Association.

Pyszczynski, T., Wicklund, R. A., Floresku, S., Koch, H., Gauch, G., Solomon, S., & Greenberg, J. (1996). Whistling in the dark. Exaggerated consensus estimates in response to incidental reminders of mortality. *Psychological Science, 7* (6), 332–336.

Quattrone, G. A. (1982). Overattribution and unit formation: When behavior engulfs the person. *Journal of Personality and Social Psychology, 42,* 593–607.

Rahim, M. A. (1983). A measure of styles of handling interpersonal conflict. *Academy of Management Journal, 26,* 368–376.

Richter, L., & Kruglanski, A. W. (1999). Motivated search for common ground: Need for closure effects on audience design in interpersonal communication. *Personality and Social Psychology Bulletin, 25*(9), 1101–1114.

Richter, L., & Kruglanski, A. W. (2003). Motivated closed mindedness and the emergence of culture. In M. Schaller & C. Crandall (Eds.), *Psychological foundations of culture.* Hillsdale, NJ: Lawrence Erlbaum.

Richter, L., & Kruglanski, A. W. (1998). Seizing on the latest: Motivationally driven recency effects in impression formation. *Journal of Experimental Social Psychology, 34* (4), 313–329.

Robinson, L. B., & Hastie, R. (1985). Revision of beliefs when a hypothesis is eliminated from consideration. *Journal of Experimental Psychology: Human Perception and Performance, 11*(4), 443–456.

Rocchi, P. (1998). Il bisogno di chiusura cognitiva e la creativita (Need for closure and creativity). *Giornale Italiano di Psicologia, XXV,* 153–190.

Rokeach, M. (1960). *The open and closed mind.* Basic Books: New York.

Rosenberg, M. J. (1965). Images in relation to the policy process: American public opinion on cold war issues. In Kelman, H.C. (Ed.), *International behavior: A social-psychological analysis* (pp. 277–334). New York: Rinehart and Winston.

Rosenblatt, A., Greenberg, J., Solomon, S., Pyszczynski, T., & Lyon, D. (1989). Evidence for terror management theory: The effects of mortality salience on reactions to those who violate or uphold cultural values. *Journal of Personality and Social Psychology, 57,* 681–690.

Ross, L. (1995). Reactive devaluation in negotiation and conflict resolution. In K. Arrow, R. Mnookin, L. Ross, A. Tversky, & R. Wilson (Eds.), *Barriers to the negotiated resolution of conflict* (pp. 30–48). New York: Norton.

Ross, L. (1977). The intuitive psychologist and his shortcomings: Distortions in the attribution process. In L. Berkowitz (Ed.). *Advances in experimental social psychology. 10,* 173–240. Orlando, FL: Academic Press.

Ross, L., Greene, D., & House, P. (1977). The false consensus phenomenon: An attribution bias in self-perception and social perception processes. *Journal of Experimental Social Psychology, 13,* 279–301.

Rubin, J. Z., & Brown, B. R. (1975). *The social psychology of bargaining and negotiation.* New York: Academic Press.

Rubini, M., & Kruglanski, A. W. (1997). Brief encounters ending in estrangement: Motivated language use and interpersonal rapport in the question-answer paradigm. *Journal of Personality and Social Psychology, 72,* 1047–1060.

Sanbomatsu, D. M., Posavac, S. S., Kardes, F. R., & Mantel, S. P. (1998). Selective hypothesis testing. *Psychonomic Bulletin & Review, 5*(2), 197–220.

Sanbomatsu, D. M., Posavac, S. S., & Stasny, R. (1997). The subjective beliefs underlying probability overestimation. *Journal of Experimental Social Psychology, 33*(3), 276–295.

Saunders, D. (1955, October). *Some preliminary interpretive material* (for the PRI Research Memorandum SS). Educational Testing Service.

Schaller, M., Boyd, C., Yohannes, J., & O'Brien, M. (1995). The prejudiced personality revisited: Personal need for structure and formation of erroneous group stereotypes. *Journal of Personality and Social Psychology, 68,* 544–555.

Scheier, M. F., & Carver, C. S. (1985). Optimism, coping, and health: Assessment and implications of generalized outcome expectancies. *Health Psychology, 4* (3), 219–247.

Schimel, J., Simon, L., Greenberg, J., Pyszczynski, T., Solomon, S., Warmonsky, J. & Arndt, J. (1999). Stereotypes and terror management: Evidence that mortality salience enhances stereotypic thinking and preferences. *Journal of Personality and Social Psychology, 77*, 905–926.

Shils, E. A. (1954). Authoritarianism: "Right" and "left." In R. Cristie & M. Jahoda (Eds.), *Studies in the scope and method of "The Authoritarian Personality"* (pp. 24–49). Glencoe, IL: Free Press.

Scott, W. A. (1965). Psychological and social correlates of international images. In H. C. Kelman (Ed.), *International behavior: A social psychological analysis.* New York: Holt, Rinehart and Winston.

Schwarz, N., & Clore, G.L. (1996). Feelings and phenomenal experiences. In E.T. Higgins & A.W. Kruglanski (Eds.) *Social psychology: A handbook of basic principles.* New York: Guilford, pp. 433–465.

Seligman, M. E. P., Abramson, L. Y., Semmel, A., & von Baeyer, C. (1979). Depressive attributional style. *Journal of Abnormal Psychology, 88*, 242–247.

Semin, G. R., Rubini, M., & Fiedler, K. (1995). The answer is in the question: The effect of verb causality on locus of explanation. *Personality and Social Psychology Bulletin, 21*, 834–841.

Shah, J. Y., Kruglanski, A. W., & Thompson, E. P. (1998). Membership has its (epistemic) rewards: Need for closure effects on ingroup bias. *Journal of Personality and Social Psychology, 75*, 383–393.

Sidanius, J. (1978). Intolerance of ambiguity and socio-politico ideology: A multidimensional analysis. *European Journal of Social Psychology, 8*, 215–235.

Sigall, H., Kruglanski, A. W., & Fyock, J. (1999). Wishful thinking and procrastination. *Journal of Personality and Social Behavior, 1*, 17–29.

Sinclair, L., & Kunda, Z. (1996). *Motivated stereotype use: Discrediting women who treat us poorly.* Paper presented at the meeting of the American Psychological Association, Toronto.

Singer, J. D. (1958). Threat perception and the armament-tension dilemma. *Journal of Conflict Resolution, 2*, 90–105.

Smelser, N. J. (1998). The rational and the ambivalent in the social sciences. *American Sociological Review, 63*, 1–16.

Smith, P. B., & Bond, M. H. (1993). Social psychology across cultures: Analysis and perspectives. Hertfordshire, England: Harvester Wheatsheaf.

Solomon, S., Greenberg., J., & Pyszczynski, T. (1991). A terror management theory of social behavior: The psychological functions of self-esteem. *Advances in Experimental Social Psychology, 24*, 93–159.

Sorrentino, R. M., & Roney, C. J. (1999). *The uncertain mind.* Philadelphia: Psychology Press.

Sorrentino, R. M., and Short, J. C. (1986). Uncertainty orientation, motivation and cognition. In R. M. Sorrentino, & E. T. Higgins (Eds.), *Handbook of motivation and cognition: Foundations of social behavior* (vol. 1), 189–206. New York: Guilford.

Stasser, G., & Stewart, D. (1992). Discovery of hidden profiles by decision-making groups: Solving a problem versus making a judgment. *Journal of Personality and Social Psychology, 63*(2), 426–434.

Stasser, G., & Titus, W. (1985). Pooling of unshared information in group decision making: Biased information sampling during discussion. *Journal of Personality and Social Psychology, 48*(6), 1467–1478.

Stasser, G., & Titus, W. (1987). Effects of information load and percentage of shared information on the dissemination of unshared information during group discussion. *Journal of Personality and Social Psychology, 53*(1), 83–93.

Steele, C. M. (1988). The psychology of self-affirmation. In L. Berkowitz. (Ed.). *Advances in experimental social psychology, 21*, 261–302. San Diego. CA: Academic Press.

Steele, C. M., Spencer, S. J., & Aronson, J. (2002). Contending with group image: The psychology of stereotype and social identity threat. In M. P. Zanna (Ed.), *Advances in experimental social psychology* (Vol. 34, pp. 379–440). San Diego, CA: Academic Press.

Stephan, W. G., & Stephan, C. W., (1996). *Intergroup relations*. Madison, WI: Brown & Benchmark Publishers.

Stillinger, C., Epelbaum, M., Keltner, D., & Ross, L. (1990). *The reactive devaluation barrier to conflict resolution*. Unpublished manuscript. Stanford University, Palo Alto, CA.

Strack, F., & Mussweiler, T. (1997). Explaining the enigmatic anchoring effect: Mechanisms of selective accessibility. *Journal of Personality and Social Psychology, 73*, 437–446.

Streufert, S., & Fromkin, H. (1969). *True conflict and complex decision making* (ONP Technical Report No. 25), Purdue University, West Lafayette, IN.

Stroebe, W., & Stroebe, M. S. (1987). *Bereavement and health: The psychological and physical consequences of partner loss*. New York: Cambridge University Press.

Sumner, W. G. (1906). *Folkways*. Boston: Ginn.

Swann, W. B., Jr. (1990). To be adored or to be known: The interplay of self-enhancement and self-verification. In R. M. Sorrentino & E. T. Higgins (Eds.). *Foundations of social behavior, 2*, 408–448.

Swann, W. B., Jr. (1984). Quest for accuracy in person perception: A matter of pragmatics. *Psychological Review, 91*, 457–477.

Swann, W. B., Wenzlaff, R. M., Krull, D. S., & Pelham, B. W. (1992). Allure of negative feedback: Self-verification strivings among depressed persons. *Journal of Abnormal Psychology, 101*, 293–306.

Tajfel, H., Billig, M.G., & Bundy, R. P. (1971). Social categorization and intergroup behaviour. *European Journal of Social Psychology, 1* (2), 149–178.

Tetlock, P. E. (1988). Structure and function in political belief systems. In A. G. Greenwald & A. Pratkanis (Eds), *Attitude structure and function* (pp. 129-151).

Tetlock, P. E. (1992). The impact of accountability on judgment and choice: Toward a social contingency model. In L. Berkowitz (Ed.), *Advances in Experimental Social Psychology* (vol. 25, pp. 331–376). New York: Academic Press.

Tetlock, P. E. (1998). Close-call counterfactuals and belief system defenses: I was not almost wrong but I was almost right. *Journal of Personality and Social Psychology, 75, 230–242*.

Tetlock, P. E. (1985). Accountability: The neglected social context of judgement and choice. In B. Staw & L. Cummings (Eds.). *Research in organizational behavior*. (Vol. 7, pp. 297–332). Greenwich, CT: JAI Press.

Thompson, E. P., Roman, R. J., Moskowitz, G. B., & Chaiken, S. (1994). Accuracy motivation attenuates covert priming: The systematic reprocessing of social information. *Journal of Personality and Social Psychology, 66* (3), 447–489.

Thompson, M. M., Naccarato, M. E., & Parker, K. H. (1992). *Measuring cognitive needs: The development and validation of the Personal Need for Structure (PNS) and Personal Fear of Invalidity (PFI) Measures*. Unpublished manuscript. University of Waterloo, Waterloo, Ontario. Canada.

Titus, H. E., and Hollander, E. P. (1957). The California F-scale in psychological research: 1950–1955. *Psychological Bulletin, 54*, 47–64.

Tjosvold, D. (1977). Commitment to justice in conflict between unequal persons. *Journal of Applied Social Psychology, 7*, 149–162.

Tomkins, S. S. (1963). Left and right: A basic dimension of ideology and personality. In R. W. White (Ed.), *The study of lives* (pp. 388-411). New York: Atherton.

Tomkins, S. S. (1965). Affect and the psychology of knowledge. In S. S. Tomkins & C. E. Izard (Eds.), *Affect, cognition and personality* (pp. 72-97). New York: Springer.

Trapnell, P. D. (1994). Openness versus intellect: A lexical left turn. *European Journal of Personality, 8*, 273–290.

Trope, Y. (1975). Seeking information about one's own ability as a determinant of choice among tasks. *Journal of Personality and Social Psychology, 32*, 1004–1013.

Trope, Y. (1986). Identification and inferential processes in dispositional attribution. *Psychological Review, 93*, 239–257.

Trope, Y. & Bassok, M. (1983). Information-gathering strategies in hypothesis testing. *Journal of Experimental Social Psychology, 19*, 560–576.

Trubisky, P., Ting-Toomey, S., & Lin, S. L. (1991). The influence of individualism collectivism and self-monitoring on conflict styles. *International Journal of Intercultural Relations, 15* (1), 65–84.

Tversky, A., & Kahneman, D. (1974). Judgement under uncertainty: Heuristics and biases. *Science, 185*, 1124–1130.

Tversky, A., & Koehler, D. J. (1994). Support theory: A non-extensional representation of subjective probability. *Psychological Review, 101*(4), 547–567.

Uleman, J. S., Winborne, W. C., Winter, L., & Shechter, D. (1986). Personality differences in spontaneous personality inferences at encoding. *Journal of Personality and Social Psychology, 51*, 396–403.

Van Oudenhoven, J. P., Prins, K. S., & Buunk, B. P. (1998). Attitudes of minority and majority members towards adaptation of immigrants. *European Journal of Social Psychology, 28*, 995–1013.

Van Wallendael, L. R. (1989). The quest for limits on noncomplementarity in opinion revision. *Organizational Behavior and Human Decision Processes, 43* (3), 385–405.

Van Wallendael, L. R., & Hastie, R. (1990). Tracing the footsteps of Sherlock Holmes: Cognitive representations of hypothesis testing. *Memory and cognition, 18* (3), 240–250.

Vermeir, I., Van Kenhove, P., & Hendrickx, H. (2002). The influence of need for closure on consumer's choice behavior. *Journal of Economic Psychology, 23*, 703–727.

Vertzberger, Y. Y. I. (1990). *The world in their minds.* Stanford, CA: Stanford University Press.

Viroli, M. (1995). *For love of country: An essay on patriotism and nationalism.* Oxford: Clarendon Press.

Vogt, W. P. (1993). *Dictionary of statistics and methodology.* Newbury Park: Sage.

Walton, R. E., & McKersie, R. (1965). *A behavioral theory of labor negotiations: An analysis of social interaction system.* New York: McGraw Hill.

Ward, T. B., Patterson, M. J., Sifonis, C. M., Dodds, R. A., & Saunders, K. N. (2002). The role of graded category structure in imaginative thought. *Memory and Cognition, 30*, 199–216.

Webster, D. M. (1993). *Groups under the influence: Need for closure effects on information sharing in decision making groups.* Unpublished doctoral dissertation. University of Maryland.

Webster, D. M. (1993). Motivated augmentation and reduction of the overattribution bias. *Journal of Personality and Social Psychology, 65*(2), 261–271.

Webster, D. M., & Kruglanski, A. W. (1994). Individual differences in need for cognitive closure. *Journal of Personality and Social Psychology, 67*, 1049–1062.

Webster, D. M., Kruglanski, A. W., & Pattison, D. A. (1997). Motivated language use in intergroup contexts: Need for closure effects on the linguistic intergroup bias. *Journal of Personality and Social Psychology, 72*, 1122–1131.

Webster, D. M. & Kruglanski, A. W. (1998). Cognitive and social consequences of the motivation for closure. *European Review of Social Psychology, 8*, 133–173.

Webster, D. M., Richter, L., & Kruglanski, A. W. (1996). On leaping to conclusions when feeling tired: Mental fatigue effects on impressional primacy. *Journal of Experimental Social Psychology, 32*, 181–195.

Webster-Nelson, D., Klein, C. F., & Irvin, J. E. (2003). Motivational antecedents of empathy: inhibiting effects of fatigue. *Basic and Applied Social Psychology, 25* (1), 37–50.

Wegener, D. T., Petty, R. E., & Smith, S. M. (1994). *Positive mood can increase or decrease message scrutiny: The hedonic contingency of mood and message elaboration.* Unpublished manuscript, The Ohio State University, Columbus, OH.

Weinstein, N. D. (1980). Unrealistic optimism about future life-events. *Journal of Personality and Social Psychology, 39*, 806–820.

Wilson, G. D. (Ed.). (1973). *The psychology of conservatism.* New York: Academic Press.

Wilson, G. D., & Patterson, J. R. (1968). A new measure of conservatism. *British Journal of Social and Clinical Psychology, 7*, 264–269.

Winter, L., & Uleman, J. S. (1984). When are social judgements made? Evidence for the spontaneousness of trait inferences. *Journal of Personality and Social Psychology, 47*, 237–252.

Yik, M. S. M., & Bond, M. H. (1993). Exploring the dimensions of Chinese person perception with indigenous and imported constructs: Creating a culturally balanced scale. *International Journal of Psychology, 28*, 75–95.

Yukl, G. (1974). Effects of situational variables and opponent concessions on a bargainer's perceptions, aspirations, and concessions. *Journal of Personality and Social Psychology, 29*, 227–236.

Zajonc, R. B. (1960). The process of cognitive tuning and communication. *Journal of Abnormal and Social Psychology, 61*, 159–167.

Zajonc, R. B., & Morrissette, J. (1960). The role of uncertainty in cognitive change. *Journal of Abnormal and Social Psychology, 61*, 168–175.

Index

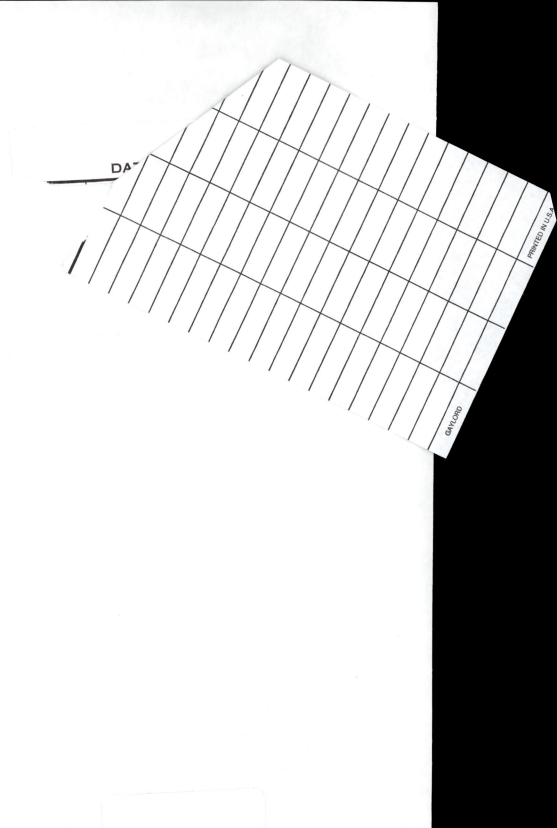